SPONSORED BY THE
JOINT COMMITTEE ON THE NEAR AND MIDDLE EAST,
SOCIAL SCIENCE RESEARCH COUNCIL

After Empire

Multiethnic Societies and Nation-Building

The Soviet Union and the Russian, Ottoman, and Habsburg Empires

EDITED BY
KAREN BARKEY AND MARK VON HAGEN

Westview Press
A Member of the Perseus Books Group

For our grandparents
who were born in the Habsburg and Ottoman empires
and lived most of their lives after empire

Copyright © 1997 by Westview Press, A Member of the Perseus Books Group

Published in 1997 in the United States of America by Westview Press, 5500 Central Avenue, Boulder, Colorado 80301-2877, and in the United Kingdom by Westview Press, 12 Hid's Copse Road, Cumnor Hill, Oxford OX2 9JJ

Library of Congress Cataloging-in-Publication Data
After empire : multiethnic societies and nation-building : the Soviet
    Union and Russian, Ottoman, and Habsburg Empires / edited by Karen
    Barkey and Mark von Hagen.
        p.   cm.
    Includes index.
    ISBN 0-8133-2963-9.—ISBN 0-8133-2964-7 (pbk)
        1. Imperialism.   2. Turkey—History—Ottoman Empire, 1288–1918.
    3. Habsburg, House of.   4. Austria—History.   5. Russia—History.
    6. Soviet Union—History.   I. Barkey, Karen, 1958–   .   II. Von
    Hagen, Mark, 1954–   .
    JC359.A53   1997
    325'.32—dc21   96-50066
                                                              CIP

The paper used in this publication meets the requirements of the American National Standard for Permanence of Paper for Printed Library Materials Z39.48-1984.

10   9   8   7   6   5   4   3   2

CONTENTS

Acknowledgments

This volume is the result of a conference convened at Columbia University in November 1994. It was sponsored by the Joint Committee on the Near and Middle East of the Social Science Research Council, the Center for the Social Sciences, and the Harriman Institute of Columbia University. Above all, we thank Lisa Anderson of Columbia's Political Science Department and Steven Heydemann of the SSRC for initiating the project on empires and Alexander Motyl for his help in organizing the conference.

We are also grateful to the participants and commentators at the conference. In addition to those who have contributed papers to this volume, we thank: Harrison White, Jack Snyder, Steve Solnick, Richard Wortman, Sukru Hanioglu, Robert Paul Magosci, Rajan Menon, and David Good. During the discussion and revision of the papers, we benefited from the critical eyes and minds of Charles Tilly, Hendrik Spruyt, Daniel Chirot, and Anthony W. Marx. Caglar Keyder and István Deák deserve special thanks for agreeing quickly and graciously to switch roles from commentators to authors.

Our editors, Margaret Sevchenko and David Gibson, worked hard for long hours to prepare the papers for publication and track down elusive footnotes and transliterations. Finally, for her help in organizing the conference we gratefully acknowledge the efforts of Hajdeja Iglic.

Karen Barkey
Mark von Hagen
Columbia University, New York

1

HOW EMPIRES END

CHARLES TILLY

From Herodotus to Montesquieu and beyond, poets, historians, and philosophers have recurrently produced one of our culture's standard literary forms: the dirge for a fallen empire. Reflection on imperial decline has world-historical resonance because it records for all to see the fallibility of seemingly unshakable human enterprises. Contrast between sometime grandeur and startling ruin has often provided the text of moral reflections on imperial decline, orations in the ruins, either by new conquerors who boast their own superiority over the defeated or by philosophers who want to warn against the excesses of hubris. (We who now pronounce on the Soviet empire's collapse should consider into which category we fall.) Among the philosophers' laments, remember Lewis Mumford's classic lines on Rome:

> From the standpoint of both politics and urbanism, Rome remains a significant lesson of what to avoid: its history presents a series of classic danger signals to warn one when life is moving in the wrong direction. Wherever crowds gather in suffocating numbers, wherever rents rise steeply and housing conditions deteriorate, wherever a one-sided exploitation of distant territories removes the pressure to achieve balance and harmony nearer at hand, there the precedents of Roman building almost automatically revive, as they have come back today: the arena, the tall tenement, the mass contests and exhibitions, the football matches, the international beauty contests, the strip-tease made ubiquitous by advertisement, the constant titillation of the senses by sex, liquor, and violence—all in true Roman style. So, too, the multiplication of bathrooms and the over-expenditure on broadly paved motor roads, and above all, the massive collective concentration on glib ephemeralities of all kinds, performed with supreme technical audacity. These are symptoms of the end: magnifications of demoralized power, minifications of life. When these signs multiply, Necropolis is

near, though not a stone has yet crumbled. For the barbarian has already captured
the city from within. Come, hangman! Come, vulture![1]

Thus Mumford applies his theory that beyond a modest limit the growth of
political power and technical virtuosity dehumanize life, bringing on their own
annihilation. Less orotund, but in the same vein, Alex Motyl declares that "absolutism engenders pathologies that lead to its own degeneration, a fact that, in territorially contiguous empires, necessarily leads to the decay of the center's control
of the periphery."[2]

Before performing learned autopsies, however, we should just be sure the body
was sick, and has actually died. Over the time that the world has known substantial states, after all, empires have been the dominant and largest state form,
carnivorous dinosaurs that nothing but a terrestrial disaster, it seems, could erad-
icate. Only now, during the twentieth century, do we seem to be leaving the age
of massive Eurasian empires that began in earnest across a band from the
Mediterranean to East Asia almost four thousand years ago. To the extent that
we regard such international compacts as the European Union, GATT, and
NAFTA as embodying imperial designs, furthermore, even today's requiem may
prove premature.

If empires are indeed disappearing, their demise raises questions just as
knotty as the dinosaurs' sudden disappearance. At the end of the world's blood-
iest and most military century, does imperial disintegration mean that interstate
military conquest will also decline, perhaps in favor of civil war and genocide?
Does the dispersal of previous empires, including the massive decolonization that
began in the 1960s, suggest what will happen to the debris of the most recent
breakdowns? How generally, when, and where, does the end of empires generate
new forms of conflict, internal and external? Do bursts of nationalism on behalf
of former imperial fragments generally accompany the dissolution of central control? Under what conditions does—or, for that matter, could—successor states to
empires form stable democratic regimes? Whether or not we have reached the
end of imperial history, previous cycles of decline present us with pressing questions and ample bases for comparison.

As we undertake such comparisons, we should avoid the smug assumption that
empires fail simply because they generally adopt unviable forms of rule. Historically, empires have been hardy beasts. Variants of the Chinese empire endured
two millennia or more, the Byzantine empire continued for more than a millennium, the Roman empire lasted for about six centuries, the Ottoman empire survived about half a millennium, various Mongol empires occupied the widest contiguous territorial range of any political organization ever to exist for some five
hundred years, while the ends of briefer but still momentous British, French,
German, Italian, Spanish, Portuguese, Belgian, Dutch, American, Russian,
Soviet, and Austro-Hungarian empires lie within the memories of living people.

Between the Roman and British juggernauts, Europe itself saw great Norman,
Lithuanian-Polish, Swedish, Burgundian, and many other empires before con-

solidated states came to dominate the continent. Around the Mediterranean, larger Muslim states organized chiefly as empires. Meanwhile, more empires arose and fell in South America, Africa, and Southeast Asia. Given the recency of imperial presence in our world, we who speak generally and definitively of empire's end run the risk of a characteristic Chinese error, mistaking the decline of a particular regime for the definitive end of a once-dominant political form. Just as we should hesitate to crow loudly about the irreversible "democratization" of a world where guerrilla, genocide, and politicide have become increasingly common practice,[3] we should hold back before declaring that empires have departed forever to live with their ancestors.

Over the roughly ten millennia during which we have some evidence for the existence of states, most states have taken one of three forms. They have appeared as city-states, agrarian military domains, empires, or various combinations of the three, as in Venice's attachment of a scattered maritime empire to a city-state or the Dutch Republic's uneasy federation among city-states. Only during the last two centuries have consolidated states—coercion-wielding organizations governing directly and rather uniformly in a series of heterogeneous and clearly bounded territories—become the dominant state form, first in the European world, and then, by conquest and emulation, in the world as a whole.

Nor should we imagine consolidated states to have such great advantages over all other political organizations that they have rendered the others obsolete; after a mere two hundred years of hegemony, Western consolidated states are already showing signs of incapacity to provide either order or public goods in the face of challenges from networks of capital, labor, drugs, arms, and terror that cross their painfully erected borders with ease.[4] A century from now, analysts may well treat consolidated states as ephemera, and empires as the historically dominant forms of political organization beyond a regional scale.

An empire is a large composite polity linked to a central power by indirect rule. The central power exercises some military and fiscal control in each major segment of its imperial domain, but tolerates the two major elements of indirect rule: (1) retention or establishment of particular, distinct compacts for the government of each segment; and (2) exercise of power through intermediaries who enjoy considerable autonomy within their own domains in return for the delivery of compliance, tribute, and military collaboration with the center.

As students of Switzerland, the United States, the German Federal Republic, Brazil, or South Africa will hurry to announce, these criteria are matters of degree rather than absolute distinctions; within their zones of competence, nevertheless, today's federal governments rule much more uniformly and directly than did the Ottoman or Mongol states. Empires rule indirectly through variable compacts because they grow chiefly through military conquest of existing polities, aided by the collaboration (however coerced) of local power-holders who retain substantial discretion within their own jurisdictions. By the same logic, they ordinarily disintegrate in some combination of external conquest and peripheral resistance, either and both often executed by former agents of the center.

Empire has proved to be a recurrent, flexible form of large-scale rule for two closely related reasons: because it holds together disparate smaller-scale units without requiring much centrally-controlled internal transformation, and because it pumps resources to rulers without costly monitoring and repression. Regional rulers use existing practices, understandings, and relationships to extract the requisite minimum of tribute, military support, and loyalty for the center's benefit. They can settle for extracting as much payment and service as the regions will bear without attempting to estimate the actual capacity of regions, localities, or individuals to pay. Just so long as regional rulers deploy some force of their own and have ready call on imperial force in emergencies, the imperial center need not build a dense system of regional policing, much less the monitoring and boundary-controlling mechanisms entailed by income taxes, property taxes, or even fine-grained excise taxes.[5] Imperial extraction of resources normally operates, to be sure, at the cost of enormous slippage, evasion, personal influence, and inequality—one reason why an emperor's sudden demand for increases in yield (or, conversely, his visible loss of coercive power) frequently generates rebellion by previously compliant subjects. But an imperial system's crude simplicity makes it adaptable to many social terrains.

In contrast to the slow accretion of power in a city-state, an agrarian domain, or a consolidated state, imperial expansion therefore sometimes occurs with startling rapidity because it combines military conquest with political co-optation, absorbing existing systems of rule into webs of tribute and military alliance. Hence the quick looming of predatory Persian, Mongol, and Ottoman empires— all of them relying initially on armed horsemen—at the horizons of their agrarian neighbors. By the same token, however, empires can collapse spectacularly. Ruin sometimes rushes in because: (1) the empire's dominated polities remain detachable by virtue of weak integration into any administrative web; (2) their viceroys enjoy autonomous power, including the power to defect; (3) subjugated populations retain distinct identities, memories, and grievances; and (4) information indicating that the center has become vulnerable spreads fast among dominated units and external enemies. The Chinese empire proved more durable than others largely because it countered all four of these threatening conditions. By extending a relatively uniform administrative structure down to the county level, by integrating county-level gentry into a system of competition for imperial favor, by rotating imperial bureaucrats frequently and refusing to station them in their provinces of origin, by stimulating internal mobility and reducing public recognition of ethnic distinctness, and by making effective shows of central force through much of its vast territory, the imperial state maintained most of its dynasties for centuries between collapses and conquests.[6]

In this light, we should remain skeptical about accounts of communism's collapse that focus on a single fatal flaw in its imperial structure, whether Alex Motyl's "absolutism" or something else. Motyl's explanation takes a common form, internalist and universal. It is *internalist* because it locates the origins of collapse within the system. It is *universal* because it claims that all such systems collapse, sooner or later, for the same reason. Similarly, Joseph Tainter bases his internal and universalist analysis of "collapse" mainly on diminishing marginal returns to central control.[7]

Many other explanations, in contrast, insist on the uniqueness of their case(s) and/or the externality of essential causes, while the most common explanations combine unique and general causes of a given decline with a balance of internal and external factors.[8] For the class of territorially contiguous empires, Motyl's internalist-universalist account posits a recurrent process by which an allegedly necessary feature of such organizations—absolutism—undermines the conditions for its own survival. Let us set aside Motyl's dubious use of "absolutism" to describe the actual operation of any state, as opposed to the ruler's claims for heaven-blessed priority over regional magnates.[9] Let us also pass by his unfortunate application of "prefect," that quintessential term of deliberately constructed direct rule, to the empowered, semiautonomous intermediaries who serve imperial regimes.[10]

Motyl's essential idea echoes Shmuel Eisenstadt's classic characterization *avant la lettre* of the principal-agent problem in empires.[11] Every empire does, indeed, face the problem of maintaining compliance and reliable information-gathering among regional agents who easily acquire ties, interests, and capacities that lead them to subvert the imperial enterprise, to ally with its enemies, or even to rebel on their own accounts. To suppose, however, that every empire succumbs to that dilemma one has to disregard the enormous variability in imperial durability and demise, and to forget the recurrent importance of external conquest.

To ask how empires end is like asking how rivers change their courses, how coral reefs go dead, how human lineages disappear. *In vitro* we might imagine a single course for empires, lineages, rivers, or reefs. Yet, verified *in vivo*, it does not occur. If empires have over four millennia been so prevalent and yet so various, we are unlikely to derive from their histories any constants less trivial than those I have already named: that some combination of external conquest and internal defection usually brings them down. Contemplating the Soviet Union, we might stretch such generalizations to stress the Afghan war's depletion of Soviet military strength and credibility, the importance of Gorbachev's declaration of nonintervention for the politics of Warsaw Pact states, or the attractions of capitalist connections to the Baltic states. But none of these will take us very far toward a systematic integration of the Soviet Union's experience with that of other empires. I don't want to spoil the game of comparing Soviet collapse with the Habsburg empire's dissolution, but I do want to warn that the search for point-by-point correspondence should in principle have very little utility. We will make more progress if we place empires and their ends in a meaningful field of variation.

Alex Motyl has actually started the essential process of differentiation by offering the distinction between territorially contiguous and scattered empires. Still, that distinction does not obviously solve our problems; given the superiority of travel by water until the last century or so, for example, it is not evident that the scattered sea-linked Venetian empire was less well-connected than the contiguous but largely land-linked Russian empire, or that Venice's suffocation through Ottoman expansion differed fundamentally from the Byzantine débâcle which Venetian-Ottoman collaboration had earlier hastened.[12] Most likely we will have to translate this dimension of variation into transaction costs, with the crude hypotheses running something like this: (1) the higher the transaction costs of maintaining central control over an imperial segment, the more likely that segment's detachment from the empire; and (2) the higher the total transaction costs of an empire's control relative to returns from all segments, the more likely the empire's disintegration.

In the absence of well-established a priori measures for transaction costs and returns from empire, a cost-benefit formulation introduces into any explanation the usual circularity of such reasoning. Still, it allows us to estimate the general effects of significant changes such as an interruption of the flow of bullion from South America to Spain or the proliferation of pirates along the trade routes connecting a maritime empire.[13] Either a decline in essential revenues or an increase in control-related costs makes an empire less viable. An empire whose lines of communication and supply are expensively long is no doubt more vulnerable to either form of disruption. Thus recast, Motyl's distinction helps identify a major dimension of imperial variation.

What other dimensions of variation should we single out? The very character of empires as large composite polities linked to central powers by indirect rule suggests candidates: size ought to make a difference, as should the character of military organization and technology, relations between the imperial center and outside powers, current organization of the international system, the degree of heterogeneity among dominated segments, the extent of inequality between center and periphery, the mechanisms employed for direct rule, and, preeminently, the center's own economic, political, and social organization. Conditions for an empire's survival, mutation, or collapse, the processes by which imperial change occurs, and the outcomes of imperial disintegration should, in principle, vary systematically according to most or all of these characteristics. Not much help, but at least a checklist for discussion.

We have some hope of going beyond checklists by means of an inverse procedure: by working back from presumed outcomes of imperial change to understandings of its regularities. Under what conditions and by what paths, for example, might we expect democratic polities to emerge from crumbling empires? Substantive and procedural definitions of democracy predominate in today's discussions of the subject—"substantive" in stressing outcomes such as equality or harmony, "procedural" in emphasizing such arrangements as free elections and succession in office.[14] I propose, however, an old-fashioned "institutional" conception of democracy focusing on relations between citizens and states. It rests on a series of concepts I must, alas, define to avoid confusion:

State: an organization controlling the principal concentrated means of coercion within a delimited territory and exercising priority in some respects over all other organizations within the same territory.

Polity: the set of relations among agents of the state and all major political actors within the delimited territory.

Rights: enforceable claims, the reciprocal of obligations.

Citizenship: rights and mutual obligations binding state agents and a category of persons defined exclusively by their legal attachment to the same state.

In this conception a polity is democratic to the degree that it establishes (1) broad citizenship, (2) equal citizenship, (3) binding consultation of citizens with respect to governmental personnel and policies, and (4) protection of citizens from arbitrary state action. No polity ever achieves full democracy by such standards, but real polities array themselves from deeply undemocratic (narrow, unequal citizenship without binding consultation or protection) to relatively democratic (high on all four values).

By these criteria, segments of empires can in principle achieve some democracy but whole empires remain undemocratic by definition; at an imperial scale their segmentation and reliance on indirect rule bar equal citizenship, binding consultation, and protection, if not necessarily breadth of membership. This definitional work helps specify what an imperial transition to democracy entails: either (a) the dismantling of the prior empire into segments within which regional institutions lend themselves to broad, equal citizenship with consultation and protection; or (b) the dissolution of indirect rule in favor of a more direct, uniform citizenship generating sets of ties between center and peripheries.

History provides a few examples of (a), but none of (b) so far. Yet on a regional scale path (b) seems to have been a necessary condition for democratization, along with subordination of military forces to civilian control, broad class coalitions in support of the state, and extensive domestic taxation entailing representation of taxpayers.[15] Without substantial dissolution of indirect rule, the rights of citizens remain weak and uneven. That observation, indeed, identifies the critical flaw in recurrent anarchist and capitalist programs of decentralization (or utter dismantling of the state) as the road to democracy; without an agency that enforces rights uniformly and effectively, rights themselves disappear.[16]

Nationalism provides another case in point. How close and general a tie exists between outbreaks of nationalism and ends of empires? The question matters not only because nationalism seems to have hastened and followed the recent disintegrations of Yugoslavia, the Soviet Union, and the Warsaw Pact, not only because intriguing analogies appear between those recent episodes and Ottoman or Austro-Hungarian decline, but also because the question identifies a zone of potentially fruitful disagreement in studies of nationalism. A wide range of analyses, not all consistent with each other, suggest that imperial decline and nationalism should generally coincide, for example because all nations resist subordination when they can, because empires actually create nationalities, and/or because as imperial disintegration begins outside powers promote separatism on the part of imperial subjects.[17]

A set of historicist analyses, equally contradictory in their causal accounts, reply that nationalism has come into being relatively recently, through a specific historical process,[18] with the additional implication of its likely disappearance as historical conditions change. Eric Hobsbawm and I, as it happens, have published interpretations of nationalism in this vein, attaching great importance to state-led attempts to define a nation and impose that definition on ordinary people, as well as to the subsequent adoption of national self-determination as a principle for the recognition of new states.[19] Thus a confrontation between generalist and historicist analyses—let's say a match between Anthony Smith and Rogers Brubaker!—holds some promise of helping us unravel not just the knotty questions of nationalism but also the tangled ends of empires.

Notes

1. Lewis Mumford, *The City in History: Its Origins, Its Transformations, and Its Prospects* (New York: Harcourt, Brace and World, 1961), 24.

2. Alexander Motyl, "From Imperial Decay to Imperial Collapse: The Fall of the Soviet Empire in Comparative Perspective," in ed. Richard J. Rudolph and David F. Good, *Nationalism and Empire: The Habsburg Empire and the Soviet Union* (New York: St. Martin's Press, 1992).

3. See Martin van Creveld, *Technology and War from 2000 B.C. to the Present* (New York: Free Press, 1989); idem, *The Transformation of War* (New York: Free Press, 1991); Helen Fein, "Accounting for Genocide after 1945: Theories and Some Findings," *International Journal on Group Rights* 1 (1993): 79–106; Ted Robert Gurr, *Minorities at Risk: A Global View of Ethnopolitical Conflicts* (Washington, D.C.: U.S. Institute of Peace Press, 1993); and Barbara Harff, "Victims of the State: Genocides, Politicides, and Group Repression since 1945," *International Review of Victimology* 1 (1990): 23–41.

4. See Stephen Graubard, ed., "Reconstructing Nations and States," *Daedalus* 122 (1993), entire issue; idem, "Europe Through a Glass Darkly," *Daedalus* 123 (1994), entire issue; idem, "What Future for the State?" *Daedalus* 124 (1995), entire issue; Hugh Gusterson, "Realism and the International Order after the Cold War," *Social Research* 60 (1993): 279–300; Istvan Hont, "The Permanent Crisis of a Divided Mankind: 'Contemporary Crisis of the Nation State' in Historical Perspective," *Political Studies* 42 (1994): 166–231; John Gerard Ruggie, "Territoriality and Beyond: Problematizing Modernity in International Relations," *International Organization* 47 (1993): 139–174; Sidney Tarrow, "La

mondialisation des conflits: encore un siècle de rébellion?" *Etudes Internationales* 24 (1993): 513–532; Janice E. Thomson, "State Sovereignty in International Relations: Bridging the Gap Between Theory and Empirical Research," *International Studies Quarterly* 39 (1995): 213–234; and Charles Tilly, "Globalization Threatens Labor's Rights," *International Labor and Working Class History* 47 (1995): 1–23.

5. Gabriel Ardant, *Théorie sociologique de l'impôt*, 2 vols. (Paris: SEVPEN, 1965); and John L. Campbell, "The State and Fiscal Sociology," *Annual Review of Sociology* 19 (1993): 163–185.

6. Kung-Chuan Hsiao, *Rural China: Imperial Control in the Nineteenth Century* (Seattle: University of Washington Press, 1960); Stuart Schram, ed., *The Scope of State Power in China* (1985); idem, *Foundations and Limits of State Power in China* (1987) (these last two volumes published for the European Science Foundation by the School of Oriental and African Studies, University of London and the Chinese University Press of Hong Kong); Vivienne Shue, *The Reach of the State: Sketches of the Chinese Body Politic* (Stanford: Stanford University Press, 1988); William G. Skinner, "Marketing and Social Structure in Rural China," *Journal of Asian Studies* 24 (1964): 3–43; idem, "The Structure of Chinese History," *Journal of Asian Studies* 44 (1985): 271–292; Frederic Wakeman, *Strangers at the Gate: Social Disorder in South China, 1839–1861* (Berkeley: University of California Press, 1966); idem, *The Great Enterprise: The Manchu Reconstruction of Imperial Order in Seventeenth-Century China*, 2 vols. (Berkeley: University of California Press, 1985); Joseph B. R. Whitney, *China: Area, Administration, and Nation Building*, Research Paper 123 (Chicago: Department of Geography, University of Chicago, 1970); Pierre-Étienne Will, "Chine moderne et sinologie," *Annales; Histoire, Sciences Sociales* 49 (1994): 7–26; Pierre-Étienne Will and R. Bing Wong, *Nourish the People: The State Civilian Granary System in China, 1650–1850* (Ann Arbor, Mich.: University of Michigan Press, 1991); and Bin Wong, "Les émeutes de subsistances en Chine et en Europe Occidentale," *Annales; Economies, Sociétés, Civilisations* 38 (1983): 234–258.

7. Joseph A. Tainter, *The Collapse of Complex Societies* (Cambridge: Cambridge University Press, 1988).

8. See, for example, Thomas A. Brady, Jr., *Turning Swiss: Cities and Empire, 1450–1550* (Cambridge: Cambridge University Press, 1985); David Strang, "From Dependency to Sovereignty: An Event History Analysis of Decolonization, 1870–1987," *American Sociological Review* 55 (1990): 846–860; and idem, "Global Patterns of Decolonization, 1500–1987," *International Studies Quarterly* 35 (1991): 429–454.

9. William H. Beik, *Absolutism and Society in Seventeenth-Century France* (Cambridge: Cambridge University Press, 1985); Nicholas Henshall, *The Myth of Absolutism: Change and Continuity in Early Modern European Monarchy* (London: Longman, 1992); Sharon Kettering, "Brokerage at the Court of Louis XIV," *Historical Journal* 36 (1993): 69–87; and Richard Lachmann and Julia Adams, "Absolutism's Antinomies: Class Formation, State Fiscal Structures and the Origins of the French Revolution," *Political Power and Social Theory* 7 (1988): 135–175.

10. Isser Woloch, *The New Regime: Transformations of the French Civic Order, 1789–1820s* (New York: Norton, 1994).

11. S. N. Eisenstadt, *The Political Systems of Empires: The Rise and Fall of the Historical Bureaucratic Societies* (New York: Free Press of Glencoe, 1963); cf. David E. M. Sapping-

ton, "Incentives in Principal-Agent Relationships," *Journal of Economic Perspectives* 5 (1991): 45–66.

12. John H. Pryor, *Geography, Technology, and War: Studies in the Maritime History of the Mediterranean, 649–1571* (Cambridge: Cambridge University Press, 1988).

13. J. H. Elliott, *Imperial Spain, 1469–1716* (London: Edward Arnold, 1963); Richard Herr, *Rural Change and Royal Finances in Spain at the End of the Old Regime* (Berkeley: University of California Press, 1989); Alberto Tenenti, *Piracy and the Decline of Venice, 1580–1615* (Berkeley: University of California Press, 1967); and Janice E. Thomson, *Mercenaries, Pirates, and Sovereigns: State-Building and Extraterritorial Violence in Early Modern Europe* (Princeton: Princeton University Press, 1994).

14. Anthony Arblaster, *Democracy* (Minneapolis: University of Minnesota Press, 1987); Ross E. Burkhart, and Michael S. Lewis-Beck, "Comparative Democracy: The Economic Development Thesis," *American Political Science Review* 88 (1994): 903–910; Robert Dahl, *Democracy and Its Critics* (New Haven: Yale University Press, 1989); Larry Diamond and Gary Marks, eds., "Comparative Perspectives on Democracy: Essays in Honor of Seymour Martin Lipset," special issue of *American Behavioral Scientist* 35 (1992); Giuseppe Di Palma, *To Craft Democracies: An Essay on Democratic Transitions* (Berkeley: University of California Press, 1990); Eva Etzioni-Halevy, *The Elite Connection: Problems and Potential of Western Democracy* (Cambridge: Polity Press, 1993); Steven M. Fish, *Democracy from Scratch: Opposition and Regime in the New Russian Revolution* (Princeton: Princeton University Press, 1995); David Held, *Models of Democracy* (Stanford: Stanford University Press, 1987); Alex Inkeles, ed., *On Measuring Democracy, Its Consequences and Concomitants* (New Brunswick: Transaction, 1991); Alberto Melucci, "Liberation or Meaning? Social Movements, Culture and Democracy," *Development and Change* 23 (1992): 43–77; Edward N. Muller and Mitchell A. Seligson, "Civic Culture and Democracy: The Question of Causal Relationships," *American Political Science Review* 88 (1994): 635–652; Guillermo O'Donnell and Phillippe C. Schmitter, *Transitions from Authoritarian Rule: Prospects for Democracy* (Baltimore: The Johns Hopkins University Press, 1986); Robert D. Putnam, *Making Democracy Work: Civic Traditions in Modern Italy* (Princeton: Princeton University Press, 1993); Dietrich Rueschemeyer, Evelyne Huber Stephens, and John D. Stephens, *Capitalist Development and Democracy* (Chicago: University of Chicago Press, 1992); and Philippe C. Schmitter and Terry Lynn Karl, "What Democracy Is . . . and Is Not," *Journal of Democracy* 2 (1991): 77–88.

15. Charles Tilly, "Democracy Is a Lake," in ed. George Reid Andrews and Herrick Chapman, *The Social Construction of Democracy* (New York: New York University Press, 1995).

16. Charles Tilly, "Globalization Threatens Labor's Rights," *International Labor and Working Class History* 47 (1995): 1–23.

17. Walker Connor, "Ethnonationalism," in ed. Myron Weiner and Samuel P. Huntington, *Understanding Political Development* (Boston: Little, Brown, 1987); Karl Deutsch, *Nationalism and Social Communication* (Cambridge, Mass.: MIT Press, 1966); Donald Horowitz, *Ethnic Groups in Conflict* (Berkeley: University of California Press, 1985); and Anthony D. Smith, *The Ethnic Revival* (Cambridge: Cambridge University Press, 1981).

18. John A. Armstrong, *Nations Before Nationalism* (Chapel Hill: University of North Carolina Press, 1982); Benedict Anderson, *Imagined Communities: Reflections on the Origin and Spread of Nationalism* (London: Verso, 1991); Ernest Gellner, *Nations and Nationalism* (Ithaca: Cornell University Press, 1983); Liah Greenfeld, *Nationalism: Five Roads to*

Modernity (Cambridge, Mass.: Harvard University Press, 1992); and Miroslav Hroch, *Social Preconditions of National Revival in Europe: A Comparative Analysis of the Social Composition of Patriotic Groups Among the Smaller European Nations* (Cambridge: Cambridge University Press, 1985).

19. E. J. Hobsbawm, *Nations and Nationalism Since 1789: Programme, Myth, Reality* (Cambridge: Cambridge University Press, 1990); and Charles Tilly "States and Nationalism in Europe 1492–1992," *Theory and Society* 23 (1994): 131–146.

2

THE END OF EMPIRES

E. J. HOBSBAWM

In the twentieth century more empires have ended than in any other; we know this, even though it is by no means clear what we mean by this statement. Like Walter Bagehot's "nation," our "empire" is recognizable even when we can't define it. The empires that have collapsed, or have been liquidated, in our century belong to several types; they seem to have little in common except that in them some outlying region or regions are ruled from a more or less remote center which is not believed to represent the interests of their inhabitants or local rulers. Even then the distinction is by no means clear. The rhetoric of separatist nationalism tends to define the situation of its constituency as "internal colonialism." Perhaps not very convincingly, but in principle, the situation of Wales vis-à-vis London is more dependent than that of Kazakhstan vis-à-vis Moscow in the Soviet era. (And how are we to classify former colonies which have been administratively integrated into the center? Puerto Rico and Martinique are almost certainly better off in their present status than they would be if they had cut all links with France and the United States, which they probably could do.) Is the relationship between London and Northern Ireland "imperial" in any sense which differs from, say, the relationship between New Delhi and some Indian state in which the president's rule has been imposed? However, I don't think these definitional obscurities need to get in our way when we actually discuss our subject. Nor have they.

The fallen empires of our century are of several types: (1) the colonial empires of the imperialist period; (2) the traditional empires of the region of European international politics; (3) the USSR, which both belongs and does not belong to my class 2; and (4) the traditional, and sometimes very ancient, empires of Asia— namely the pre-communist Chinese empire and the modern version of the Persian empire.

Our papers have dealt exclusively with groups 2 and 3, though from them the German empire, twice fallen in the century, has been omitted and may be treated as a special case. It may also be reasonable to omit pre-communist China and pre-Islamic Iran. However, in purely quantitative terms, the fall of the colonial empires of the imperialist period is much the largest phenomenon of its kind. The fall of the Ottoman, Habsburg and Russian empires (tsarist and Bolshevik) generated about thirty new states in all; the fall of the colonial empires generated three times as many. It would therefore have to be considered, if only for comparative purposes.

I would prefer to say nothing about the *causes* of the fall of empires; the broken empires of our century have too little in common in this respect. One can reasonably place Ottomans, Habsburgs, and Romanovs into the same pigeonhole; all were obsolescent political entities in an era of nation-state building, to which they offered no alternative. All were weak (relative to their official size and resources) and therefore endangered players in the international power game. All were regarded as doomed, or at least as on the slide, for many decades before they actually fell. On the other hand, tsarist Russia and the USSR cannot be so easily equated. Although World War I broke the back of the Habsburg, Romanov, and Ottoman empires, the October Revolution actually reconstituted the tsarist empire on a new basis—i.e., it provided exactly what the old empires had failed to do, namely an "un-national" (the word was applied to the USSR in C. A. Macartney's *National States and National Minorities*, a Chatham House publication of 1934) alternative to the nation-state. The causes of the USSR's collapse are quite different from those of the Romanov empire. Its internal tensions were quite different, and so was its situation in the world and the international situation in which it disintegrated. And, by the way, it had not been seriously expected or predicted, even by those who regarded its system as increasingly inviable. In short, there is not much in common between the fall of the pre-1914 empires and imperialist colonial empires. To find a common cause or set of causes for all of these would require us to operate on a level of generalization or abstraction that would virtually bypass or eliminate concrete historical analysis, and I can't find much interest in a comparative study of different causes.

On the other hand, a comparative study of *consequences* strikes me as much more useful. Here the distinction between the colonial-imperialist empires and the others is instructive. With the single exception of Portugal, the break-up of the imperialist empires had no political effect on the metropoles. This is so even in Italy and Japan, the states which lost their colonial empires as a consequence of total defeat in World War II. They went on as before, except insofar as they were transformed by their dependencies. They were, in fact, states whose basic structure or infrastructure was sufficiently firm to survive major internal or external shocks. Moreover, as rich and advanced countries of the developed world, the ex-metropoles often retained political, moral, and economic influence in their

former dependencies. Neither of these depended essentially on the political control exercised by the metropole. This may explain the puzzling phenomenon of Britain, where one might have expected the loss of an empire that covered one quarter of the globe to have left more of a political scar than it did. The country simply did not believe for a very long time—probably not until the 1970s—that the end of the empire had fundamentally undermined its international position as a world power.

There were only three ways in which the loss of an *external* empire such as a colonial one could impinge directly on metropolitan politics. First, through its impact on the armed forces, where these had tried to resist colonial liberation. This was plainly the case in France and Portugal, in both of which army coups were attempted or achieved, though under very different political colors. Yet what is even more striking is how soon, in both countries, the army returned to the barracks, and the unchallenged supremacy of a functioning constitutional civilian government was restored. In both countries the army simply ceased, once again, to be an independent factor in politics. Again, in Britain where the army has waged a very frustrating sub-war in Northern Ireland for a quarter of a century, there has been so far no signs of military politicking, though perhaps some signs of political dissidence among the undergrowth of the intelligence services.

Second, the loss of empire had its effect through the impact of the mass repatriation of citizens or others from the former colony to the metropolis—e.g., groups of refugees and emigres such as the Algerian *pieds-noirs*. This has clearly had a long-term effect—for instance, in France, by strengthening xenophobia and right-wing extremism. But, once again, the direct impact does not seem to have been dramatic in the short run, certainly much less than, say, the impact of the mass immigration, first of refugee Oriental Jews, later of Soviet Jews, on Israeli politics.

Third, it had its effect on the former center through the reverse phenomenon, namely the mass immigration of former natives of the colonies. Once again, this had surprisingly little impact—perhaps more in the Netherlands than elsewhere—but in the longer run it certainly helped restrictive and xenophobic policies to triumph in the receiving countries. And yet, we must ask ourselves whether the fact that, in formerly imperial countries, these immigrants came so often from the metropole's former colonies—from the Maghreb to France, from South Asia and the Caribbean to Britain—is not trivial. It was the size of the immigration of workers from poor and backward regions to rich European countries that created the tensions, whether or not they came from the country's own former colonies. Canada, Australia, and the United States (at least before Proposition 187) form an exceptional group of countries that have so far not seriously restricted Third World immigration.

Neither the pre-1914 empires nor the USSR drew the sharp imperialist distinction between metropoles and dependencies. The end of empire thus had to disrupt the basic state structure, if only by dividing a single state into several, and a single non-national multiethnic entity into a number of notionally "national,"

but in fact equally multiethnic, states. It also revolutionized their political systems, substituting nominally liberal democracies generally lacking adequate roots for monarchies or communist states. Equally important, it broke what had been the web of internal relations within a single state into incoherent fragments. In the case of the USSR, which had developed as a planned all-union economy with an all-union division of labor, the immediate results were particularly disastrous, leaving—to take one example—Lithuania with the plant capacity to produce 90 percent of the USSR's light bulbs, but cut off from its old markets. However, lesser problems were traumatic enough. The fall of the Habsburgs automatically turned the 25 percent of the Viennese population born outside the frontiers of the new Austria into foreigners, unless they chose to opt for citizenship. I don't think this aspect of the end of empires has been quite sufficiently taken account of in our discussions.

The consequences of the end of the empire for the former imperialist colonies were, almost without exception, even more dramatic than for the center, except where they involved the formal independence of mainly white settler countries, which had already become virtually independent—e.g., the British "dominions"—and where the mass of settlers did not coexist with a majority, or a large bloc, of indigenous inhabitants. Most of the imperialist dependencies consisted not of established states conquered by the Europeans, but of territories to which only the new imperial administration had given structure and definition. Their borders, their existence as administrative units, their political identity, indeed often the language of their politics and administration, were given to them through their colonial status. They possessed no political elites or potential cadres of government other than those created during and by the colonial era; and insofar as they had such elites here and there, the new leaders of the independent states rejected them, for reasons into which we need not go. The last thing the new Ghana or the new India wanted was indirect government via Ashanti elites or princely states. With rare exceptions, such as the Indian succession states, the post-colonial states started with nothing except their borders. Hence the obvious contradiction between their formal constitutions and political models—inherited from the metropoles or inspired by revolution—and their political realities. Hence also their tendency to drift into military government, which is striking, even in the would-be communist states, whose political essence since 1917 has been the rigid subordination of armed forces to party.

Here the comparison with the end of the old European empires is instructive. Where these had obvious inheritors, often with an available infrastructure of government and administration, the transition was simple, as in most of the Habsburg succession states. The major problem was whether and how to unify and standardize the institutions of the new states composed of units with very different provenance, e.g., Serbia, ex-Austrian Slovenia, and ex-Hungarian Croatia, or a Poland with a triple administrative and legal heritage. Compared to the post-colonialist entities, not many states were set up without any historic precedent, i.e., governmental continuity—for instance, presumably, but I don't know,

3

THINKING ABOUT EMPIRE

ALEXANDER J. MOTYL

Common sense tells us that empires rise and fall. We know that the Roman, Habsburg, Ottoman, and Romanov realms were called empires, and we know—from history or, more precisely, from historians—that they had temporally identifiable beginnings and ends. Not surprisingly, we conclude that the history of entities called empires must hold the explanatory key to the rise and fall of empires.

The intuition is correct, but only up to a point. It is of course trivially true that historical knowledge about self-styled empires is indispensable to theorizing about empires.[1] But, as the case of the Soviet Union shows, empires in name are not all there is to empire. For if we may, as we in fact do, term the USSR an empire, even though its leaders never called it that, then, surely, we are equally entitled to go against the terminological preferences of self-styled emperors and insist that their realms really may *not* have been empires.[2]

Coming to grips with the rise and fall of empires as a class of objects with certain properties must also involve something so obvious—and so obviously tedious for most historians—as a conceptual analysis.[3] Only after the concept of empire (as well as of rise and fall, but that is a subject for another essay) has been delineated and defined, with respect to its semantic field and in terms of history, experience, knowledge, intuition, and the like, is an empirical inquiry appropriate. On its own, historical investigation, no matter how rich, detailed, and nuanced, is powerless either to explain why empires rise and fall or even to identify the class of entities that rise and fall. After all, induction, like deduction, presupposes the ability to distinguish ravens from non-ravens and black from non-black.

This argument does not dispute the ontological reality of historical events, but it does assume that they are knowable only through the mediation of our own language and concepts.[4] It may thus be interesting to ask why and how historical subjects perceived their reality as they did, but it is manifestly impossible—*pace* Leopold von Ranke's aspirations—for us to recreate or experience it.[5] The work of Robert Darnton shows that a sense of bewilderment inevitably accompanies our confrontation with historical actors.[6] We may study their language, their texts, and their opinions, but we can never break out of our own hermeneutic circle and enter theirs. More important, if we could pull off such a trick, our understanding of history would actually be impaired. As Arthur Danto has persuasively argued, the conceptual distance imposed upon us by the passage of time makes history possible.[7] It is precisely *because* our perspective is rooted in the future that we can comprehend the past, and not merely chronicle past events.

What Empire Might Be

Let us begin the conceptual analysis of empire by unpacking what may be its two least unacceptable defining characteristics.[8] Most scholars would probably agree that every empire consists of something called a core and something called a periphery.[9] And most might agree that both core and periphery, whatever they are, are situated in geographically bounded spaces inhabited by culturally differentiated elites and populations.[10] By "culturally differentiated" I mean that core elites and populations share certain cultural characteristics and are different, with respect to these characteristics, from their counterparts in the periphery. It matters not whether these characteristics are physically real or merely imagined.

If cores are situated in bounded spaces, what, then, is situated inside cores? A sensible answer, and for two reasons, is *organizations*, and not, as one might expect, institutions. One reason is that such a notion of core echoes Max Weber's classic definition of the state, and empires *are* states. Another is that, thanks to the "new institutionalists," institution has come to mean virtually everything under the sun, thereby becoming almost useless as a concept.[11]

The organizations that constitute a core must, I suggest, be (1) political, economic, and sociocultural (multidimensional); (2) located in a bounded geographic space (territorially concentrated); (3) supportive of one another (mutually reinforcing); and (4) endowed with significant decisionmaking authority (centralized). In sum, a core is a multidimensional set of territorially concentrated and mutually reinforcing organizations exercising highly centralized authority in a state. In contrast to cores, peripheries are the territorially bounded administrative outposts of central organizations. While there can only be one core in an empire, there must be at least two peripheries for empires to be distinguishable from bifurcated states, such as the former Czechoslovakia.

Not surprisingly, the relationship of core to core elite is already implicit in the two concepts. Thus, we expect core elites to run core organizations. By the same logic, peripheral elites run peripheral organizations. The running of core organizations manifests itself in a variety of ways, some typical of nonimperial states and some peculiar to empires. We expect core elites, like all state elites, to craft foreign and defense policy, print the currency, and control borders. But imperial elites must also have other prerogatives to be worthy of the modifier. They direct the finances of peripheries; they appoint peripheral governors or prefects; and they are not accountable to the periphery, which, in turn, has no legal basis for influencing the appointment of core officials and the choice of core policies. While the relationship of core elite to peripheral elite must therefore be termed dictatorial, that of core elite to core population and of peripheral elite to peripheral population is indeterminate.[12] I emphasize that this understanding of empire, in its exclusive emphasis on the core-periphery relationship, has nothing specific to say about the regime either of the core polity or of the peripheral polity.

While a species both of multinational state and of dictatorship, an empire is not merely a dictatorial multinational state, but a peculiar kind of dictatorial multinational state. Figure 3.1 situates the concept of empire within a family of related polities. Ethnoterritorial federations, such as Canada, former socialist Yugoslavia, and post-Soviet Russia, have culturally distinct administrative units, but no core institutions. Such multinational dictatorial states as Franco Spain and Saddam Hussein's Iraq have cores, but lack culturally bounded administrative units. Multinational nondictatorial states and territorial federations such as the United States and Switzerland possess neither cores nor distinct cultural subunits. In empires, meanwhile, territorially bounded cores and peripheries are coterminous with culturally distinct administrative units. More than a simple dictatorial multinational state, an empire is a highly centralized, territorially segmented, and culturally differentiated state within which centralization, segmentation, and differentiation overlap.[13]

Although I am certain that this definition, like all definitions, will not meet with universal acclaim, I am equally certain that it makes some sense conceptually and even fits the facts historically. Because the Persian, Roman, early Byzan-

		Core	
		Present	Absent
Administrative units	Culturally distinct	Empire	Ethnoterritorial federation
	Nondistinct	Multinational dictatorial state	Multinational nondictatorial state; territorial federation

FIGURE 3.1   Types of Multinational States

tine, Mongol, Ottoman, Habsburg, Romanov, French, British, and Soviet polities possessed the defining characteristics of empire, we are justified in saying that they were indeed empires. In each, the organizations clustered in a culturally distinct region usually centered on a capital city and its hinterland exercised direct control over the finances and elites of the rest of the empire.

Fully appreciative of the historian's delight in historical richness, we are not surprised that the degree of cultural distinctiveness, like the degree of control, varied, that all real empires only approximated the definitional ideal type. The Ottomans of Constantinople, Rumelia, and Anatolia shared Islam with most imperial elites; ethnic Germans formed a sizeable portion of tsarist Russia's ruling elite; after 1867, Habsburg control over Hungary declined in a manner reflective of the dynamics of "imperial decay";[14] all elites shared a Soviet Russian culture in Leonid Brezhnev's USSR, while republican elites enjoyed a fair degree of genuine autonomy.

Unwilling to reify historical richness and the representations, signs, and names that constitute it, however, we are equally unsurprised by the fact that parts of empires may be definitionally imperial, while others may not, and that, hence, the same territory, with the same core state, may or may not be termed an empire at various times in history, regardless of what it is officially called and how it emerged. Accordingly, it would be illogical to call Byzantium an empire on the eve of Constantinople's seizure by the Ottomans in 1453, or fail to recognize that Moscow's relationship with the USSR's East European satellites was no less imperial than its relations with the non-Russian republics.

How Empires Rise

As a mental category that serves only to distinguish one class of objects from other classes of objects, the concept of empire says nothing about the causes or consequences of imperial rise or imperial fall.[15] To smuggle an explanation into the concept of empire is a sleight of hand that conveniently proposes unsubstantiated theories as definitions and typically results in claims that something cannot be an empire if it is not the product of imperialism or the cause of exploitation.[16] But once the definition of empire is cleansed of hidden causes and effects, the question of how and why empires rise and fall leads to illuminating answers quite different from those generally encountered in the literature.

For the sake of simplicity, let us pare the concept of empire of most of its complicating baggage and, in light of the just completed definitional exercise, focus only on three defining characteristics: (1) a distinct core elite and a distinct peripheral elite; (2) a distinct core population and a distinct peripheral population; and (3) a dictatorial relationship between the core elite and the peripheral elite.

This list suggests a simple procedure for identifying how—but not *why*— empires rise and fall. As these three defining characteristics "make" an empire, anytime they come together in some political entity, regardless of its past or future, we can, in the spirit of the conceptually inspired inductivism of this essay, confidently assert that an empire has emerged. And anytime any entity with these three characteristics loses all or any of them, then we can just as confidently claim that an empire has disappeared. There is no reason why, logically, all three characteristics cannot come together or fall away simultaneously—in which case utterly new entities may be said to have emerged or disappeared. There is also no reason why only one or two of these characteristics cannot appear or disappear for the entities possessing them to gain or lose the status of empire.

Consider the implications of these observations. We generally assume that empires come into existence only as a result of the extension of core control over some potential periphery. Naturally, a core elite can extend its power into territories with already existing distinct elites and populations via military campaigns, wars, and subsequent conquest and thus engage in straightforward imperialism. History is rife with examples of just this sort of military expansionism and of the empires to which it frequently gave rise. Rome may be the classic example.

But military conquest surely is not the only manner in which core elites can expand the scope of their sovereignty. History offers just as many examples of dynastic unions between powerful and weak monarchs resulting in the incorporation of the latters' realms on imperial terms. The rise of the Habsburg empire and the emergence of the Polish-Lithuanian Commonwealth are two such cases. There is also no reason why, logically, "ready-made" peripheries cannot be bought or otherwise acquired, perhaps by thievery or stealth—as was Bosnia in 1908 by the Habsburgs, in clear violation of the resolutions of the Congress of Berlin.

The above examples concern only the third defining characteristic of empire, the dictatorial relationship between a core elite and a peripheral elite. But empires can also emerge if the other two characteristics involving distinct elites and distinct populations undergo change. Logically, there is no reason why nondictatorial states with distinct elites and distinct populations should not be termed empires if they become dictatorial or why dictatorial states cannot be transformed into empires by virtue of the emergence of territorially bounded distinct elites and/or territorially bounded distinct populations.

In the first instance, empire would be the product of an ethnoterritorial federation's development of, as Figure 3.1 suggests, dictatorial relations between its units. In the second and third instances, empire would result from a multinational dictatorial state's development of culturally distinct administrative units. All three developments could also take place more or less simultaneously, if multinational nondictatorial states were to develop culturally distinct administrative units and cores for any number of internally specific political, social, or economic reasons.

Post-Soviet Russia may soon be an example of the first possibility. At present, the Russian state occupies the second quadrant of Figure 3.1. As an ethnoterritorial federation, it has culturally distinct administrative units—the various republics—populated by distinct populations and run by distinct elites. Inasmuch as Moscow's relationship with these units is democratic at best and chaotic at worst, it cannot be deemed imperial. If current trends continue, however, that judgement may have to change. Boris Yeltsin has already abandoned many of the policies that contributed to his early democratic reputation; reactionary forces, on the left and on the right, are not insignificant; and "men on horseback" lurk in the wings. Should democratization be abandoned, de facto if not de jure, and should Moscow's relations with the provinces then become dictatorial, the Russian Federation will have become, and rightly be deemed, an empire.

The USSR illustrates the second tendency, how an empire might emerge after a dictatorial state acquires distinct peripheral elites and populations. In creating the Union of Soviet Socialist Republics, the Bolsheviks purposefully transformed revolutionary Russia's simple dictatorship over its newly acquired territories into a complex web of imperial relationships premised on non-Russian administration of symbolically sovereign republics inhabited by distinct non-Russian populations. As politics is at the core of my definition of empire, the fact that many of the republics underwent modernization and that Russia paid a high price economically for its political dominance does not detract from the imperial nature of the Soviet state.

Showing how empires emerge—via expansion and the four possible moves suggested by Figure 3.1—cannot explain their emergence, but, it does underscore the magnitude of the explanatory task, suggest the kinds of theoretical questions that should be asked, and imply what the future of empire may be.

First of all, it is probably safe to say that a nontrivial theory of imperial emergence, one that explains all five patterns, will be, at best, immensely difficult to formulate. Indeed, a universal theory may be logically impossible, inasmuch as the explanada involved are quite different. Although the defining characteristics of empire do provide for identical initial conditions, the explanatory task seems either to require very different covering laws or to imply very different causes or combinations of necessary and sufficient conditions. Probabilistic accounts would be afflicted with the same problems.[17]

While a "theory of everything" may therefore be beyond our grasp, there is no reason why more focused theoretical enterprises, such as providing plausible accounts of imperial emergence via territorial expansion, regime change, elite formation, and societal transformation, should not be possible. Indeed, there already exist rich social science and historical literatures on all of these issues. Peripheries, for example, may form as a result of modernization, education, uneven development, and the subsequent emergence of excluded ethnic entrepreneurs and "internal colonies."[18] The task before students of empire is to apply these insights, with the appropriate modifications, to imperial settings.

Finally, by having identified acquisition, union, war, dictatorial regimes, social differentiation, and excluded elites as possible sources of empire, we are in a position to speculate, more or less knowledgeably, about the likelihood that empires will continue to arise even in a "post-imperial" age. Somewhat unexpectedly perhaps, the picture is mixed.

Despite some fluctuations, most of the international sources of empire have declined in importance over the last two centuries. Land purchases became virtually impossible after the division of the world into a seamless web of states, and dynastic unions became irrelevant with the introduction of effectively non-monarchical regimes in all states. In contrast, war is still a going concern, even though some scholars question its utility.[19] Less questionable, perhaps, is that one of the traditional goals of war, extensive territorial expansion, has become significantly more difficult to attain and sustain.

Two formidable obstacles stand in the way. Because modern states serve as the international system's organizing principle, the inviolability of state boundaries is a generally accepted international norm and even "failed states" are usually preferred to territorial division. To be sure, norms do get violated and the reconfiguration of states does occur, but, as the fall of the USSR and Yugoslavia suggests, usually as a last resort. In any case, if and when aggressors threaten security and regional stability, great-power intervention or geopolitical balancing generally suffices to stifle or keep expansion within reasonable limits. In sum, the reduction in opportunities for, and the growth of disincentives to, traditional imperialism suggest that empires are unlikely to emerge in this manner in the foreseeable future.

But recall that there are two other ways for empires to come into being. There is, first, no reason to think that existing non-dictatorial systems will never break down and become dictatorial and that all transitions to democracy will succeed. Quite the contrary, we know from history, from the extensive literature on democratic breakdowns, and from the transparent teleology of the concept of transition that democracies do end and that democratization can fail.[20]

The second internal source of empire, differentiation, is even more likely in the near future. All that modernization is supposed to entail—industrialization, education, urbanization, and so on—not only occurs unevenly, thus creating pockets, if not whole areas, of backward development, but also leads to social differentiation and elite frustration. And if, as the history of modernization leads us inductively to expect, these continue to breed ethnic assertiveness, regional patriotism, and communal identities, then the probability that distinct elites and populations, unsuccessful separatist movements, nondemocratic relations between cores and peripheries, and thus empires will emerge should remain correspondingly high.

These remarks do not constitute a theory of imperial emergence, but they do suggest that, although the sources of empire have undergone a shift in the last century or so, the emergence of empire is, *ceteris paribus*, unlikely to be affected in any substantive way. Although the international sources of empire may have declined in importance, the internal sources are not only present, but, arguably, have assumed greater salience. And because empires can emerge silently—without noisy campaigns or bombastic proclamations of manifest destiny—they should continue to exist in everything but name for some time to come.

How Empires Fall

As the foregoing remarks intimated, the fall of empires can proceed along lines very similar to those of the rise of empires, involving both externally and internally generated processes that transform interstate relationships, regimes, societies, and elites. First on our list, although not necessarily primary in importance, are wars and national liberation struggles, both of which can produce long-term processes of decline by attrition, as in the case of the Ottomans, or complete and instantaneous collapse, as was true of the Romanovs, Habsburgs, and Soviets.[21] Inasmuch as liberation struggles are commonplace and war has hardly disappeared, both should continue to exert a corrosive influence on putative empires.

While dynastic divorces and family squabbles have contributed to the breakup or diminution of realms in the past, they are much less likely to do so now and in the future. After all, dynasties are out of fashion and, even if they were not, core elites would surely prevent peripheral elites from leaving an empire with their erstwhile realms in hand. In contrast, while parts of empires have been sold in the past—Louisiana and Alaska come to mind—there is reason to think that, if economic globalization truly diminishes the value of territorial holdings, such entrepreneurial practices may revive in the future.

Just as the emergence of a dictatorial relationship between core and periphery can transform an ethnoterritorial federation into an empire, so, too, the demise of such a relationship can transform an empire into an ethnoterritorial federation. Although I prefer to characterize Vienna's post-1867 relations with Budapest as an example of imperial decay, it is admittedly possible to claim that a qualitative change had taken place after the *Ausgleich* and that, with Budapest's acquisition of approximate political parity, the late Habsburg empire ceased being fully imperial across much of its territory.[22]

Similar reasoning holds for the other entities populating Figure 3.1. If peripheral or core populations or elites lose their distinctiveness, or if regime change accompanies population and elite shifts, then empires cease to exist. In the middle of the nineteenth century, for instance, when Ukraine's formerly distinct Cossack elite had disappeared and its population seemed to be only a Little Russian variant of the Great Russian people, "imperial" cannot be the best modifier for the Russo-Ukrainian relationship.

As with the silent emergence of empires, such internal realignments can occur as the result of economic development, demographic movement, and the resultant intermixing and assimilation of ethnic groups.[23] In addition, the actions of core elites—such as forcible assimilation, population resettlement, and ethnic cleansing—can play, and historically have played, a major role in promoting, in effect if not in intent, the transformation of imperial peripheries into mere regions of dictatorial multinational states.[24] The Soviet Union provides examples of each of these policies. Thus, non-Russians were subjected to varying degrees of cultural and linguistic Russification; Russians were settled throughout all the republics; and Volga Germans, Crimean Tatars, Koreans, Chechens, and Ingush were effectively cleansed from their homelands. Not surprisingly, the creation of national states in Western Europe, or for that matter in North America, would also be inexplicable without reference to equally brutal actions aimed at eradicating core-periphery distinctions.

The Future of Empire

As with the rise of empire, identifying the forms of imperial decline does not amount to an explanation, but it does suggest that a unified theory explaining so many different hypotheses is probably impossible, that theories accounting for particular forms of decline are perfectly possible and, indeed, may already exist in the social science literature, and that educated guesses about the future sustainability of empire can be made.

As there is no reason to repeat my remarks about the first two points, let us proceed directly to an evaluation of the forces working for and against empire, now and in the future. I start with the observation that, by and large, the same factors that can bring empire into existence can also end it. While seemingly banal, this proposition does have one important implication. If other things are held equal, we have no grounds for claiming, finally and conclusively, that empire is no longer possible. Scholars and policymakers who speak of the passing of the "age of empires" may be premature in their judgement.

But, as we saw, other things are not equal. One important difference was that, wilfully or not, the core elites of empires have frequently pursued policies—such as assimilation, resettlement, and genocide—aimed at ending the core-periphery distinction. That contemporary elites have been especially prone to act in this manner may mean that empire is an inefficient organizational system,[25] and that modern administration proceeds more smoothly if populations speak the same language and if local elites lose their collective character and are absorbed into the state as individuals, and not as groups.[26] Inasmuch as assimilation presumably furthers the effective administration of empire, modern core elites would seem to have a direct, if perhaps unwitting, interest in the demise of the very empires they rule.

Do these arguments spell the end of empire? For better or for worse, the answer is "no." Although the logic of the modern bureaucratic state may be incompatible with that of empire, it does not follow that state elites actually have the capacity, wherewithal, or skills either to eliminate empire or to do so in a manner that will not aggravate core-periphery relations or even create core-periphery distinctions. The literature on the crisis of the state in general and of the national state in particular provides ample grounds for paying heed to the limitations on elites. This caveat is of particular relevance today, when the language of human rights and self-determination dominates international discourse, when identity may have become the key criterion of political loyalty, and when state attempts to deal with ethnic diversity are almost invariably represented as encroachments on cultural authenticity and thus become inducements to ethnic mobilization. Where do these remarks leave us? On the one hand, somewhat less uncertain about the rise and fall of empire. On the other hand, quite certain that the forces promoting the silent emergence of empires and the incapacity of modern states to cope with an increasingly assertive multinationality could even work in favor of empire. Terminological conventions and political niceties may dictate that such entities not be called empires, but, by meeting not unreasonable definitional requirements, they will be just that. Ironically, although imperialism may belong to the past, empire may belong to the future.

Notes

1. See Arthur L. Stinchcombe, *Theoretical Methods in Social History* (New York: Academic Press, 1978).

2. For an excellent discussion of these conceptual issues, see John Wilson, *Thinking with Concepts* (Cambridge: Cambridge University Press, 1963).

3. Much of my thinking about concepts has been influenced by Giovanni Sartori, *Social Science Concepts* (Beverly Hills: Sage, 1984), 15–85.

4. See Karl R. Popper, *The Poverty of Historicism* (New York: Harper Torchbooks, 1964), 135.

5. Von Ranke's famous dictum was, of course, that history should be written "wie es eigentlich gewesen sei."

6. See, for instance, Robert Darnton, *The Great Cat Massacre and Other Episodes in French Cultural History* (New York: Basic Books, 1984).

7. Arthur Danto, *Narration and Knowledge* (New York: Columbia University Press, 1985).

8. This section draws on Alexander J. Motyl, "After Empire: Competing Discourses and Interstate Conflict in Postimperial Eastern Europe," in ed. Barnett Rubin and Jack Snyder, *Political Order in the Former Soviet Republics*, forthcoming.

9. See Jean Gottmann, ed., *Centre and Periphery: Spatial Variation in Politics* (Beverly Hills: Sage, 1980).

10. I employ the concept of culture developed in Clifford Geertz, *The Interpretation of Cultures* (New York: Basic Books, 1973).

11. For a striking example of how broadly—and uselessly?—the concept is used, see Douglass North, *Institutions, Institutional Change and Economic Performance* (Cambridge: Cambridge University Press, 1990).

12. I discuss this relationship in "From Imperial Decay to Imperial Collapse: The Fall of the Soviet Empire in Comparative Perspective," in ed. Richard L. Rudolph and David F. Good, *Nationalism and Empire* (New York: St. Martin's, 1992), 15–43.

13. This definition clearly resonates with Michael Doyle's: "Empire . . . is a relationship, formal or informal, in which one state controls the effective political sovereignty of another political society" (*Empires* [Ithaca: Cornell University Press, 1986], 45).

14. On imperial decay, see Motyl, "From Imperial Decay," pp. 17–24.

15. Recall that definitions are semantically equivalent statements of the "A is B" variety, whereby any sentence containing concept A could be written with concept B, and vice versa, without any change in meaning. In contrast, explanations are roughly of the "If X, then Y" form and posit some kind of causal connection between X and Y. The resulting error can be written as "A is (If X, then Y)" or "(If X, then Y) is B."

16. For a related critique of the concept of revolution, see Alexander J. Motyl, "Concepts and Skocpol: Ambiguity and Vagueness in the Study of Revolutions," *Journal of Theoretical Politics* 4, no. 1 (1992): 93–112.

17. See David-Hillel Ruben, ed., *Explanation* (Oxford: Oxford University Press, 1993); Ernest Sosa and Michael Tooley, eds., *Causation* (Oxford: Oxford University Press, 1993); and Merrillee H. Salmon, "Explanation in the Social Sciences," in ed. Philip Kitcher and Wesley C. Salmon, *Scientific Explanation* (Minneapolis: University of Minnesota Press, 1989), 384–409.

18. Michael Hechter, *Internal Colonialism* (Berkeley: University of California Press, 1977).

19. John Mueller makes this case in *Retreat from Doomsday: The Obsolescence of Major War* (New York: Basic Books, 1989).

20. In particular, see Juan J. Linz, *The Breakdown of Democratic Regimes: Crisis, Breakdown, and Reequilibration* (Baltimore: The Johns Hopkins University Press, 1978).

21. For a discussion of attrition and collapse, see Alexander J. Motyl, "Imperial Collapse and Revolutionary Change," in ed. Juergen Nautz and Richard Vahrenkamp, *Die Wiener Jahrhundertwende* (Vienna: Boehlau, 1993), 813–819. See also Rein Taagepera, "Patterns of Empire Growth and Decline: Context for Russia," unpublished paper, March 1995.

22. Alan Sked, *The Decline and Fall of the Habsburg Empire, 1815–1918* (London: Longman, 1989), 187–234.

23. The classic statement of this view is Karl W. Deutsch, *Nationalism and Social Communication* (Cambridge, Mass.: MIT Press, 1966).

24. R. D. Grillo, *Dominant Languages: Language and Hierarchy in Britain and France* (Cambridge: Cambridge University Press, 1989); Joshua Fishman, "Language Maintenance and Ethnicity," *Canadian Review of Studies in Nationalism* no. 2 (Fall 1981): 229–247.

25. This, essentially, is the argument of Robert Gilpin, *War and Change in World Politics* (Cambridge: Cambridge University Press, 1981); Douglass North and Robert Paul Thomas, *The Rise of the Western World* (Cambridge: Cambridge University Press, 1973); and Joseph Tainter, *The Collapse of Complex Societies* (Cambridge: Cambridge University Press, 1990).

26. Ernest Gellner, *Nations and Nationalism* (Ithaca: Cornell University Press, 1987).

4

THE OTTOMAN EMPIRE

CAGLAR KEYDER

Accounts of the decline and fall of the Ottoman Empire vie on an ideological battlefield, with political commitments largely determining the reasons one offers for the collapse. As the dominant versions of history written since the end of the Great War have consciously or unwittingly adopted the perspective of the nation state, the collapse of the empire has often been viewed as the inevitable fulfillment of the destiny of a nation.[1] Now that the nation-state has itself lost favor, however, the search has turned to accounts outside the nationalist paradigm. One way of doing this is to abandon any effort to recount the story of state formation, and take refuge instead in the history of the subaltern;[2] another is to problematize the formation of nation states by exploring the alternatives at the moment of collapse of empires.[3] This last is the road I propose to take. What recommends it is a nostalgia for the "what-if" counterfactual or "optimists'" reading[4] of imperial history. From this viewpoint, a constitution providing universal and equal citizenship combined with ethnic and territorial autonomy might just have saved the empire and avoided the excesses of nationalism and of the nation-state. In the first part of this paper, I will show that there were two separate dynamics in the dissolution of the Ottoman Empire, the first a function of the patrimonial nature of the state; and the second of national separatism, due to the Empire's confrontation with European capitalism. These dynamics ultimately derived from social and political structure. In the second part of the paper I will discuss the final years before the World War, trying to show that some plausibility could be attached to the "optimist reading" in the counterfactual.

Dynamics of Dissolution

The two basic models used to understand the structural reasons for the decline of the Ottoman Empire cover most of the macrosociological alternatives for all empires. The first is the patrimonial-crisis model which assumes that the classical empire is basically agrarian, governed by a strong center that uses non-hereditary tax-collecting administrators to control peripheral areas. The crises that might arise within this model have to do with the potential centrifugal forces inherent in any peripheral administration: provincial officials may find it expedient to retain a portion of revenues for their own gain, possibly in alliance with local notables. An understanding between the functionary and the local notables then may well develop into an alliance that can mean the loss of a province and its revenue to the imperial center. Since the revenue-extracting potential of the imperial center is extensive rather than intensive, these losses translate into further weakening of the empire's ability to maintain its territories intact. Recentralization remains a possibility, however. In fact, the cyclical model of Chinese dynastic history hinges precisely on this possibility, whereby a previously wayward provincial governor becomes the progenitor of a new, strengthened dynastic center.

Ottoman history provides examples of both centrifugal breaks and one failed attempt at recentralization, which settled the second-best alternative of centrifugal success. Throughout the eighteenth century provincial notables (*ayan*) increased their autonomy vis-à-vis the imperial center. Some were originally tax collectors and governors, who subsequently became locally entrenched and involved in the economic and social life of the province. Some were local notables, mainly merchants, who gained sufficient economic weight and political standing to be able to force the palace to appoint them first as tax-farmers then as quasi-hereditary local governors. During this period of de facto devolution of power, the Ottoman sultans had to bargain and negotiate with these newly arisen notables in order to raise provincial armies and claim their share of the tax revenue.[5]

During the first decades of the nineteenth century, however, the Ottoman center embarked on a relatively successful recentralization project, at least in what might be considered the heartland of the empire—Anatolia and the near Balkans.[6] One province which totally avoided recentralization and achieved de facto separation was Egypt, a paradigmatic centrifugal case in which a late but very powerful *ayan* succeeded in converting his warlord status into a hereditary khedivate. Muhammad Ali, originally from Macedonia, had been appointed—in the true Ottoman tradition of sending bureaucrats to provinces where they would not be likely to establish local constituencies—to govern Egypt. He was soon able, however, to eliminate the tax-farming structure and to establish an independent administration; and subsequently to create a sufficient structure of interest around his rule. Thus he provides the perfect historical example of a successful dismantling of empire via the dynamics of patrimonial crisis.

That the Egyptian case belongs under the rubric of crisis dynamics of classical empires is also evidenced in the subsequent history of Muhammad Ali. In the typical fashion of a provincial official first establishing his independence from a weakened center, he then turned to the project of conquering the center in order to resume the patrimonial cycle with a new and strengthened dynasty. This was not, however, an isolated Chinese empire. The Ottoman Empire figured prominently in great-power balances, being the object of intense imperial rivalry; besides, it had already started its modernizing reforms when the confrontation occurred, and it was both pliable and promising as an arena for free-trade imperialism. As a result, bargains between Britain and Russia finally decided the pretender's fate.[7] Muhammad Ali's success in establishing autonomy and an Egyptian royalty could not be translated into founding a new Ottoman dynasty.

Ottoman recentralization during the first half of the nineteenth century coincided with the beginnings of administrative modernization. In other words, its success also heralded the advent of a new kind of rule characterized by the deployment of greater state strength based on an infrastructure of governance.[8] If successful, this modernization would bring the Ottoman entity closer to the centralized, territorial state model of Europe. In fact, the Tanzimat reforms, starting in 1839 and continuing through the century despite Abdulhamid's despotic style of rule, aimed precisely at achieving this goal.[9]

Success in the modernization of the state elicited different responses, however. While the ayans of Anatolia and the near Balkans were decisively defeated, permitting the gradual formation of unitary rule, the early nineteenth-century recentralization did not have much impact from the point of view of replacing the dominance of the local notables in the Arab provinces.[10] The notables of Damascus, Aleppo, Beirut, and Jerusalem continued to keep attempts by the Ottoman center to establish unitary rule at bay. They found the imperial framework acceptable as long as its demands remained limited to the exercise of limited sovereignty.

The story unfolded differently in most of the European possessions of the empire. The same global wave of commercialization and monetization in the eighteenth century that allowed provincial notables to accumulate economic power also created the preconditions for the rise of merchant groups, new urbanites, and an educated middle class, especially in the lands close to the European pole of growth.[11] It was this development which eventually brought about various nation-based movements intent on separation from the empire. In its European possessions Ottoman power could not be re-asserted; the course of devolution remained unreversed.

While the patrimonial model is situated in a timeless universe of imperial dynamics working out the internal balance of forces in isolation, the nationalist model of secession is premised on the confrontation between the empire, its precapitalist essence, and an expanding capitalist economy—a confrontation that leads, again, to imperial dismantlement. Given an agrarian patrimonial empire where the primary concern was to perpetuate a revenue system based on land tax, the classical Ottoman system did not look too kindly on the accumulation of wealth in private hands. A legal framework designed to uphold the ideological fiction of all land belonging to the sultan was the principal factor in this perpetuation. Thus, appropriation of land and mercantile accumulation remained uncertain propositions, easily reversed by a change in the strength or policy of a given ruler. This was not an environment where capitalism could flourish; and, in fact, "modernization" during the Tanzimat period aimed precisely at accommodating the incorporation of the empire into the capitalist logic of expanding Europe.

Before the reforms of the nineteenth century could take root, however, capitalist accumulation had already created its own autonomous space in most of the Balkans, thanks to the inability of the center to impose its precapitalist logic. In other words, differentiation and class formation had already gained momentum by the beginning of the nineteenth century. The economic dimension of this uneven development dates from the previous century, when the landlords who attained a degree of independence from the center were able to reinforce their autonomy through access to trading networks in Central Europe. Through the century these provinces became wealthier, new educated middle classes came into being, and their proximity to the European mainland accelerated their political development and nationalist aspirations. That most of these newly enriched groups in the Balkans were non-Muslim was a significant factor in attracting the protection, encouragement, and support of various European powers, who both helped prepare the political and intellectual case for nationalism, and provided crucial diplomatic and military assistance. This is the story of Greek, Serbian, and Bulgarian nationalisms.

In all these cases nationalism resulted from a mercantile-bourgeois impulse, and was a reaction to the slow pace of economic and political change in the core of the empire. These provinces increasingly came under the economic gravitational pull of the European market. Their merchants enjoyed the protection Austria, Russia, France, and Britain extended through the capitulatory regime,[12] and they found international support in their bid for independence. Political and legal reforms came too late and were too tentative to satisfy these demands. Had they been prompt and determined, would the nationalist dismantling have taken a different course? Political reform toward recognition of all imperial subjects as citizens with equal status might have gone a long way toward blunting nationalist sentiments, as well as permitting economic activity consonant with accumulation within the purview of the European economy. Furthermore, if political and legal change had occurred earlier, peripheral incorporation of the empire as a whole might have emerged as an attractive option, where a merchant bourgeoisie of Balkan extraction might have given its support to the project, with a view to attaining class domination in the empire as a whole. This situation would then have eliminated some of the political-economic factors leading to nationalist separatism.

Balkan nationalism culminated in a massive loss of territory following the 1877–78 war with Russia. The empire lost more than a third of its land, especially the provinces where its non-Muslim population had constituted the majority. Social and economic conditions shifted radically, as did the causes of the empire's dismantling. Two important dimensions of this difference have to be highlighted. First, the only significant non-Muslim populations remaining in the empire after 1878 were the Greeks and Armenians, who together constituted no more than one-fifth of the population.[13] There was no identifiable territory in the empire where either could claim a majority. Slightly more than half the Armenian population lived in eastern Anatolian provinces (but even here they were a minority);[14] the rest were divided between Cilicia and western Anatolia, including Istanbul. The Greek population lived mainly in western Anatolia, Istanbul, Thrace and Macedonia, but was also scattered in the interior and in Cappadocia. There was, in other words, no longer a geographical basis for separatism.

Second, the Tanzimat reforms had signalled a major transformation in the ancien regime, a political and legal change which began to define a modern environment of citizenship and accumulation-oriented economic activity. In this context it was possible to envisage a rapidly modernizing state with legal guarantees for individual citizens, religious freedom, and some ethnic autonomy. This vision was nurtured by the substantial economic growth that had taken place since the opening up of the empire to free trade in 1838. As the world economy expanded, trade served as the engine of transformation and commodification: centuries of low-level equilibrium in most of the Ottoman countryside yielded to technological change and growth. By the eve of the Great War one-fourth of the Empire's population lived in cities; the countryside was no longer a subsistence economy, and perhaps fifteen percent of the output of the economy went to exports.[15]

Unlike Egypt, neither Anatolian nor Syrian agriculture was based on large plantations owned in part by foreign investors. Instead the productive sphere was composed of small producers whose surpluses were appropriated by merchants, creditors, and other middlemen. Some of the successful petty commodity producers were Greeks and Armenians; but also belonging to these Christian groups was the overwhelming majority of intermediaries—those who oriented the producers towards market demand; who collected, financed, purchased and sold the surpluses; and who marketed and retailed imports coming from the opposite direction.[16] By the end of the nineteenth century, cities and towns in Anatolia and the Arab provinces were prospering, and population growth was especially high in the port cities.[17] In the empire as a whole, the share of prosperity accruing to the Christians was disproportionately large, but in Anatolia the situation was more polarized than elsewhere. In the burgeoning Anatolian cities, a Greek and Armenian middle class emerged that was wealthy and educated; active in defining an urban public space of associations, clubs and publications, and increasingly willing to participate in the administration of the provinces and the empire. For this nascent bourgeoisie, a separatist nationalism did not hold much attraction.

The circumstances that led to the emergence of a non-Muslim bourgeoisie and to the increasing disparity in income and consumption between it and the rest of the population made a reactive project originating in the palace effective at the popular level. Abdulhamid II, the last sultan to rule the empire, had disbanded Parliament in 1878, soon after the promulgation of the Constitution in

1876, and had gradually established an absolute rule distinguished by a despotic and paranoid style. Although the Constitution had been suspended, only to be reactivated in 1908, the break with the Tanzimat reforms was more in style than in content. The spirit of 1839 and 1856, bent on establishing a legal and administrative framework for a unitary empire, lived on.[18] An authoritarian liberalism characterized social and economic policies. The major reversal was in the political system: the long-awaited constitutional and parliamentary underpinning to the evolving system of rule of law was now frozen, earning for Abdulhamid the vilification of Europeans, and later the Young Turks. The vilification was, however, counterbalanced by his growing popularity among the Muslim population.

The composition of the First Ottoman Parliament of 1876 had been impressive in its diversity, perhaps unique in the history of multiethnic empires: out of 125 deputies 77 were Muslim, 44 Christian, and four Jewish.[19] Despite the closing of the Parliament non-Muslims continued to be well represented in the Ottoman administration, both in the central and provincial bureaucracy, and in the palace which gradually replaced the Porte as the real seat of power.[20] The higher schools which had started in Istanbul to educate military personnel and functionaries for the civil service grew in scope and started to attract students from all corners of the empire.[21] Education and careers were molding a unified imperial elite that reflected the multiethnic, multi-confessional composition of the population, while sharing a common perspective that came to be known as Ottomanism. Albanians, Macedonians, Greeks, Armenians, various Muslim groups from the Russian empire, Arabs from Baghdad, Syria and Palestine, Kurds, and Turks made up this elite. For the first time in its history, the empire appeared to be genuinely multiethnic.

There was a parallel story, however, unfolding at the popular level, that was considerably less benign. During the 1877–78 war, when the empire lost most of its remaining territory in Europe and in the Caucasus, close to a million Muslims had been uprooted and forced to emigrate—mostly to the secure heartland of Anatolia. This influx was of sufficiently huge proportions to radically change the ethnic balance, since the entire population of the area that later became Turkey was perhaps 10 to 12 million.[22] These people had also come from economically more advanced regions, with greater experience of markets and technology, and they were, on the whole, better educated than the Anatolian Muslims. They did not remain ethnically secluded: unions between immigrants from geographically distant provinces were common, as well as marriage into the indigenous population, especially in urban areas. An underappreciated dimension of the present-day population of Turkey is its ethnic mix: individuals from all the former Muslim provinces—now in Russia, the Caucasian Republics, and the Balkans—and from Turkish-speaking areas of the Tsarist empire have blended together with Anatolian populations, themselves of diverse origin, and become "Turkified." Except in the more egregious versions of ethnic discourse, therefore, the appellation "Turk" refers simply to assimilability under the Turkish language and Muslim religion.

Intermarriage between Christians and Muslims (except under duress) was rare, even when language was not a barrier, as, for example in the case of the Turkish-speaking Greek Orthodox population in the Anatolian interior. In the less fluid society that existed before the nineteenth century, populations lived in isolated villages or well-defined and segregated neighborhoods in cities, and differences in material or social conditions were not an issue. As ethnic groups came into contact through the accelerated pace of economic change and urbanization, the social schismosis also became apparent. Not only religious practice, but also schools and community organization, patterns of consumption and levels of Westernization, material culture and lifestyles increasingly diverged. Although it was by no means the entire Christian population that participated in the economic ascendancy mentioned above, cultural, educational, and missionary activities, which gradually came to awaken ethnic consciousness, took under their sway entire populations. In addition, the empire in the late nineteenth century had become an arena for religious and secular missionaries of all persuasions and nationalities. Most of them ignored the Muslim population, and targeted instead Christians and Jews with their education, alms, and sermons.[23] Against this background Muslims became aware of their rapid decline. New immigrants from the more developed areas of tsarist Russia and the Balkans, their sense of outrage and hostility fresh, were instrumental in articulating this awareness.

Nonetheless, it is not clear that Abdulhamid's turn to Islamism was dictated by the growing resentment of the Muslim population. He seems to have been a cautious and timid ruler, with a penchant for playing balance-of-power diplomacy with the Great Powers in order to benefit from imperialist rivalry over Ottoman territories. Especially since there were no attempts to limit the economic ascent of non-Muslims during his reign, and no indication that he preferred any policy other than economic liberalism, it seems likely that his Islamism was primarily directed at consolidating the allegiance of the Arab subjects of the Empire. Although, it may also be argued that the intricate mechanisms of control, built around a free-trade treaty (of 1838 vintage), capitulatory concessions, and the Public Debt Administration (which had been established in 1881 to oversee the repayment of the debt after the empire declared bankruptcy) would hardly permit any leeway in policy.[24] Independent of the sultan's intentions, Islamism resonated strongly in a Muslim population having to cope with the effects of the rapid transformation of traditional balances and punishing social dislocation.

Was the Nation-State Inevitable?

The Young Turks first became visible on the European political scene not too long before their incredible success in forcing the Sultan to revive the Constitution and agree to immediate elections for a Parliament in 1908.[25] There had been various organizations of dissident Ottomans in Europe, engaged mostly in publishing anti-absolutist essays, although without the intellectual sophistication, for instance, of Russian revolutionaries. In fact, most of Abdulhamid's critics had chosen exile because they felt themselves unfairly passed over and were ready to return and serve the country once a deal was struck. Essentially, the Young Turks were the activist and radical faction of the Ottoman elite. They had attended schools which trained the elite for imperial service, and their perspective on reform was confined to achieving more effective administration. They were surprisingly ignorant of political economy, and of all third-world revolutionary movements theirs was the least anti-imperialist. The Young Turks saw themselves as players in the European arena rather than as nationalists voicing resentment against the West. For this reason, their success did not occasion any concern in European capitals; on the contrary, it was celebrated as putting an end to the last autocratic regime in Europe.

The Young Turk organization which succeeded in reinstating the Constitution in 1908 was known as the Committee of Union and Progress (CUP). Organized in Salonica, its members included disgruntled military officers. It formed in an environment colored by the Macedonian problem, a seemingly intractable struggle between Greeks, Bulgarians, Serbs and Macedonian nationalists, which the Ottoman army had been unable to control, and which provided a perfect battleground for the imperial rivalry raging between Austria and Russia, with appearances by Britain on the Russian and by Germany on the Austrian side. The officers, despairing of containing nationalist guerrillas of various stripes, apparently decided that political freedoms where all views could be expressed in a parliament working for the common good might be an option to try, and they rebelled against the authority of the sultan. Surprising everyone, Abdulhamid capitulated, and agreed to recall the Parliament and to reinstate the Constitution. Within a few months an elected parliament was functioning which reflected in composition the population's ethnic mix.[26]

The accepted reading of the ideological history of the CUP is that it started as Ottomanist, but turned Turkish-nationalist under the force of circumstances. The difficulty with this interpretation is that even before it turned to nationalism, the CUP was essentially centralist, apparently believing that the empire could be turned into a unitary nation-state, a "Japan of the Near East," secular and with universal legal norms and citizenship.[27] Against a background of ethnic and sectarian particularism, made concrete in the *millet* system, this was a radical platform. The history of ethnic relations in the empire, as well as increasing ethnic consciousness, seemed to dictate the viability of a rule of law, only if in conjunction with some degree of ethnic and sectarian autonomy. "[M]ost non-Muslims, and many non-Turkish Muslims, meant by liberty and equality liberty for the community and equality between communities, and saw their own interest not in strengthening the power and increasing the intervention of the central government, but in maintaining the rights of the communities and strengthening the administrative autonomy of the provinces."[28]

Events strengthened the nationalist hand. Within months after the 1908 elections, Austria declared its annexation of Bosnia-Herzegovina, Bulgaria declared its independence, and Greece took over Crete. An attempt at counterrevolution followed in the spring of 1909, but was defeated when the army, over which the CUP had secure control, marched into the capital and formally ousted the sultan. A two-year respite was followed by a rebellion in Albania and the Italian declaration of war over Tripoli (in September 1911); and then the decisive Balkan War (November 1912) which signaled the beginning of a series of engagements that finally killed the empire.

The period between the fall of 1909 and elections in March 1912 offered perhaps an indication of the direction that politics in a multiethnic empire could take when circumstances permitted. The parliament functioned properly, the Constitution was in place, and hopes were high; also, it was during this time that the Liberals, another wing of the Young Turk movement, began to gain ground against the CUP. Their intellectual leader was an Ottoman prince (the grandson of Sultan Abdulmecid), and their platform consisted of political and economic liberalism and administrative decentralization.[29] Compared to the statist centralism of the CUP, the federalism of Prince Sabaheddin had already before 1908 attracted Greek and Armenian groups active in Europe. With the opening of the Parliament and freedom of the press, a growing number of deputies and intellectual figures, among them Arab notables, Greek and Armenian politicians, and various Islamic groups, gravitated to the Liberal platform. They were increasingly wary of CUP designs for a unitary state, which they variously feared would become Turkish-nationalist, militantly secularist, or uncompromising in imposing a single blueprint in matters where the millets had been autonomous, such as education. The CUP, on the other hand, found its constituency among the aspiring Turkish intelligentsia and provincial merchants, statist and activist, and resenting the ascendance of a non-Muslim bourgeoisie—the classic composition of a nationalist constituency.

Communitarian devolution and federalism in all probability held greater promise for the integrity of the empire, at least in the short term. There is no indication that the liberals were aware of the contemporaneous discussion in Austria-Hungary revolving around the alternatives of "atomized" versus "organic" citizenship.[30] The program of the Entente Liberale, as it came to be known, defended a communitarian version of organic citizenship. In addition to decentralization, its second pillar was "private initiative," connoting anti-statism and economic and political liberalism. The Liberals asked for proportional representation of ethnic groups in the Parliament, and they made formal agreements with the Greek constitutionalists and Armenian Hunchaks based on the defense of church autonomy and official recognition of the equivalence of confessional schools. In addition to Arab and Christian political classes and Turkish Islamicists, the Ottoman Socialist Party, accusing the CUP of nationalism, also supported this platform.[31]

It is not clear whether the Entente would have won the elections in 1912 had they not been rigged. In the Arab provinces of Syria, Beirut, and Aleppo, and the sanjak of Jerusalem, twenty-four out of the thirty deputies had already switched to the Entente, and before the CUP began to use state resources to manipulate the campaign, the urban vote seemed poised to bring in the Liberals as the majority party.[32] The CUP, however, successfully scared some candidates, intimidated especially rural voters, and used the ongoing war with Italy as an excuse for asking that voters stand behind the government. Combined with fears that the Liberals intended to increase the representation of Christians in the Parliament, these led to a CUP victory. Elsewhere in the empire the CUP was accused of using the "big stick" and state officials to get its way, and the elections were widely condemned as returning an unrepresentative legislature.

In investigating the ramifications of a counterfactual Liberal victory, the attitudes of the Greek and Armenian communities toward the post-1908 Ottoman state become crucial. The viability of the empire as a multiethnic entity, before it was to become a Turkish nation-state in the succeeding decade, depended on the relations established between the state and the non-Turkish communities. Of these, the Greeks were the most crucial, not only because of their disproportionate numbers in Istanbul and their economic importance, but also because of the hostility over Greek independence and to various clashes with the Greek state since. Accordingly, the main problem for Ottoman Greeks was how to distance themselves from the Greek state. The Greek Orthodox patriarchate located in Istanbul shared the same concern, and could therefore provide an alternative. The patriarchate had to chart a narrow course between keeping the Ottoman government satisfied that it was not acting as an extension of the Greek state and not alienating its own flock.[33]

Athens had a much less ambiguous agenda. The Greek state actively sought to increase its influence among Ottoman Greeks. Soon after independence, Greek consuls were instructed to offer Greek citizenship to all Ottoman Greeks who were deemed to have somehow contributed to Greek independence. Hence, a fifth column was formed, which became the principal client of Greek irredentism. The Greek state also endeavored to instill a sense of ethnic identity among the Ottoman Greeks, especially by sending Greek nationals to the empire to teach in various Greek schools. There is no question that these policies worked to some degree, and a nationalist consciousness was gradually raised.[34] Nonetheless, most Ottoman Greeks seem to have realized that the dispersal of their population made a territorial annexation by Greece problematic, and other policies that could benefit from the new constitutional regime were needed.

One revealing episode of these crucial years was the establishment of an influential political organization designed not as a political party, but as an ethnic association to serve as a forum for political discussion. The Constantinople Office (CO, also translated as the Constantinople Organization or Society) was founded in 1908 in Istanbul and occupied a prominent position among Greek notables until the onset of the Balkan War in late 1912, when its platform became moot.[35] The CO defended a staunchly Ottomanist position, reflecting the interests of the Greek bourgeoisie of Istanbul, who were "eager to support a strong Ottoman state reinforced by the consensus of its non-Muslim bourgeoisie."[36] The political notables participating in the restitution of the constitutional regime shared the same view. A Greek deputy from Izmir asserted that the national idea for Ottoman Greeks lay in the effort "to contribute with all the moral and material capital of our Nation to the civilization of the Empire."[37] The CO's diagnosis of the situation was that Greeks had to accept coexistence with Muslims, and that the Ottoman constitution provided an adequate umbrella: a new era had begun, "one that might lead eventually to full equality with the Turks and possibly even co-rule of the Empire."[38] Hence, the Greeks should benefit from the new legal framework to secure positions in the bureaucracy and should ultimately aim to participate fully in the government of the empire. The CO and the Greek deputies supporting its platform were naturally attracted to the Liberal Party "because it combined the promise of liberalization with the preservation of the *millets'* cultural identities."[39]

The importance of the CO lies in establishing the availability of an alternative to nationalism—even if the window of opportunity opened only briefly. There was a political and intellectual platform to which Ottoman Greeks could rally in defiance of the Greek state and its irredentist policies. More importantly, as the de facto bourgeoisie of the empire, the Greek notables of the capital found it in their interest to devise a modus vivendi with the Turks, rather than opt for political adventure. In fact, this divergence of interest surfaced even after the empire had been torn apart and the Aydin vilayet was under Greek occupation, between the Greek notables of Izmir and the occupation authorities, and, more tellingly, between Sterghiades, the Greek governor who came to sympathize with the Ottoman Greeks, and Athens.[40] Anatolian Greeks who were forced to relocate to Greece after the Greek occupation forces were driven out seem to affirm their social and cultural difference and reluctant coexistence with Greeks of the mainland, to this day.[41]

First the elections, then the onset of the Balkan war spelled the end of the Liberal interlude. When the Bulgarian armies came within a cannon shot of Istanbul, with Salonica falling to Greece, and Edirne, a former capital city and a site of symbolic significance, to Bulgaria, the nationalism that CUP policies had adumbrated found a ready constituency. Once again, there was a large immigration of Turks from the newly lost territory, with fresh resentment against Christians, and great jubilation when Edirne was taken back in the summer of 1913, thus validating CUP's claims. At around the same time the first serious clashes started between Turkish and Greek peasants, with raids organized against Greek villages in western Anatolia, probably with the tacit approval of the authorities. These first clashes were the harbinger of the ethnic wars and massacres that were to occur, first in 1915 against the Armenian population, then in the period

1919–1922, against the armies of the Greek state. There could no longer be a turning back to Ottomanism as an official policy.

The evolution of official nationalism determined the response it received as well. "By reaction against the new Turkish nationalism, that of the Armenians was strengthened, that of Arabs, Albanians, and Kurds came to political life."[42] In the historiography of Arab nationalism, the CUP victory over the Entente and the Balkan wars are seen as the watershed when intellectuals turned away from Ottomanism and began to search for ways to promote Arab nationalism. "As far as Arab political nationalism is concerned, it can safely be asserted that it was the national and racial policies of the Young Turks which fanned its flames."[43] "Whatever doubts the CUP still had as to which policy should be the basis of the building up of a new Turkey were settled by [Balkan] wars. . . . The anti-Arab and anti-Muslim spirit of this new Turkish nationalism expressed itself openly and violently on the eve of the First World War"[44]

Indeed the disintegration of the empire had become inevitable after 1913. The conjuncture, within which diverse elements of the imperial mosaic rallied around the liberal platform as a possible path toward a *Nationalitätenstaat*, had passed, both because of external aggression, which strengthened the Turkish-nationalist sentiment within the empire, and because the Young Turk revolution had been led by centralists committed to charting an efficient course of modernization from above. The advance of Turkish nationalism could only elicit similar responses from the other nationalities of an already mobilized society. All nationalisms exact great tolls in human suffering, and Turkish nationalism was no exception. Its geographical claim implied a massive ethnic cleansing. When the empire's estate was fully partitioned a decade after the start of the Balkan wars, the world had been remade in the image of nation-states pursuing Wilsonian principles. Under the hegemony of nationalist ideologies, not many mourned the empires or investigated counterfactual possibilities.

Notes

1. The recent rewriting of the history of nationalisms does not substantially change this preference. While it deconstructs nationalism's own history by pointing to the constructedness of the national ideal or the initial alienness of an ideology which eventually came to dominate, the story still focuses on the formation of the nation-state. In this version the masses no longer inherently share and willingly participate in the nationalist identity or the belief in the nation's destiny; instead an elite with state-building aspirations succeeds in propagating its own project. The burden of the inevitability of the national construct is shifted from the *Volk* to the nationalist intelligentsia, but historical alternatives remain uninvestigated.

2. Gyan Prakash, "Writing Postorientalist Histories of the Third World: Perspectives from Indian Historiography," *Comparative Studies in Society and History* 32, no. 2 (1990): 383–408.

3. In this task, Islamicist commentators were ahead of their secular counterparts. Their analysis of the decline and fall of the Ottoman Empire revolves around the abandonment of the Islamic essence of the state. Thus the blame is placed not on nationalism, but on reformist bureaucrats, subservient to their European and Christian masters, whose mistake was to import alien forms of governance and thus to disrupt the balances of the golden age of the empire. According to this line of thought, the alternative that an Islamic empire could make it into the modern world was always there.

4. Arthur Mendel, "On Interpreting the Fate of Imperial Russia," in ed. T. Stavrou, *Russia Under the Last Tsar* (Minneapolis: University of Minnesota Press, 1969), 13–41.

5. See Halil Inalcik, "Centralization and Decentralization in Ottoman Administration," in ed. T. Naff and R. Owen, *Studies in Eighteenth Century Islamic History* (Carbondale: Southern Illinois University Press, 1977); Andrew G. Gould, "Lords or Bandits? The Derebeys of Cilicia," *International Journal of Middle East Studies*, 7, no. 4 (1976): 485–506.

6. For a fuller discussion of the development of ayans and recentralization in the empire, see my *State and Class in Turkey: A Study in Capitalist Development* (London: Verso, 1987), ch. 1; and idem, "The Agrarian Background and the Origins of the Turkish Bourgeoisie," in ed. Ayse Oncu, Caglar Keyder, and Saad Eddin Ibrahim, *Developmentalism and Beyond: Society and Politics in Egypt and Turkey* (Cairo: American University in Cairo Press, 1994), 223–255.

7. See Allan Cunningham, *Eastern Questions in the Nineteenth Century: Collected Essays*, 2 vols. (London: Frank Cass, 1993), vol. 2., pp. 72–107, 108–129, for insightful accounts of Ottoman relations with the Great Powers as seen from the Foreign Office perspective.

8. Cf. Haldun Gulalp, "Capitalism and the Modern Nation-State: Rethinking the Creation of the Turkish Republic," *Journal of Historical Sociology* 7, no. 2 (1994): 155–176.

9. Roderick Davison, *Reform in the Ottoman Empire, 1856–1876* (Princeton: Princeton University Press, 1963); Stanford J. Shaw and Ezel K. Shaw, *History of the Ottoman Empire and Modern Turkey*, 2 vols. (Cambridge: Cambridge University Press, 1977), vol. 2, is a comprehensive overview.

10. The classic account is Albert Hourani, "Ottoman Reform and the Politics of Notables," in ed. W. R. Polk and R. L. Chambers, *Beginnings of Modernization in the Middle East: the Nineteenth Century* (Chicago: University of Chicago Press, 1968), 41–68.

11. A fundamental essay in interpretation which covers most of this ground is Kemal H. Karpat, "The Transformation of the Ottoman State, 1789–1908," *International Journal of Middle East Studies* 3, no. 3 (1972): 243–281.

12. Roderick Davison, "Nationalism as an Ottoman Problem and the Ottoman Response," in ed. W. W. Haddad and W. Ochsenwald, *Nationalism in a Non-National State: The Dissolution of the Ottoman Empire* (Columbus: Ohio University Press, 1977), 25–56.

13. Kemal H. Karpat, *Ottoman Population, 1830–1914: Demographic and Social Characteristics* (Madison: University of Wisconsin Press, 1985).

14. See Richard G. Hovannisian, *Armenia on the Road to Independence* (Berkeley: University of California Press, 1967), 37.

15. Vedat Eldem, *Osmanli Imparatorlugunun Iktisadi Sartlari Hakkinda Bir Tetkik* (Istanbul: Is Bankasi Yayinlari, 1970), was the first book to draw attention to the remarkable economic development during the last period of the empire. The principal source for

a quantitative evaluation of the impact of trade and foreign investment is Sevket Pamuk, *The Ottoman Empire and European Capitalism, 1820–1913: Trade, Investment, and Production* (Cambridge: Cambridge University Press, 1987).

16. For a fuller discussion, Keyder, *State and Class*, ch. 2.

17. Caglar Keyder, Eyup Ozveren, and Donald Quataert, eds., "Port-Cities in the Eastern Mediterranean," Special Issue of *Review* 16, no. 4 (1993), contains an overview of social change in nineteenth-century port cities in the empire.

18. See Ilber Ortayli, *Imparatorlugun En Uzun Yuzyili* (Istanbul: Hil, 1983).

19. There were 71 Muslims, 44 Christians, and 4 Jews in the first Parliament of 1876; the changing composition of the population of the empire is reflected in the 1908 parliament, where there were 234 Muslims (147 Turks, 60 Arabs, and 27 Albanians), 50 Christians, and 4 Jews (see Shaw and Shaw, *History of the Ottoman Empire*, p. 278).

20. Mesrob K. Krikorian, *Armenians in the Service of the Ottoman Empire, 1860–1908* (London: Routledge, Kegan Paul, 1978).

21. Selim Deringil, "Legitimacy Structures in the Ottoman State: The Reign of Abdulhamid II (1876–1909)," *International Journal of Middle East Studies* 23, no. 3 (1991): 345–359; also Rashid Khalidi, "Society and Ideology in Late Ottoman Syria: Class, Education, Profession and Confession," in ed. John P. Spagnola, *Problems of the Modern Middle East in Historical Perspective: Essays in Honour of Albert Hourani* (Reading, Mass.: Ithaca Press, 1992), 119–131.

22. Justin McCarthy, "Foundations of the Turkish Republic: Social and Economic Change," *Middle Eastern Studies* 19 (1983).

23. There are several studies of missionary activity in the empire. See, e.g., Uygur Kocabasoglu, *Kendi Belgeleriyle Anadolu'daki Amerika: 19. Yuzyilda Osmanli Imparatorlugu'ndaki Amerikan Misyoner Okullari* (Istanbul: Arba, 1989).

24. Pamuk, *Ottoman Empire and the World Economy*; also Roger Owen, *The Middle East in the World Economy* (London: Methuen, 1981). For a documentary account, see Charles Issawi, *The Economic History of Turkey, 1800–1914* (Chicago: University of Chicago Press, 1980).

25. For the CUP a classic source is Ernest Edmondson Ramsaur, *The Young Turks: Prelude to the Revolution of 1908* (Princeton: Princeton University Press, 1957).

26. Feroz Ahmad, *The Young Turks, the Committee of Union and Progress in Turkish Politics, 1908–1914* (Oxford: Oxford University Press, 1968).

27. Ibid., also Feroz Ahmad, "The Late Ottoman Empire," in ed. Marian Kent, *The Great Powers and the End of the Ottoman Empire* (London: George Allen and Unwin, 1984), 5–30.

28. Albert Hourani, *Arabic Thought in the Liberal Age, 1798–1938* (Cambridge: Cambridge University Press, 1983), 281.

29. Ali Birinci, *Hurriyet ve Itilaf Firkasi* (Istanbul: Dergah Yayinlari, 1990), is comprehensive; also Nezahat Nurettin Ege, *Prens Sabahaddin, Hayati ve Ilmi Mudafaalari* (Istanbul: Gunes Yayinevi, 1977).

30. Uri Ra'anan, "Nation and State: Order out of Chaos," in ed. Uri Ra'anan, Maria Mesner, Keith Armes, and Kate Martin, *State and Nation in Multi-ethnic Societies: The Breakup of Multinational States* (New York: Manchester University Press, 1991), 3–32.

31. Birinci, *Hurriyet ve Itilaf*, p. 141.

32. Rashid Ismail Khalidi, "The 1912 Election Campaign in the Cities of Bilad al-Sham," *International Journal of Middle East Studies* 16, no. 4 (1984): 461–474; Hasan Ka-

yali, "Elections and the Electoral Process in the Ottoman Empire, 1867–1919," *International Journal of Middle East Studies* 27, no. 3 (1995): 265–286.

33. Evangelos Kofos, "Patriarch Joachim III (1878–1884) and the Irredentist Policy of the Greek State," *Journal of Modern Greek Studies* 4, no. 2 (1986): 107–120.

34. Paschalis Kitromilides, "Imagined Communities and the Origins of the National Question in the Balkans," in ed. Martin Blinkhorn and Thanos Veremis, *Modern Greece: Nationalism and Nationality* (Athens: Sage-Eliamep, 1990), 23–66, especially pp. 44–51.

35. For histories of the CO, see Gerasimos Augustinos, "Consciousness and History: Nationalist Critics of Greek Society, 1897–1914," *East European Quarterly* (Boulder, Colo.: 1977); also Thanos Veremis, "From the National State to the Stateless Nation," in ed. Blinkhorn and Veremis, *Modern Greece*, pp. 9–22.

36. Ibid., p. 18.

37. Quoted in Alexis Alexandris, *The Greek Minority of Istanbul and Greek-Turkish Relations, 1918–1974* (Athens: Center of Asia Minor Studies, 1983), 39.

38. Augustinos, *Consciousness and History*, p. 131.

39. Ibid.

40. See a regrettably unpublished dissertation on this most interesting period, Victoria Solomonides, "The Greek Administration of the Vilayet of Aidin, 1919–1922," Ph.D. diss., University of London, 1984.

41. See, for example, Renee Hirschon, *Heirs of the Greek Catastrophe: The Social Life of Asia Minor Refugees in Piraeus* (Oxford: Clarendon Press, 1989).

42. Hourani, *Arabic Thought*, p. 282.

43. Zeine N. Zeine, *The Emergence of Arab Nationalism* (Delmar, N.Y.: Caravan Books, 1973), 82.

44. Ibid., p. 99.

5

THE HABSBURG EMPIRE

SOLOMON WANK

Alluding to Austria in *The Philosophy of History*, Hegel writes: "Austria is not a kingdom but an empire, i.e. an aggregate of many political organizations (*Staatsorganizationen*) that are themselves royal (*königlich*)."[1] With his typical perspicacity, Hegel put his finger on the defining feature of the Habsburg empire[2] from its rise in the early sixteenth century to its collapse in 1918, i.e., its imperial structure. Research agendas concentrating on the nationalities problem and attendant cultural and social issues miss the significance of the Habsburg empire *qua* empire. Historians pursuing those agendas usually take the imperial structure for granted and overlook the theories of empire developed by, among others, S. N. Eisenstadt, Michael Doyle, Alexander Motyl and Imanuel Geiss. In the formulations of these theorists, empire is a form of political structure *sui generis* with an inherent dynamic that leads, over time, to its decline and disappearance.[3] Empires provide a picture of "massivity, stability and endurance," but also of "long declines and, sometimes, precipitous falls."[4] From that theoretical perspective, the imperial structure of the Habsburg empire, and not the presence on its territory of diverse nationalities—the latter was inherent in the former—was its most basic feature and the one that ultimately determined its destiny.

Of course there are historians who deride the whole notion of the "decline and fall" of the Habsburg empire, let alone its inevitability. For example, Alan Sked, dismisses all such talk as "misplaced determinism," even though *Decline and Fall* is part of the title of his recently published book.[5] Rather than a long process of decline leading to the empire's dissolution, Sked and others see a quite different historical trajectory. After almost falling apart in the Revolution of 1848, the Habsburg empire rebounded and rose rather than declined. On the eve of the First World War the empire was, according to Sked, more stable and prosperous than at any time in its modern history, and the nationality problem had abated.[6] This sanguine picture relies heavily on the positive assessments of Habsburg economic growth contained in the works of recent economic historians such as David Good, Richard Rudolph, and John Komlos.[7]

There is some validity to this rosy picture, although, in my view, much more with regard to prosperity than to stability or the abatement of the nationality problem. Elsewhere I have argued that a considerable amount of instability existed beneath the surface, and not very far beneath it at that.[8] Suffice it to mention here a few observations in that regard. Can the empire be described as politically stable and the nationality question as attenuated when the constitutions of Istria, Croatia, and Bohemia were suspended in 1910, 1912 and 1913 respectively, and the Austrian parliament (Reichsrat) was sent packing in March 1914, with no inclination on the part of the prime minister, Count Karl Stürgkh, to recall it any time soon? Is it evidence of stability to claim as many historians do, that only two things held the empire together—veneration of old Emperor Francis Joseph and the loyalty and devotion of his army?[9] At least one Habsburg army officer, Major (later General) Ulrich Klepsch found it very worrisome that loyalty to the old emperor, to the extent that it existed, was to him personally and not part of a larger loyalty to a Habsburg or Austrian state. In a letter to a friend in 1887, Klepsch wrote, "It seems to me as if only the love of the peoples for the person of the emperor was the bond, the *only* one, which held Austria together." He felt, "*that is not good.*"[10] With regard to the army as the other prop holding the empire together, one might ask: Is a state that relies primarily on its army for its existence stable in a deeper political sense?

The stability on the surface could be interpreted as resignation on the part of the leaders of the various nationalities in the face of existing political and diplomatic realities in the years before 1914, rather than loyalty to or acceptance of the empire as such. Chief among the internal political realities was the Habsburg army—"trained and equipped primarily to maintain order at home"[11]—and the readiness of the emperor and his advisers to use it to put down challenges to the existing imperial structure. Diplomatically, as Hans Mommsen writes, "Without some impulse from without, that is without some change in the European power constellation which set aside the foreign policy compulsion to preserve the dualistic state, no resolution of the nationalities problem was possible."[12] Part of that foreign policy compulsion is related to a strong Germany committed to the status quo in the Habsburg empire and its preservation as a great power.[13] Thomas Masaryk spoke for many non-German and non-Magyar national leaders when he stated in 1913: "Just because I cannot indulge in dreams of its [the Habsburg empire's] collapse and know that whether good or bad, it will continue, I am most deeply concerned that we should make something of this Austria."[14] From its enunciation in 1848 by Francis Palacký the Czech national patriot, Austro-Slavism's affirmation of the Habsburg empire, embodied in Palacký's 1848 declaration that if the Austrian empire had not existed it would have been necessary to create it, was conditioned on federalization and national autonomy for all of the nationalities.[15] Despite the restraints imposed by political and diplomatic realities, nationalities such as the Czechs, Croats, Poles and Slovenes sought independent representation among European nations in areas such as the Second International, the Olympic games and other international sports organizations, and in professional organizations of scholars and scientists.[16] At the 1908 Olympic games, the Czech team marched in alphabetical order in the opening procession between Belgium and Brazil under the name of Bohemia and behind its own flag, the red and white banner of the Bohemian crownland with "Bohemia" (*Bohême*) written on it.[17]

In the end, Sked, and those who share his viewpoint, maintain that the most that can be said is that the Habsburg empire disintegrated in 1918 "because it lost a major war."[18] If the Central Powers had won the war, the empire "would have survived intact and probably expanded."[19] Sked's argument, however, is a bit confusing, quite apart from its begging the question of why losing a war should have had as a consequence the complete dismantling of the Habsburg empire. He also states that if the Central Powers had won the war, the empire would have been reduced to a military and economic appendage of Germany, "with little future as an independent state."[20] Survival in that condition would have been tantamount to the end of the Habsburg empire as an imperial political construct.

If one grants that the Habsburg empire was more prosperous and, at least superficially, stable in 1914 than at any other time in its recent history, one is left with a curious paradox. On the one hand, there is the picture of a relatively stable and prosperous Habsburg empire and, on the other, that of an imperial political elite described on the eve of war as imbued with a sense of the empire's imminent dissolution, even by those historians who assess the empire's social and economic progress positively.[21] The sense of "impending doom" strongly influenced the imperial elite's political calculations in favor of war in July 1914. Four days before Austria-Hungary's declaration of war on Serbia, Count Alexander Hoyos, a high foreign ministry official and one of the architects of the war policy, declared in a tone of anguished bravado: "We are still capable of resolve! We do not want to be or ought to be a sick man. Better to be destroyed quickly."[22] In a more subdued tone, Baron Leopold von Andrian-Werburg, the highly respected and influential Austro-Hungarian consul-general in Warsaw (1911–1914), summed up this mind-set in his account of the beginning of the war written in 1918 and only recently published.

> Before the murder of the archduke and also after the murder, there prevailed under the impression of our weak behavior during the Balkan war, deep depression among our military leaders and in the diplomatic milieu surrounding the [foreign] minister. . . . We are heading for collapse and partition and do not defend ourselves. . . . After Turkey comes Austria. That is the catchword in Eastern Europe.[23]

Emperor Francis Joseph's pessimism is well known. Shortly before his death in 1916, the old emperor said to an Austro-Hungarian diplomat, "I have been aware for a long time of how much of an anomaly we are in the modern world."[24] Was the pessimism of the emperor and elite pessimism justified, or simply a figment of their collective imagination? This paper will argue that it was justified.

There is, in my view, no contradiction between a generous assessment of the Habsburg empire's positive qualities and the elite's perception that it was in a critical state bordering on dissolution. The effects of relatively rapid and uneven economic growth on social and nationalist movements since 1848 strengthened the centrifugal forces in the empire, while at the same time they weakened the ties between the imperial center at Vienna and the peripheral regions. Some form of reorganization along federal lines might have given the Habsburg state a new lease on life. But even if that were possible, Otto Brunner is correct in pointing out that such a reform would have spelled the end of the Habsburg empire and the imperial concept no less than if they had been destroyed by war and revolution. Neither Francis Joseph nor Francis Ferdinand, Brunner continues, could have sponsored such a reorganization, even if they possessed the freedom to do so.[25] From the perspective of the Habsburg ruler and his advisers, the deterioration of the relationship between Vienna and the various crownlands was indeed cause for deep pessimism. In the end the fall of the Habsburg empire was the logical consequence of the dynamics of its imperial structure. For the sake of practicality, the discussion here of that process is limited largely to the period 1848–1918.

The Habsburg empire, like all historical empires, was a collection of formerly independent or potentially independent historical-political entities that came under the sway of the Habsburgs. The Habsburg empire, again like all historical empires, was not really a state in the sense of a society "characterized by the integration of its components" into a community of "social interaction and cultural values."[26] An imperial government, states Michael Doyle, "is a sovereignty that lacks a community."[27] The lack of a coherent *Staatsidee* binding together the domains of the Habsburg empire was recognized by a prominent adviser to Emperor Francis Joseph, Foreign Minister Count Gustav Kálnoky, who opined in a memorandum written in the mid-1880s:

> Since the time when the Habsburg territorial possessions were first united, the monarchy has developed more in the sense of a power (*Macht*) than in the sense of a state (*Staat*). Power and purpose in external matters were more recognizable than its purpose as a state.[28]

The absence of any coherent internal purpose derives from the way in which empires are created. The following outline of the pattern of imperial decay and decline is derived from the works of the previously mentioned theorists of empire.[29]

Empires, Alexander Motyl states, are formed, by transforming "distinct societies with autonomous institutions and regional elites into politically subordinate civil societies."[30] The distinctiveness of the subordinated societies continues to exist, but their political sovereignty has been extinguished or sharply reduced. In effect, the elites of the subordinated societies are reduced to the status of vassals. The relationship between the imperial center—in the Habsburg case the hereditary lands with their seat in Vienna[31]—and the peripheral societies is one of power and long duration. The object of that relationship is the establishment of an imperial peace within the subordinated territories that allows the extraction of adequate resources from the peripheral societies to maintain the political unity and military capacity necessary to support the imperial ambitions of the ruler and his advisers. The policies of the emperor and his advisers aim at maximizing their independence by freeing them from the restraints imposed by traditional elites and power centers and gaining control over men, money and resources.[32] The survival of the political system of empires requires the continuous existence of a delicate balance between traditional and non-traditional elements and between the limited political participation of segments of the population—traditional aristocracy, some urban groups, religious groups, parts of the peasantry (in some cases)—and the non-involvement of the majority.[33]

Imperial decay—the erosion of the hegemonic center-periphery relationship—inevitably sets in when the ruler, in order to preserve the integrity of his state and the longevity of his empire, accords some or all of the peripheral territories a greater degree of autonomy vis-à-vis the center. This strategy contradicts the absolutist basis on which imperial rule rests and therefore ultimately backfires, increasing the regional identification of vassals and their claims on financial and material resources, and the demands of proto-nationalist regional elites. Maintaining the delicate political balance between forces and interests necessary for the independence of the center becomes increasingly difficult. Together, these developments decrease resources drawn from the provinces, weaken the independence of the center, delegitimize the imperial ideology, and accelerate imperial decay. Imperial decay leads to a weakening of the power of the state and its capacity to compete internationally. The decay of state power in turn leads to territorial diminution by a process of attrition as rival powers pick off peripheral lands. The strategies of the ruler and his advisers to arrest decline all tend to be counterproductive and lead to crises. Eventually the linked processes of imperial decay and decline result in the severing of the bonds between the center and the periphery as well as the emergence or re-emergence of the previously subordinated historical-political entities.[34] That concisely describes what happened to the Habsburg empire in the last seventy years of its existence.

Like all empires, the Habsburg empire was created—in the sixteenth and seventeenth centuries—by war and conquest, although the process was helped along by some brilliant marital contracts.[35] By the late seventeenth century, the Habsburg empire emerged as a European Great Power from wars against Bohemia, Hungary, France, and the Ottoman empire. However, despite the development of some institutions of centralization and a standing army, the political unity of the empire was tenuous. "It was," writes R.J.W. Evans, "a complex and subtly-balanced organism, not a 'state' but a mildly centripetal agglutination of bewilderingly heterogeneous elements."[36] As such, it was unable to compete with other centralized and proto-national states in the more aggressive and competitive eighteenth-century international arena. Prussia's invasion of the Habsburg duchy of Silesia in 1740 was a herald of this new world. The response of the Habsburg dynasty was to reform.

For over a hundred years, from 1740 until 1848, the Habsburg rulers vigorously pursued a policy of centralized royal absolutism as they strove to build a modern autocratic state. After the revolutions of 1848, and the pressure of modernizing forces, the Habsburgs reversed course. In order to ensure the prolongation of their empire in increasingly difficult political circumstances, the Habsburgs inadvertently sponsored a degree of pluralism and diversity while continuing to rule over a hierarchical and undemocratic state. Their rule had become overextended and their ability to extract resources from the provinces had diminished. Holding on to their possessions now compelled them to decentralize their power. In keeping with that policy, the Habsburg ruler and his advisers acknowledged nationalism in a limited sense, but even in that limited sense, decentralization led to the formation of constituencies among the nationalities that vied with the imperial center in Vienna for power and delegitimized the supranational imperial ideology, both of which accelerated imperial decay.

The most obvious example of the limited response to nationalism is, of course, the Compromise of 1867, which Emperor Francis Joseph concluded with the Magyar oligarchy. The compromise gave the empire a deceptive stability for fifty years, but at the price of alienating most of the Slavs, with the exception of the Poles. In return for their acceptance of the compromise with the Magyars, the Polish magnates were granted their own "compromise" with the Habsburgs in 1869, which gave Galicia virtual autonomy under their control and made Polish the official language. This did not alter the fact that the Poles always aimed at secession and the re-establishment of an independent Poland. Beyond the Compromise of 1867, the emperor and his advisers sought to preserve their independence by playing one nationality off against another, "to maintain a more-or-less balanced and equitable distribution of dissatisfaction."[37] That strategy, otherwise known as divide-and-rule, was counterproductive; it strengthened national elites and stoked the fires of national rivalry which disrupted internal tranquility.

After 1867, the Habsburg dynasty found it difficult to justify its ostensibly supranational rule vis-à-vis national elites and masses, its supranational ideology notwithstanding. The dynasty, itself, "was in some irreducible sense German,"[38] and the members of the imperial elite, regardless of ethnic origin, felt themselves bound to the German *Kulturnation*. Consequently, the dynasty, the court and the imperial government increasingly appeared German. In December 1911, the British vice-consul in Ragusa (Dubrovnik), W.N. Lucas-Shadwell, a reliable diplomat sympathetic to the Habsburg authorities, reported to the foreign office on the political atmosphere in Dalmatia:

> The bulk of the population is anti-dynastic, because it looks upon the dynasty as being anti-Slav and as an essential part of the present regime. The feeling toward the Emperor is one of complete indifference; he is looked upon as a German with German sentiments and as being completely out of touch and sympathy with his Slav subjects.[39]

The Habsburg ideal of government, sometimes referred to as the *österreichische Staatsidee* was that of a centralized, unified state run by German-speaking bureaucrats and military leaders, however much Emperor Francis Joseph was forced to modify that ideal in the course of the nineteenth century to hold on to the dynasty's possessions. The supranational ideology was further weakened by the fact that in practice the Habsburgs ruled in a national sense in favor of the Germans and Magyars. This was implicit in the Compromise of 1867. In early February 1867, as the negotiations with the Magyar oligarchy were nearing their end, Baron (later Count) Friedrich Beust, the foreign minister, stated:

> I am quite aware that the Slavic peoples of the Monarchy will view this policy [dualism] with distrust; but the government cannot ever be fair to all the nations. Therefore we have to rely on the support of those with the most vitality and those are the Germans and the Hungarians.[40]

When Count Richard Belcredi, the prime minister, protested that the Slavs could not be so easily ignored and that the government should not rely on individual nationalities but be above all of them,[41] Emperor Francis Joseph countered: "It might be that the way suggested by Count Belcredi is the more correct one, but that of Baron Beust ought more quickly lead to the desired goal,"[42] i.e., the preservation of the empire's status as a Great Power. Count Kálnoky, the Austro-Hungarian foreign minister, made what was implicit, explicit in his previously mentioned memorandum of the mid-1880s:

> The governance of the empire, which is based, on the one hand, on that nationality [the Magyars] whose interests are most securely tied to its continued existence and, on the other, on that nationality [the Germans] whose moral defection would involve the question of the very existence of the monarchy, is the logical justification for the dualistic system from the standpoint of foreign policy.[43]

That strategy also was counterproductive. It alienated non-Germans and non-Magyars and strengthened demands for national autonomy.

By 1914, Vienna was declining as an imperial city: the policies of the emperor and his advisers no longer represented the whole empire or even the Austrian half of it, except in military and foreign affairs, and not even in those areas completely. So, for example, the right conceded to the Hungarian government to sign international commercial treaties in its own name compromised that formerly exclusive monarchical prerogative.[44] Quite apart from Budapest, power had shifted to the peripheries of the empire, to new nationalist political forces in the new power centers of Prague, Cracow, Zagreb, and Lvov which were pulling away from the center, i.e., Vienna and the Habsburg hereditary lands. The emperor and the court became more and more unable to relate to the most important conflicting forces in the empire. The imperial state became an abstraction, and the emperor's strength more symbolic than real.

The relative economic backwardness of the Habsburg empire compared to the other Great Powers, made it difficult to draw subsidies from the periphery to serve the center, and the organizational inefficiency of the imperial structure diminished its military capacity and undermined its prestige as a Great Power. From the point of view of the emperor and his advisers, the ability of the empire to play the role of a Great Power was the sole justification for its existence, even though it lacked the requisite political and economic conditions. Any other policy, such as withdrawal or disengagement—i.e., accepting the status of a middling power which would have accorded with perceptions of it within the European Concert—was rejected because such moves would be a sign of weakness and convey the wrong signal to all of the domains under Vienna's control. It was the determination of the ruler and his advisers to preserve the shaky imperial structure and restore the empire's reputation as a Great Power that motivated them to seek salvation in war in 1914, as they had in 1859 and 1866. In that sense the war was not an accident, of which the collapse of the Habsburg empire was an unfortunate by-product; rather, it was a symptom of the systemic crisis of the imperial structure.

The decay of the center-periphery relationship and the attendant decline of state power would have led in time to the slow demise and eventual disappearance of the Habsburg empire through a gradual process of territorial attrition. The empire, as Count Kálnoky noted, was surrounded by nationally homogeneous states which would have liked to strengthen themselves by incorporating Habsburg territories inhabited by their co-nationals.[45] Some attrition did take place in the nineteenth century; Lombardy and Venetia were lost to the new kingdom of Italy. The process, however, was held in check by the operation of the international system. As Hans Mommsen states, there was in the European power constellation "a foreign policy compulsion to preserve the Habsburg empire."[46] The international system "sheltered"—to use Alexander Motyl's term—the Habsburg empire from the worst consequences of its political and military weakness.[47]

On its own, the Habsburg empire would not have been able to survive in the competitive world of Great Power politics, but it was not on its own. Its continued existence was considered a necessity to prevent a power vacuum in East Central Europe which could lead to a war among the Great Powers to fill. In an international system composed of sovereign states, the disappearance of a major state endangered the proper functioning of the balance-of-power system. After 1815, Russia provided support for the security of the Habsburg empire, but withdrew it as a consequence of Habsburg policy during the Crimean War. The Habsburg empire was defeated by France (and Sardinia-Piedmont) in 1859 and Prussia in 1866, but in neither case was its continued existence as a state at issue. Bismarck eschewed marching into Vienna and showed no interest in incorporating the Habsburg empire's nine million Germans into the new German state. The preservation of the Habsburg empire was more useful to Bismarck than the annexation of its German-inhabited territories. The alliance with Germany in 1879, while not unproblematic, protected the Habsburg empire from the thrust of imperialist pan-Slavism under the aegis of the Tsar. When, in the last quarter of the nineteenth century, Bismarck proved unwilling to incur Russian ill will by supporting Vienna's more aggressive anti-Russian Balkan policies, England came to the aid of the Habsburgs against Russian designs in Bulgaria and Constantinople. In short, the Habsburg empire depended for its security on other Great Powers, and throughout the nineteenth century it received the support of at least one of them.[48]

The European international system underwent a significant change after 1900. The fluidity and flexibility that characterized international relations earlier was replaced by a more rigid system of alliances. The policy of Great Britain also changed drastically. Traditional British policy after 1815 eschewed assuming any obligations in Europe. A free hand and the control of the balance of power were considered the best means to protect British interests. England, however, could not but regard the buildup of the German navy as a direct challenge to its security. In response, Great Britain moved closer to France and Russia—its traditional enemies—and assumed obligations in Europe. Increasingly, England and its allies viewed the Habsburg empire as a German satellite, and were no longer as thoroughly convinced that Austria-Hungary's existence was a European necessity as they had been before 1900. The reckless choice of war to restore the prestige of the empire as a Great Power proved as counterproductive as domestic policies to prevent imperial decay and state decline.

The decision for war against Serbia precipitated the crisis that led to the collapse of the empire. It lost its sheltered position and became expendable "when the specter of a German dominated Mitteleuropa began to haunt the allies in 1916. At that time plans for a 'new' East Central Europe replacing Austria-Hungary received serious consideration."[49] What that meant in practice was that the Allies would allow events to follow a more or less natural course as the empire began to break up in the fall of 1918.[50] Paradoxically, the complete dismantling of the imperial relationship between the core and periphery was conditioned by the sheltered international position that the Habsburg empire enjoyed for a hundred years. Only that protected status allowed the decay and decline to develop to a degree where the imperial state no longer had sufficient strength to resist the political defections that came from all sides in the last month of the war.

The consequences of the collapse of the Habsburg empire is the subject of a separate paper in this volume. However, a few observations in this regard may be permitted to round off the analytical framework here. The disintegration of the Habsburg empire, along with the similarly multinational Russian and Ottoman empires, led logically to "Balkanization" in East Central Europe. That was the other side of nation-state building. As stated previously, imperial orders do not cause subordinated states to disappear, nor do they resolve conflicts between the disparate nationalities forced into political unity by overriding authority; the emperor and his advisers merely suppressed and/or manipulated such conflicts for the purpose of enforcing an imperial peace as a foundation for their political ambitions.

With the collapse of the imperial order the old historical structures and the suppressed conflicts re-emerge, modified by factors associated with the extinct empire.[51] Not the least of these in East Central Europe was the persistence of empires until well into the twentieth century (assuming that the defunct Soviet Union had some structural features of an empire). This historical factor interrupted, delayed and distorted the process of state formation and the development of nationalism in the region. The aggressive and destructive tendencies of East Central European nationalism from 1918 to the present are, in part, the awful consequences of those circumstances. Nevertheless, in the present absence of empires, the process of nation-state formation in East Central Europe is nearing its belated end. Every Habsburg successor state is more national than it was in 1918. The terrible splintering of Yugoslavia represents one of the final steps in the process. Whatever the future of the Danubian area, it now appears likely that it will be shaped by the decisions of independent states that, with a few exceptions, include whole nations—barring, of course, the rise of a new empire or the reconstitution of an old one.

Notes

1. G.W.F. Hegel, *Vorlesungen über die Philosophie der Geschichte*, ed. S. Brunstad (Leipzig: Felix Meiner, 1924), 559.

2. In this paper, Habsburg empire refers to the "German" Habsburg empire which split off from the Spanish Habsburg empire in 1521. The Spanish Habsburg line became extinct in 1700.

3. S. N. Eisenstadt, *The Political System of Empires* (New York: Free Press, 1963); Michael W. Doyle, *Empires* (Ithaca: Cornell University Press, 1986); Alexander Motyl, "From Imperial Decay to Imperial Collapse: The Fall of the Soviet Empire in Comparative Perspective," in ed. Richard L. Rudolph and David F. Good, *Nationalism and Empire: The Habsburg Monarchy and the Soviet Union* (New York: St. Martin's Press. 1992), 15–43;

idem, "Imperial Collapse and Revolutionary Change: Austria-Hungary, Tsarist Russia, and the Soviet Union in Theoretical Perspective," in ed. Jürgen Nautz and Richard Vahrenkamp, *Die Wiener Jahrhundertwende: Einflüsse-Umwelt-Wirkungen* (Vienna: Böhlau Verlag, 1993), 813–832; Imanuel Geiss, "Great Powers and Empires: Historical Mechanisms of Their Making and Breaking," in ed. Geir Lundestad, *The Fall of Great Powers: Peace Stability, and Legitimacy* (Oxford: Oxford University Press, 1994), 23–43.

4. S. N. Eisenstadt, ed., *The Decline of Empires* (Englewood Cliffs, N.J.: Free Press, 1967), 1.

5. Alan Sked, *The Decline and Fall of the Habsburg Empire, 1815–1918* (London: Longman, 1989), 187.

6. Ibid., 264. See also István Deák, *Beyond Nationalism: A Social and Political History of the Habsburg Officer Corps 1848–1918* (New York: Oxford University Press, 1990), 3, 8–9.

7. David Good, *The Economic Rise of the Habsburg Empire 1750–1914* (Berkeley: University of California Press, 1984); John Komlos, "The Habsburg Empire as a Customs Union," in *Economic Development in Austria-Hungary in the Nineteenth Century*, Eastern European Monograph, no. 128 (New York: Columbia University Press, 1988); Richard Rudolph, *Banking and Industrialization in Austria-Hungary* (Cambridge: Cambridge University Press, 1976).

8. See Solomon Wank, *The Nationalities Question in the Habsburg Monarchy: Reflections on the Historical Record*, Working Paper no. 93–3, Center for Austrian Studies, University of Minnesota, 1993. See also idem, "The Growth of Nationalism in the Habsburg Monarchy," *East Central Europe*, 10, pts. 1–2 (1983): 165–179.

9. E.g., Deák, *Beyond Nationalism*, p. 4.

10. Klepsch to Baron (after 1909 Count) Alois von Aehrenthal, St. Petersburg, 28 December 1887. Printed in Solomon Wank, ed. *Aus dem Nachlass Aehrenthal: Briefe und Dokumente zur österreichisch-ungarischen Innen- und Aussenpolitik 1885–1912* (Graz: Neugebauer, 1994), no. 19, p. 21. Aehrenthal, who later became foreign minister (1906–1912), was at the time chef-de-cabinet for the foreign minister, Count Gustav Kálnoky.

11. István Deák, "The Fall of Austria-Hungary: Peace, Stability, and Legitimacy," in ed. Geir Lundestad, *The Fall of Great Powers: Peace, Stability and Legitimacy* (Oxford: Oxford University Press, 1994), 81–101. The quotation is on p. 90.

12. Hans Mommsen, "Die Arbeiterbewegung in Deutschland und Österreich: Eine Vergleichende Betrachtung," in ed. Robert A. Kann and Friedrich E. Prinz, *Deutschland und Österreich: Ein bilaterales Geschichtsbuch* (Munich: Jugend und Volk, 1980), 437.

13. See Solomon Wank, "The Impact of the Dual Alliance on the Germans in Austria and Vice-Versa," *East Central Europe* 7, no. 2 (1980): 288–309, esp. 293–294, 304–309, and the works cited therein.

14. Quoted in H. Gordon Skilling, "T. G. Masaryk, Arch-Critic of Austro-Hungarian Foreign Policy," *Cross Currents: A Journal of Central European Culture* 11 (1992): 213–233, here 214.

15. See Jiří Kořalka and R. J. Crampton, "Die Tschechen," in ed. Adam Wandruszka and Peter Urbanitsch, *Die Habsburgermonarchie 1848–1918*, 6 vols. (Vienna: Verlag de Österreichischen Akademie der Wissenschaft, 1980), vol. 3, pp. 502, 520–521. Palacký's letter containing his declaration is printed in Robert A. Kann, *The Multinational Empire: Nationalism and National Reform in the Habsburg Monarchy, 1848–1918*, 2 vols. (New York: Columbia University Press, 1950), vol. 1, pp. 176–177.

16. The Czechs were successful in obtaining recognition in several of these areas. See Jiří Kořalka, *Tschechen im Habsburgerreich und in Europa 1815–1914: Sozialgeschichtliche Zusammenhänge der neuzeitlichen Nationsbildung und Nationalitätenfrage in den böhmischen Landern* (Vienna: Verlag für Geschichte und Politik, 1991), 280–291.

17. Ibid., p. 291. The Austrian government successfully put pressure on the International Olympic Committee to disallow the participation of a separate Bohemian team in the 1912 Olympics. However Czech members of the 1912 Austrian Olympic team were identified as Austrians followed by their nationality in parentheses: *Autrice* (*Tcheque*). At the awards ceremonies for Czech medalists, the Bohemian flag flew under the Austrian imperial flag (ibid. pp. 291–292).

18. Sked, *Decline and Fall of the Habsburg Empire*, p. 264. See also Deák, "The Fall of Austria-Hungary," pp. 81, 82.

19. Sked, *The Decline and Fall of the Habsburg Empire*, p. 187.

20. Ibid., p. 259. F. R. Bridge, in his authoritative diplomatic history of the Habsburg empire, states that during the course of the war, Germany reduced the monarchy to the position of "a helpless satellite" for which a German victory would have meant the end of its existence "as an independent Great Power." Bridge, *The Habsburg Monarchy Among the Great Powers 1815–1918* (New York: Berg, 1990), 341, 380.

21. Sked, *Decline and Fall*, pp. 254–256; Bridge, *The Habsburg Monarchy Among the Great Powers*, pp. 336–338; Deák, "Fall of Austria-Hungary," pp. 82–83.

22. Josef Redlich, *Schicksalsjahre Österreich. Das politische Tagebuch Josef Redlichs*, ed. Fritz Fellner, 2 vols. (Graz: Böhlau, 1953–1954), vol. 1, pp. 238–239. The quotation is on p. 239. On Hoyos, see Fritz Fellner, "Die Mission Hoyos," in ed. Wilhelm Alf, *Deutschlands Sonderweg von Europa 1862–1945* (Frankfurt-am-Main: P. Lang, 1984), 283–316.

23. The memorandum is appended to John Leslie, "Österreich-Ungarn vor dem Kriegsausbruch: Der Ballhausplatz in Wien im Juli 1914 aus dem Sicht eines österreichisch-ungarischen Diplomaten," in ed. Ralph Melville et al., *Deutschland und Europa in der Neuzeit: Festschrift für Karl Otmar Freiherr von Aretin zum 65. Geburtstag* (Wiesbaden: Franz Steiner Verlag, 1988), 663–684, appendix 675–684. The quotation is on p. 675. See also Solomon Wank, "Desperate Counsel in Vienna in July 1914: Berthold Molden's Unpublished Memorandum," *Central European History* 26, no. 3 (1993): 281–310.

24. Quoted in Carl J. Burckhardt, *Reden und Aufzeichnungen* (Zurich: Manesse Verlag, 1952), 109.

25. Otto Brunner, "Das Haus Habsburg und die Donaumonarchie," *Südostforschungen* 14 (1955): 123–124, 126–127, 140–144.

26. Ibid., p. 36.

27. Doyle, *Empires*, pp. 35–36.

28. Gustav Graf Kálnoky, memorandum entitled, "Die Nationalitätenfrage in Oesterreich-Ungarn in ihrer Rückwirkung auf die aeussere Politik der Monarchie." The memorandum is printed in two places: Barbara Jelavich, "Foreign Policy and the National Question in the Habsburg Empire: A Memorandum of Kálnoky," *Austrian History Yearbook* 6–7 (1970–1971): 147–159, and Ernst Rutkowski, ed., *Briefe und Dokumente zur Geschichte der österreichisch-ungarischen Monarchie*, 2 vols. (Munich: R. Oldenburg, 1983), vol. 1, pp. 490–500. The memorandum is discussed in Solomon Wank, "Foreign Policy and the Nationality Problem in Austria-Hungary, 1867–1914," *Austrian History Yearbook* 3, no. 3 (1967): 38–41, 45.

29. See above, n. 3. The two articles by Alexander Motyl have been especially suggestive.

30. Motyl, "From Imperial Decay to Imperial Collapse," p. 19.

31. As used here the term covers substantially the same area as the present-day Austrian Republic.

32. Eisenstadt, *Political System of Empires*, pp. 116–119.

33. Ibid., pp. 132–137, 199.

34. For some suggestive reflections on this point, see Imanuel Geiss, "Decolonisation et conflits post-coloniaux en Afrique: Quelque Reflections," *Colloque international: Les deux guerres mondiales; les analogies et les differences*, Warsaw, September 12–14, 1984 (Warsaw: Comité des Sciences historiques, 1985), 1–22. Geiss's article contains several references to the Habsburg empire and the successor states. See also, Geiss, "Great Powers and Empires: Historical Mechanisms of Their Making and Breaking," pp. 38–42.

35. See in general, R.J.W. Evans, *The Making of the Habsburg Monarchy, 1550–1700* (Oxford: Oxford University Press, 1979).

36. Ibid., p. 447.

37. Dennison Rusinow, "Ethnic Politics in the Habsburg Monarchy and Successor States: Three Answers to the National Question," in *Nationalism and Empire*, pp. 243–267. The quotation is on p. 254.

38. Evans, *The Making of the Habsburg Monarchy*, p. 275.

39. F. R. Bridge, "British Official Opinion and the Domestic Situation in the Habsburg Monarchy, 1908–1914," in ed. B.J.C. McKercher and D. J. Moss, *Shadow and Substance in British Foreign Policy 1895–1939: Memorial Essays Honouring C. J. Lowe* (Edmonton: University of Alberta Press, 1984), 77–113. The quotation is on pp. 99–100.

40. Horst Brettner-Messler, ed., *Die Protokolle des österreichischen Ministerrates 1848–1867*. VI Abteilung, *Das Ministerium Belcredi*, 2 vols. (Vienna, 1971, 1973), vol. 1, Ministerrat, 1. February 1867, p. 401.

41. Ibid., p. 403.

42. Ibid., pp. 405–406.

43. See n. 28.

44. Éva Somogyi, *Die Protokolle des gemeinsamen Ministerrates der österreichisch-ungarischen Monarchie, 1896–1907* (Budapest: Akademiai Kiado, 1991), no. 73 (October 9, 1907), 507.

45. See his memorandum cited in n. 28 above.

46. See above, n. 12.

47. Moytl, "Imperial Collapse and Revolutionary Change," pp. 816–819.

48. The dependent international position of the Habsburg empire is elaborately described in Bridge, *Habsburg Monarchy Among the Great Powers*.

49. Piotyr Wandycz, *The Price of Freedom: A History of East Central Europe from the Middle Ages to the Present* (New York: Routledge, 1992), 196. See also, Henry Cord Meyer, *Mitteleuropa in German Thought and Action 1815–1945* (The Hague: Nijhoff, 1955), 215, 240, 250–1.

50. Fritz Fellner, "The Dissolution of the Habsburg Monarchy and Its Significance for the New Order in Central Europe: A Reappraisal," *Austrian History Yearbook* 4–5 (1968–1969): 3–27, esp. 8–9, 10–12.

51. For some conflicting observations on the legacy of the Habsburg empire, see, Steven Beller, *Reinventing Central Europe*, Working Paper no. 92–95, Center for Austrian Studies, University of Minnesota, 1991, pp. 17–18; and Deák, "Fall of Austria-Hungary," pp. 95–99.

6

THE RUSSIAN EMPIRE

MARK VON HAGEN

Curiously, for all the considerable literature devoted to the fall of the Old Regime in Russia in 1917, very little scholarship has focused on the collapse of the empire as such, by which I mean the breakup of that polyethnic empire into the array of proto-states and regional autonomies that began in February/March 1917 and ended most everywhere by late 1921/1922 with the consolidation of the Soviet Union under Bolshevik rule. I suggest several reasons for that general oversight. The very fact that the empire seemed to collapse only temporarily (if the consolidation of the USSR under the leadership of new political elites a few years later is understood as its restoration in some important senses) undoubtedly reinforced a well-entrenched interpretation of the Russian empire as a nation-state (at least in formation) rather than as a genuinely multinational state. A persuasive spokesman for that interpretation was Peter Struve, the legal Marxist-turned-liberal and Kadet Party leader, who posed the dilemma for Russia in 1911 as one between the undesirable (from his point of view) evolution toward the Habsburg *Nationalitätenstaat* and the desirable (and in his view inevitable) progress toward the nation-state along the lines of Germany or other West European models.[1] For later historians who adopted this view, the short, albeit tragic, years of revolution and civil war merely interrupted a longer-term process of nation-building that somehow culminated in the Soviet state.

This historiographical tradition that sees Russian history as the realization of the nation-state dates to as early as Nikolai Karamzin's history of the Russian state,[2] but had its most influential development in the scholarship of the Russian "state school" and its successors (who were influenced in turn by German Hegelian historical thinking in mid-century and German positivism later in the century).[3] Under the influence of this powerful model of a centralizing, unitary Russian state, any non-Russian or noncentralizing traditions (including a brief and virtually unresearched federalist or regionalist alternative) were viewed as ephemera; for historians of 1917, they were considered only insofar as they contributed to the anarchy that helped defeat the liberal-moderate socialist coalition of the period of Dual Power in 1917 (the Provisional Government and Petrograd Soviet) and secure the triumph of the Bolshevik dictatorship.[4] This is certainly the view of Richard Pipes and E. H. Carr, the two historians of the revolution who have tried most systematically to incorporate the "national question" into their narratives of the fall of the Old Regime and the rise of the Bolsheviks to power.[5] With a sense of amazement, and in places incredulity, both Pipes and Carr describe the rapid and largely unexpected rise of nationalist and regionalist movements in 1917. But theirs is a story of gradual Bolshevik triumph over these historical "accidents" and temporary obstacles as the Russian state subsequently resumed its centralizing, dictatorial (and for Carr modernizing) path.[6] For those states that succeeded in breaking more or less permanently with the Russian empire, Poland and Finland, their histories have for the most part become detached from that of the empire; the case of the Baltic states presented more problems of integration with the overall narrative of Russian and Soviet history (they survived as independent states for the interwar period until their reannexation to the Soviet Union in 1940).

Still, no historian today (with the exception perhaps of some overly inspired by the national movements, including Russian nationalists who would blame the collapse of the empire on the non-Russian secessionist movements and their sponsors from abroad) would trace the fall of the Old Regime directly or primarily to the "national question,"[7] just as few today would blame the national question for the collapse of the Soviet Old Regime. Instead, most historians have sought the causes for the breakup of empire in the conditions of dismantling the Old Regime, not the other way around. For scholars who have attempted to identify the causes for the fall of the autocracy, the debate has been waged between those who favor a more circumstantial or accidental view of the fall of the Old Regime (a view dubbed by Arthur Mendel[8] as the optimists' history and which saw a Russia emerging from the revolutionary years of 1905–1907 with a demi-constitutional monarchy and significant strides toward the rise of a moderate civil society and property-owning peasantry to bolster that regime) and those whose views are framed more by a sense of the profound structural weaknesses and the dilemmas of a European Old Regime state carrying out a rapid and fatally destabilizing modernization (Mendel's "pessimists" see 1905–1907 as the harbinger of 1917, especially in the failure of the liberal alternative and the hardening of positions among radical left and radical right).

Each of the two camps situates the Great War accordingly in its explanatory model: the optimists (who favor the accidental) see the war as the primary cause for the collapse of the largely promising developments since 1907 and for bringing about a revolution that might otherwise have been avoided, whereas the pessimists (prone to downplay personality and short-term events) view the war as only delaying the inevitable social conflagration and exposing even more starkly than before the glaring contradictions that pervaded all levels and aspects of the imperial order. In short, historians have largely concentrated their energies on evaluating the relative chances for success of a reformist or revolutionary outcome of 1917; social historians have tended to favor (by implications of their research at least) a revolutionary outcome, while more narrowly political or institutional historians have favored the reformist. Both camps however, whether looking at major social groups or at imperial institutions, have largely assumed that the empire worked as a nation-state and have devoted marginal, at best, attention to the "national question."

I do not propose a way out of that important debate, but hope to raise a new perspective that, by integrating the national question into the explanatory model, allows for a more complicated (and this is not to suggest that the existing explanatory models are simple-minded) reconsideration of the empire's collapse. After all, what brings together the four comparative cases treated in this volume is that, unlike previous falls of Old Regimes in France or Britain (and even the contemporary fall of the Old Regime of Wilhelmine Germany), the Russian, Ottoman, Habsburg, and Soviet states broke up into a multitude of new state formations, organized primarily around the national principle. The fall of the Old Regimes in France, Britain, and even Germany (to a lesser extent), on the contrary, resulted in the reinforcement of the national idea within the largely preexisting boundaries. By contrast, the Habsburg, Ottoman, and, temporarily, Russian empires and the Soviet state can be seen from this perspective as failed nation-state projects. In other words, the "national idea" had not been successfully integrated into the institutions and political cultures of what remained, at the time of their collapse, very much polyethnic states. (Significantly, when the Soviet Union restored the polyethnic state in its 1922 constitution, its elites rejected an ethnic or national title for the new formation.) In what follows I shall combine elements of the structural and conjunctural approach with a reconsideration of the Great War (and thereby wandering tentatively into the circumstantial camp) in order to begin to explain why the empire collapsed *after* the fall of the Old Regime and how its collapse was largely shaped by the way in which the Old Regime was dismantled.[9]

The Structural Crisis of the Old Regime

The argument for structural crisis, favored until recently by Soviet historians and still by several Western scholars,[10] centers on the incongruence between the imperial political order, with its Orthodox-based autocracy and premodern estate system, and the combined pressures of socioeconomic transformation loosely summed up as modernization, a modernization that was largely driven and certainly exacerbated by international military and economic competition.[11] That crisis was the product of several overlapping structural features.

First, at the base was a socioeconomic crisis that Leon Trotsky formulated as "uneven development";[12] a premodern largely agrarian economy afflicted by rural overpopulation and very low productivity coexisted with a rapid, state-sponsored industrialization drive. The industrialization drive was financed by taxation of the agrarian population, supplemented by extensive foreign borrowing. The heavy tax burden aggravated the already desperate situation of much of the empire's peasantry and placed the "accursed peasant question" at the center of oppositionist politics. This socioeconomic development perspective is only reinforced when we examine the ethnic or national patterns of development. Most of those areas undergoing the most rapid modernization, in the sense of industrialization, urbanization, and the transition to capitalist markets, were also borderland areas (most notably the western borderlands, the Kingdom of Poland, the Baltic provinces, Finland, parts of the Ukrainian lands; also Baku in Transcaucasia), where class and ethnic divisions reinforced one another in potentially explosive mixtures.[13] The first dramatic illustration of the destabilizing consequences of these developments was the Revolution of 1905–1907, which was initially and generally much more violent and protracted in the peripheral provinces (again Poland, the Baltic regions, Ukraine, and Transcaucasia) than in the central Russian ones. Even in the areas less touched by industrial development, violent agrarian disorders frequently pitted Russian, Ukrainian, Latvian, or Belorussian peasants against Polish, Jewish, or German landowners or money lenders.[14]

Second, the state-sponsored industrialization drive was primarily inspired by considerations of security and a fierce international imperial and military competition; Russia's elites entertained great-power ambitions that were not matched by the empire's military and naval resources. Some military planners tried desperately to prepare Russia for the revolution in warfare that transformed the global order in the late nineteenth century, but the necessary changes demanded greater socioeconomic transformations and were stymied by the reluctance of the autocracy to loosen its hold over society. In the event of a major war, such as the Great War would prove to be, the comparative disadvantage of the Russian empire in what Bruce Menning calls "linkages" (including a shortage of young general-staff officers and inattention to wireless communications) would prove nearly fatal against the German military machine.[15] These weak linkages between policy and military capability were part and parcel of late imperial decision-making, which continued to be marked by fragmentation, discontinuities, bureaucratic and personal rivalries, and an overall lack of coordination. For a policy area which so vitally affected the survival of the regime, late imperial military politics was shaped by the ill fit of an outdated dynastic rule and ruling ideology with modern institutions and professional demands.[16]

The uneven development of the empire's resources was reflected in the perceptions of uneven loyalties among the non-Russian peoples; the seeming progress in military modernization continued to rest on a very unstable manpower pool and backward organizational resources. Despite a law (the cornerstone of War Minister Dmitrii Miliutin's military reform of 1874) that had ambitions of universal military service (and was inspired by the recent successes of the Prussian army against Austria and France), in fact the regime continued to rely most heavily on the Slavic peasant population of the empire and exempted large groups of non-European subjects from military service. Here, too, the unwillingness to integrate large sections of the population was most apparent for the borderland regions of the empire.[17] At the same time, the officer corps remained far more representative of the empire's polyethnic population, with Baltic Germans, Finns, Georgians, and Poles especially prominent; but the social chasm that separated the elites, especially the relatively cosmopolitan aristocracy, from the largely Slavic peasantry, was replicated in the army.

Third, that the imperial elites could not rely on the loyalties of the exempted communities was only part of a larger problem of under-institutionalization of the Old Regime. Despite (or perhaps because of) the imperial bureaucracy's ambitions for control and centralization of power, the regime remained remarkably incapable of mobilizing the societal and economic resources it needed to sustain its great-power ambitions. Even after the Great Reforms of the 1860s that were intended to integrate society into the political order of the empire, various threatened elites tried to thwart any real devolution of power away from the emperor and his ministers or loyal gentry servitors in the countryside.[18] Here too, the institutions that were envisioned by the reformers to expand the sphere of local self-government in the empire, the zemstvos, were restricted to the Russian heartland; attempts after 1905 to extend them to the borderlands came up against fierce resistance from the largely Russian gentry.[19]

Insofar as the zemstvos took root in rural society,[20] even that degree of imperial integration at the local level was absent in most of the borderland provinces, where the institution of governor-general often combined civil and military rule in one person. In other words, in several of the borderland regions, where social and ethnic tensions were at their most explosive and where the local population was not trusted to bear the burdens of military service, the imperial state had put down its least secure roots. Even where the zemstvo had been introduced, the lasting legacy of societal distrust in imperial bureaucrats (especially the Interior and War ministries) framed the setting for the conflicts that emerged during the Great War between representatives of "society" in the Union of Towns and Zemstvos and the Red Cross, on the one hand, and the martial-law authorities in occupied and front-line zones, on the other.[21]

Fourth, shaping the socioeconomic, security, and institutional crises of the Old Regime was a looming crisis in imperial ideology that continuously pitted state and society against one another. The tsar, his immediate entourage, certain imperial ministries, and the leadership of the Orthodox hierarchy (including the Holy Synod) tenaciously held onto a set of increasingly anachronistic views about dynastic, autocratic rule that brought them into ever sharper conflicts with modernizing sections of the imperial bureaucracy itself, but also with the rising oppositionist movements in educated society. The tsar and his loyalists came out of the experience of revolution in 1905 ever more determined to hold onto autocracy, empire, and Orthodoxy, even with the advent of the quasi-constitutional monarchy of the Duma period; but even the tsar and his defenders were muddying the waters in the last decades by identifying the autocracy increasingly with the Russian "people" and thereby undercutting the transnational pretensions of ruling elites. The autocracy, certainly reluctantly and probably unconsciously, responded to the pressures of constitutionalism at home and modern nationalism elsewhere in Europe (including the example of other "nationalizing" monarchs) by trying to act "more Russian" and thereby to claim some popular sovereignty by virtue of the national principle.[22]

Over the course of the nineteenth century and at an accelerated pace after 1905, loyalties to imperial transnational identities and institutions suffered considerable erosion. In an era of nationalism and imperialist competition, secular counter-elites challenged the dynasty's hegemony with a variety of alternative ideas and ideologies: liberal and conservative nationalism, liberal imperialism, anti-imperial nationalism, federalism, and varieties of revolutionary socialism.[23] The intrusion of mass politics into the empire's life saw not only the rise of liberal and revolutionary parties, but the consolidation of conservative and reactionary movements as well (the gentry reaction, the rise of a radical Russian national and religious right, especially in the ethnically mixed borderlands). The rise of this conservative politics, combined with the evolution of a large part of the liberal constitutionalist movement in the direction of Russian statist nationalism,[24] effectively foreclosed any serious renegotiation of the polyethnic state in the Duma, especially after the coup d'état of Prime Minister Petr Stolypin on June 3, 1907, that narrowed the electoral franchise and thereby excluded not only most of the radical peasant and worker parties, but nearly all participation by non-Russian peoples in legal political activity.[25] In the meantime, however, in the conditions of relative liberalization of political activity after 1905, the excluded national and revolutionary movements were nonetheless able to expand their popular bases for the next confrontation in 1917.

The 1905 Revolution, as the starting point of a conjunctural transformation, revealed these crises in sharp relief. The regime felt itself as never before isolated from society and betrayed by its presumably loyal peasant subjects; the army suffered disastrous defeats at the hands of a "backward" Asian power and proved temporarily incapable of suppressing domestic unrest; the borderland regions erupted in social and ethnic conflict; and the educated elites in and outside of government were divided and confused in their loyalties. The October Manifesto opened a new era in imperial political life, but not a less troublesome one. The non-Russian political leaders lost faith in their liberal Russian counterparts, as did native Russian socialists after a brief period of a united front of oppositionists.

Despite the emergence of movements and parties of nationalist opposition among the non-Russian (and Russian) communities, the peoples of the empire continued to coexist in relative peace until the outbreak of the Great War. In everyday practice, the minority communities of the empire combined adherence to local languages, religions, and cultures with loyalty to the tsar and imperial state. With varying degrees of qualification, Baltic Germans, Jews, Tatars, Ukrainians, and Poles formed a cosmopolitan elite whose loyalties were focused on the transnational state and the autocrat.[26] But because the fates of the ethnic and national communities were integrally tied to the structural crises of the Old Regime, any event that destabilized the structures of the autocracy, such as the Great War would prove to be, inevitably wrought a transformation in the relations among those communities as well.

The Great War, the Revolutions of 1917, and Imperial Collapse

Such, then, was the picture of the empire on the eve of the Great War. The war not only exacerbated all these tensions, but qualitatively transformed them, especially those related to the polyethnic composition of the Russian empire. The war itself, whose origins and significance have produced a large and divided literature in European history (but not among Russian historians), was at least partly the consequence of what might well be conceived as an international structural crisis, a longer-term reshaping of international relations occasioned by the rise of Germany, new industrial and military technologies, and the breakdown of Central and East European dynastic alliances in the new conditions of imperial competition, the rise of the nation-states of Western Europe, and the pan-European constitutional challenges to autocratic rule. In other words, the war itself might also be interpreted as a symptom or component part of the overall crisis of the Old Regime(s) (rather than primarily as a largely accidental circumstance contributing to its collapse).

The beginnings of the collapse of the empire proper date from the war, when German and Austrian armies reversed the initial Russian successes and occupied all of Russian Poland, much of the Baltic provinces, and the western borderlands by 1915.[27] The war pitted the multinational Russian empire against two other multinational empires, the Ottoman and Habsburg, and was paradoxically waged from the start in the rhetoric of national liberation. Wartime propaganda and practice had the consequence of internationalizing the empires' ethnic problems, including the legitimizing of a practice of appealing to the subject national minorities within the enemy's territory to overthrow their imperial regimes, financing emigré nationalist political organizations and their publication apparatuses under the slogan of national liberation.[28] Pan-Germanism, pan-Slavism, and pan-Turkism took on new life as occupation regimes came and went on the borderlands of the empires. Specific wartime policies targeted ethnic groups and served to overlay many social and political conflicts with a national patina, whereas ethnic identities in the empire were politicized and militarized in new and dangerous ways.[29] For example, the Germans, Austrians, and Russians experimented with the formation of national military units within their respective armies made up of emigré volunteers and then prisoners of war specifically for deployment against their respective oppressor empires.

Occupation regimes proved especially destructive for the mixed ethnic populations of the borderlands of the belligerent empires. In the name of military security, martial-law authorities claimed broad powers over censorship, detention of suspected spies and other politically reliable persons, and general movement in and out of the military zones. Discriminatory legislation either privileged or disadvantaged one ethnic group over another in matters of language and schooling, religious practice, obligations for military service, property rights, and other economic warfare measures. Churches, synagogues, schools, and publishing houses were closed under some regimes and reopened under others; property was confiscated from suspect communities and redistributed among those deemed more loyal; men and women who were identified with the "wrong" national identities were deported out of the security zones, often arrested, tortured, or executed on the slightest pretext.[30] The evacuations visited even more frightful destruction on the unwitting communities of the borderlands; scorched-earth policies were coupled with forced mass population transfers to deny the enemy any further advantages from their occupation. All the belligerent governments were unprepared to cope with the flood of refugees, but the Russian Old Regime was particularly inept and generally turned over relief efforts to nongovernmental organizations, most of which promptly devised national identity tests and distributed meager aid only to those who could "prove" they belonged to the correct ethnic community.[31] The refugees themselves, powerless in their homeless conditions, were ever more inclined to respond favorably to the appeals of radical parties, while the communities that were forced to receive them also struck out in riots and other violence against the unwelcome newcomers.[32]

The mobilization of the Russian nationalist right and the harsh policies of the military authorities had the further unintended consequence of encouraging the consolidation of more radical anti-Russian movements throughout the Russian empire. Even before the catastrophic evacuation of the summer of 1915, the occupation policies of the Galician regime had begun to make their impact felt in other parts of the empire. The continual deportations of politically unreliable individuals and large groups was transforming Kiev, among other major cities, into a cauldron of conspiratorial societies and revolutionary circles.

By 1917 the effects of these policies were to severely constrain the generally more fluid prewar options for identities and loyalties within the empire; in particular it meant that membership in one ethnos or nation or another was no longer necessarily compatible with loyalty to the empire's institutions, at least as far as that was interpreted by local military or civilian authorities. In the case of the Russian empire, the acceptable loyalty came to be ever more closely identified with Russian nationality; Germans, Jews, Poles, Turks, and Ukrainians were viewed increasingly as real or potential traitors. The Russian nationalist right generally viewed the war as an opportunity to rebuild and revive their organizations under the slogans of patriotism, but even liberals were susceptible to outbursts of chauvinist (*kvasnoi*) patriotism that the war made acceptable. The retreats and failures of the first year of the war also set in motion a murderous dynamic of suspicion and a veritable obsession with treason and traitors that focused on ethnic "others." Beyond the severe narrowing of identity options, the stakes attached to those options were raised by the politics of war, which translated into deportations, property confiscations, arrests, torture, murder, and a range of repressions against non-Russian cultural and political life.[33]

Although the Russian imperial elites, as did the other belligerent empires, blamed the enemy for fomenting ethnic and national discontent within its borders, their own wartime policies did far more to inject the national element into imperial politics than the enemy did by reinforcing the importance of ethnicity as a weapon and policy instrument.[34]

Katherine Verdery, in her insightful explorations of national sentiment and nationalism in post-Soviet eastern Europe, looks not only to those policies and attitudes that sustained ethnic identities during the Soviet Old Regimes, but also at the "conditions of exit" from those Old Regimes.[35] Analogous conditions can help explain the collapse of the Russian empire after the February/March Revolution of 1917. The Provisional Government, too, introduced democratization of the imperial order by repudiating many of the former imperial elites, destroying repressive institutions, and devolving central authority to local representatives of educated society (*obshchestvo*) who shared the Petrograd leadership's liberal agenda. Immediately organizations dominated by educated society that had been active during the war, especially the Unions of Towns and Zemstvos, began assuming many of the functions previously performed by central ministries.[36] In these conditions, ethnic and regional movements quickly filled the political vacuum left by the withdrawal of central authority. In all the borderlands and many of the heartland regions, such new powers went hand in hand with demands for greater autonomy and for a federalist reworking of the empire's political order.

Such aspirations caught the new regime in Petrograd by surprise; the Dual Authority pursued a politics of procrastination and postponement with regard to the claims for greater autonomy and self-rule by the borderlands and looked for scapegoats, whether foreign powers or local revolutionaries, to blame for the ethnic tensions. Both the liberals and moderate socialists firmly believed that ethnic discontents were the consequence of imperial nationality policies and expected such tensions to disappear with the declaration of constitutional freedoms.[37] The liberals in power were ready to accede to what they perceived as the justified demands of Polish and Finnish nationalists, but balked at such demands from Ukrainians, Tatars, or the peoples of Transcaucasia.[38]

The war dragged on, the social and ethnic conflicts grew sharper, but the Provisional Government adhered to a strict, albeit selectively strict, legalism and called for patience until the Constituent Assembly would resolve all the outstanding problems. In the meantime, the national and regional movements took advantage of the confusion to appeal to broader social constituencies, while those constituencies pressured their fledgling leaders into ever more radical positions.

A particularly dramatic example was soldiers. The wartime experiments with national military formations[39] set a precedent for soldiers serving the cause of national liberation, even if they had been meant for breaking up the enemy's empire. With their newly won freedoms, soldiers began demanding a revolution in their own conditions; for non-Russian soldiers and officers, this often meant extending the principle of national military formations to their nations and allowing them to be transferred closer to their native homelands.[40] The imperial high command split over whether to permit the extension of the earlier experiments, but individual commanders on the ground frequently sanctioned them even without waiting for authorization from their superiors; they justified their innovations as a way to combat the rapidly spreading "democratization" and Bolshevization of the ranks and naively hoped that they would be better able to cope with the nationalization of units than they would with socialists and revolutionaries. Not only did such experiments contribute to the further disintegration of the imperial army, still facing a formidable German-led coalition force, but returning soldiers forced local and regional civilian politicians into radical and belligerent positions vis-à-vis Petrograd.[41] The soldiers demanded peace, a national solution to the land question, cultural and intellectual freedoms for their nations, and real political autonomy (eventually upgraded to secession from the Russian state).[42]

During 1917 the Bolsheviks supported all these planks and often worked hand in hand with the nationalist organizations, including the most separatist émigré ones,[43] but once they came to power in November they refused to recognize the existing national and regional governments because of their "bourgeois" character and tried to install regimes more sympathetic to Bolshevik power.[44] This hostile stance on the part of the Bolsheviks forced the still vacillating borderland elites into secession, but many refused to abandon their hopes for cooperating with a genuinely democratic, revolutionary Russia. Once the borderlands seceded, the armed forces created grudgingly by the Provisional Government provided the necessary military support that allowed the regimes briefly to survive repeated attacks from the Central Powers, the Bolsheviks, the White Armies, and domestic insurgent forces. The relatively greater tactical flexibility of the Bolsheviks regarding the national aspirations of many borderland elites contributed to their victory over the anti-Bolshevik White movement, whose leaders persistently defended their understanding of the Provisional Government's nationality policy as the preservation of Russia, "one and indivisible."[45]

Conclusion

The collapse of the empire followed on the fall of the Old Regime, but shared many of the same structural and conjunctural causes, especially once the national question is factored in. The impression of uneven economic development is reinforced when one extends the survey of important trends to the borderlands. The patterns of uneven development are reflected in the empire's hesitant integration of its peoples and social groups, including in such key areas of national security as military conscription policy. The failure of imperial ideology at the very top of the political apex to transform itself into a set of more modern ideas, together with the ideology of Russian counter-elites who would come to power in 1917 and had evolved into a neo-pan-Slavic and statist Russian nationalism, also proved dysfunctional when confronted with challenges from regional and national sub-elites. Finally, the conditions of exit from the Old Regime provided the immediate causes for the breakup of the empire when the Provisional Government destroyed much of the imperial political and administrative structure and naively placed its hopes in the restorative powers of society to preserve the empire in its new democratic version.

Nationalism as such did not bring down the empire; rather, the practices of wartime regimes accelerated trends toward relocating identities and loyalties around national symbols by raising the stakes that followed from those identities. In the political space that the Provisional Government opened up after the fall of the Romanov dynasty, nation became one of several powerful sets of symbols, together with class, around which oppositionist movements crystallized against the Petrograd proto-government. The Provisional Government's insistence on preserving the empire in the name of its European great-power ambitions and its policies of procrastination and selectively strict legalism during a breakdown in state institutions and the erosion of traditional elites served to push initially moderate sub-national and regional elites reluctantly into more and more extreme positions of secession and independence.

When the multinational Russian state went to war against other multinational states, the under-institutionalized and poorly integrated structures proved a major liability. The same structures may also go some way toward explaining the failure of the proto-states to survive, absent other geopolitical advantages (distance from the Bolshevik center) and international support (Baltic states and Poland in particular).[46]

Notes

1. See his "Raznyia temy," *Russkaia mysl'* no. 1 (January 1911): 184–187.

2. *Istoriia Gosudarstva Rossiiskogo*, 12 vols. (Moscow: Izd. A. A. Petrovicha, 1903).

3. For a survey of some of the most important features of the state school, which included Sergei Solov'iev, Boris Chicherin, Pavel Miliukov, and Alexander Kizevetter, see the essay by Miliukov, *Glavnye techeniia russkoi istoricheskoi mysli* (St. Petersburg: Izd. M. V Aver'ianova, 1913); also chapters in N. Rubinshtein, *Russkaia istoriografiia* (Moscow: Gospolitizdat, 1941).

4. For a recent critique of the historical approach to the Russian empire as a nation-state and an ambitious alternative narrative of imperial Russia, see Andreas Kappeler *Russland als Vielvölkerreich* (Munich: C. H. Beck Verlag, 1992).

5. *The Formation of the Soviet Union* (Cambridge, Mass.: Harvard University Press 1964); and *The Bolshevik Revolution, 1917–1923*, 3 vols. (New York: Macmillan, 1950), vol 1., esp. pt. 3.

6. Pipes' title, *Formation of the Soviet Union*, shapes his narrative in a teleological tone, with the first two chapters chronicling the disintegration of the Russian empire and the remaining devoted to the Soviet conquest of the various breakaway regions. Carr entitles pt. 3, "Dispersal and Reunion," with the constitution of the USSR as the final chapter in his history of 1917–1923.

7. Pipes, too, sees the rise of nationalist movements as a consequence, not the primary cause, of the anarchy unleashed by the fall of the old regime and the incapacity of the Provisional Government to contain the disorder.

8. "On Interpreting the Fate of Imperial Russia," in ed. T. Stavrou, *Russia Under the Last Tsar* (Minneapolis: University of Minnesota Press, 1969), 13–41.

9. In so doing, I shall adapt some of the hypotheses formulated by Andreas Kappeler in his masterful study, *Russland als Vielvölkerreich*.

10. See Ronald Grigor Suny, "Toward a Social History of the October Revolution," *American Historical Review* 88 (February 1983): 31–52; and his "Revision and Retreat in the Historiography of 1917: Social History and Its Critics," *Russian Review* 53 (April 1994): 165–82.

11. Variants of these arguments have been made by Theda Skocpol, *States and Social Revolutions* (Cambridge: Cambridge University Press, 1979); Theodore von Laue, *Why Lenin? Why Stalin?* (Philadelphia: J. B. Lippincott, 1971); and the authors' collective in *Krizis samoderzhaviia, 1895–1917* (Leningrad: Nauka, 1984).

12. For the classic formulation, see *The Russian Revolution*, ed. F. W. Dupee, trans. Max Eastman (New York: Doubleday, 1959), preface and ch. 1.

13. Kappeler, *Russland*, ch. 8.

14. Kappeler, *Russland*, ch. 9; Z. Lenskii, "Natsional'noe dvizhenie," and K. Zalevskii, "Natsional'nyia dvizheniia," in ed. L. Martov, *Obshchestvennoe dvizhenie v Rossii v nachale XX-go veka*, 4 vols. (St. Petersburg: Obshchestvennaia Pol'za, 1911), vol. 4, pts. 1–2; Abraham Ascher, *The Revolution of 1905* (Stanford, Calif.: Stanford University Press, 1988); Teodor Shanin, *Russia 1905–07: Revolution as a Moment of Truth* (New Haven: Yale University Press, 1986); see also the collection of documents compiled by I. D. Kuznetsov, *Natsional'nye dvizheniia v period pervoi revoliutsii v Rossii. Sbornik dokumentov iz arkhiva byv. Departamenta Politsii* (Cheboksary: Chuvashskoe Gos. Izdvo, 1935); and L. M. Ivanov, A. M. Pankratova, and A. L. Sidorov, *Revoliutsiia 1905–07 gg. v natsional'nykh raionakh Rossii. Sbornik statei* (Moscow: Gospolitizdat, 1955).

15. On the problems of backwardness and modernization in military affairs, see William C. Fuller, Jr., *Strategy and Power, 1800–1914* (New York: The Free Press, 1992); and Bruce Menning, *Bayonets before Bullets* (Bloomington: Indiana University Press, 1992).

16. In addition to the linkages discussed above, Russia suffered from a chronic shortage of noncommissioned officers, especially when compared to the German army. The poorly developed primary educational network and weak career incentives for NCOs were rooted in the socioeconomic backwardness of the empire.

17. On Miliutin's anxieties about the loyalties of non-Russian ethnic groups, see P. A. Zaionchkovskii, *Voennye reformy 1860–1870 godov v Rossii* (Moscow: Moscow University, 1952), 261ff., 304–305, 308, 312; Robert F. Baumann, "Universal Service Reform and Russia's Imperial Dilemma," *War and Society* 4, no. 2 (September 1986): 31; and

Forrestt A. Miller, *Dmitrii Miliutin and the Reform Era in Russia* (Nashville, Tenn.: Vanderbilt University Press, 1968), 152–168.

18. S. Frederick Starr, *Decentralization and Self-Government in Russia, 1830–70* (Princeton: Princeton University Press, 1972).

19. On the "gentry reaction," see Roberta Manning, *The Crisis of the Old Order in Russia: Gentry and Government, 1861–1914* (Princeton: Princeton University Press, 1981); and Leopold H. Haimson, ed., *The Politics of Rural Russia, 1905–1914* (Bloomington, Ind.: Indiana University Press, 1979).

20. And here, the volume edited by Terence Emmons, *The Zemstvo in Russia* (Cambridge: Cambridge University Press, 1982), casts considerable doubt on the success and viability of these institutions even in those areas that had the longest experience with them.

21. Daniel Graf, "Military Rule Behind the Russian Front, 1914–1917: The Political Ramifications," *Jahrbücher für Geschichte Osteuropas*, N. F. 22, no. 3 (1974): 390ff.

22. See Richard Wortman, "Moscow and Petersburg: The Problem of Political Center in Tsarist Russia, 1881–1914," in ed. Sean Wilentz, *Rites of Power: Symbolism, Ritual and Politics since the Middle Ages* (Philadelphia: University of Pennsylvania Press, 1985).

23. The literature on the socialist and liberal movements is by now extensive and well-known. For some of the other important political trends, see Georg von Rauch, *Russland: staatliche Einheit und nationale Vielfalt; föderalistische Kräfte und Ideen in der russischen Geschichte* (Munich: Isar-Verlag, 1953); Dmitri von Mohrenschildt, *Towards a United States of Russia: Plans and Projects of Federal Reconstruction of Russia in the 19th Century* (Rutherford, Va.: Fairleigh Dickinson University Press, 1981); Serge A. Zenkovsky, *Pan-Turkism and Islam in Russia* (Cambridge, Mass.: Harvard University Press, 1960).

24. William G. Rosenberg, *Liberals in the Russian Revolution: The Constitutional Democratic Party, 1917–1921* (Princeton: Princeton University Press, 1974); Richard Pipes, *Struve: Liberal on the Right, 1905–1944* (Cambridge, Mass: Harvard University Press, 1980).

25. See Geoffrey Hosking, *The Russian Constitutional Experiment: Government and Duma, 1907–1914* (Cambridge: Cambridge University Press, 1973); Robert Edelman, *Gentry Politics on the Eve of the Russian Revolution: The Nationalist Party, 1907–1914* (New Brunswick, N.J.: Rutgers University Press, 1980).

26. Jeffrey Brooks has argued that Russian popular literature revealed a relatively more tolerant and cosmopolitan attitude toward non-Russians, especially when contrasted to contemporary American and British popular fiction, after the turn of the century. See his *When Russia Learned to Read* (Princeton: Princeton University Press, 1985), ch. 6. Similarly Paul Bushkovitch (in an unpublished paper, "What is Russia? Russian National Consciousness and the State, 1500–1917") observed that Russian national politics at the end of the old regime remained backward vis-à-vis its Western and Central European variants, where a more militant and chauvinist politics was becoming the norm before the outbreak of the Great War.

27. For the history of the war and its major campaigns, see W. Bruce Lincoln, *Passage Through Armageddon* (New York: Touchstone, 1986); and Norman Stone, *The Eastern Front, 1914–1917* (New York: Scribner, 1975).

28. Marc Ferro, "La politique des nationalites du gouvernement provisoire, fevrier-octobre 1917," *Cahiers du monde russe et sovietique* 2 (1961): 131–65; also Helene Carrere

d'Encausse, *The Great Challenge: Nationalities and the Bolshevik State, 1917–1930*, trans. Nancy Festinger (New York: Holmes and Meier, 1991).

29. Robert W. Coonrod, "The Duma's Attitude toward War-time Problems of Minority Groups," *ASEER* 13 (1954): 30–38; Heinz-Dietrich Loewe, *Antisemitismus und reaktionäre Utopie* (Hamburg: Hoffmann und Campe Verlag, 1978); Ingeborg Fleischhauer, *Die Deutschen im Zarenreich* (Stuttgart: Deutsche Verlags-Anstalt, 1986), 479–522.

30. For a hostile description of Russian occupation policies in Galicia, see Marzell Chlamtacz, *Lembergs politische Physiognomie während der russischen Invasion* (Vienna, 1916).

31. For the chaos of relief efforts, see Evgenii Nikol'skii, "Bezhentsy v Velikuiu voinu," unpublished manuscript, Hoover Institution Archives; also P. P. Gronskii, "The Effects of the War on the Central Government Institutions of Russia" (unpublished manuscript, Hoover Institution Archives); and T. I. Polner, et al., *Russian Local Government During the War and the Union of Zemstvos* (New Haven: Yale University Press, 1930).

32. Among the dilemmas created for the Russian government by the evacuation was the de facto breaching of the Pale of Settlement for the empire's Jewish population for the first time. Local governors in the inner provinces were overwhelmed by the arrival of so many refugees and warned that they could not be responsible for the safety of the new inhabitants, "because the people are worked up and there is agitation for pogroms, particularly on the part of soldiers coming back from the front." Arkadii N. Iakhontov, *Prologue to Revolution: Notes of A. N. Iakhontov on the Secret Meetings of the Council of Ministers, 1915*, ed. and trans. Michael Cherniavsky (Englewood Cliffs, N.J.: Prentice-Hall, 1967), 58, 102.

33. I explore these transformations more comprehensively in an unpublished paper, "The Great War and the Mobilization of Ethnicity in the Russian Empire."

34. For similar explanations of the rise of national movements outside the Russian empire, see Pierre Birnbaum, *States and Collective Action* (Cambridge: Cambridge University Press, 1988); John Breuilly, *Nationalism and the State* (Chicago: University of Chicago Press, 1993).

35. "Nationalism and National Sentiment in Post-Socialist Romania," *Slavic Review* 52, no. 2 (1993): 179–203. Verdery has in mind primarily the processes generally known as democratization and marketization.

36. See Daniel T. Orlovsky, "Reform During Revolution: Governing the Provinces in 1917," in ed. Robert O. Crummey, *Reform in Russia and the USSR: Past and Prospects* (Urbana, Ill.: University of Illinois Press, 1989); and Robert Paul Browder and Alexander F. Kerensky, eds., *The Russian Provisional Government 1917*, 3 vols. (Stanford, Calif.: Stanford University Press, 1961), vol. 1, pt. 2, chs. 5–7.

37. The Georgian Menshevik Iraklii Tsereteli described the stubborn indifference to the national strivings of the subject peoples of the Russian empire on the part of the socialist intelligentsia members of those very peoples. See his discussion of the national question in I. I. Tsereteli, *Vospominaniia o Fevral'skoi revoliutsii*, 2 vols. (Paris and The Hague, 1963), vol. 2, pp. 69–161.

38. P. Galuzo, "Iz istorii natsional'noi politiki Vremmenogo Pravitel'stva (Ukraina, Finlandiia, Khiva)," *Krasnyi arkhiv*, 30 (1928): 46–79; Wolodymyr Stojko, "Ukrainian National Aspirations and the Russian Provisional Government," in ed. Taras Hunczak, *The Ukraine, 1917–1921: A Study in Revolution* (Cambridge, Mass.: Harvard University

Press, 1977), 5–32. For Kadet positions on the national question, see B. Nol'de, *Natsion-al'nyi vopros v Rossii* (Petrograd: Tipografiia T-va A. S. Suvorina, 1917); and F. F. Kokoshkin, *Oblastnaia avtonomiia i edinstvo Rossii* (Moscow: G. Lissner, 1906); and C. J. Smith, "Miliukov and the Russian National Question," *Harvard Slavic Studies* 4 (1957): 395–419.

39. By 1917 the Russian General Staff had agreed to the formation of separate units of Czechs, Slovaks, Croats, Slovenians, Serbs, Poles, and Armenians.

40. See Allan Wildman, *The End of the Russian Imperial Army*, 2 vols. (Princeton: Princeton University Press 1980); and M. S. Frenkin, *Russkaia armiia i revoliutsiia 1917–1918* (Munich: Logos, 1978).

41. The relations between the Ukrainian Central Rada in Kiev and a host of Ukrainian soldiers' congresses at the northwestern, southwestern, and Romanian fronts, as well as the three All-Ukrainian Soldiers' Congresses in 1917 are the most dramatic illustration of this dynamic. See O. I. Shchus', "Vseukrains'kyi viys'kovi z'izdy," *Istorychni zoshyty* no. 7 (1992).

42. Richard Pipes argues that "the national question in 1917 had perhaps its most rapid development in the army," *The Formation of the Soviet Union*, p. 56.

43. For examples of Bolsheviks collaborating with the Union for the Liberation of Ukraine, which operated out of Germany and Austro-Hungary, see the Andry Zhuk collection, National Archives of Canada. See also Stefan T. Possony, *Lenin: The Compulsive Revolutionary* (Chicago: Regnery, 1964), 169–170.

44. For a summary of much of the literature on the "national revolutions" in 1917, Ronald Grigor Suny, *The Revenge of the Past* (Stanford, Calif.: Stanford University Press, 1993), ch. 2; and Suny's contribution to this volume. On Ukraine, see John-Paul Himka, "The National and Social in the Ukrainian Revolution of 1917–20: The Historiographical Agenda," *Archiv für Sozialgeschichte* 34 (1994): 95–110.

45. Anna Procyk, *Russian Nationalism and Ukraine: The Nationality Policy of the Volunteer Army During the Civil War* (Toronto: Canadian Institute of Ukrainian Studies Press, 1995).

46. For further exploration of these matters, see my "The Dilemmas of Ukrainian Independence and Statehood, 1917–1921," *The Harriman Institute Forum* 7, no. 5 (1994): 7–11.

7

THE SOVIET UNION

VICTOR ZASLAVSKY

The sudden dissolution of the Soviet Union in 1991 was one of the most unusual events in world history; it is probably the only case of a superpower and its empire collapsing in peacetime, and seemingly for largely internal reasons. In the few years that have passed since the Soviet Union ceased to exist, there has been no dearth of explanations for this fateful event, though thus far analysts have often confused the causes of Soviet collapse with what precipitated it, by attributing Soviet disintegration to perestroika and other reckless policies of Gorbachev's administration—a position still espoused by the Russian right. More recently, however, scholars have begun to examine the deeper forces that shaped the destiny of Soviet society. In trying to identify a host of causes that led to Soviet disintegration, some have stressed the failure of the ruling party to find a mobilizing task and prevent its own corrupt routinization;[1] others insist that the loss of ideological legitimacy rather than economic decline was at the root of the Soviet failure;[2] still others argue that it was caused in large part by the growing demands of the Soviet nationalities for independence and autonomy.[3]

All these causes and a number of others singled out by researchers are undoubtedly relevant, but an overview of the growing literature on the subject still leads to the conclusion that in dealing with the profound systemic crisis that hit Soviet society, most scholars tend to concentrate on those aspects and manifestations that particularly suit their discipline and interests. As a result, they identify and analyze economic, political, ideological, ethnic, and cultural aspects of the Soviet crisis, but often ignore their numerous interconnections and fail to investigate the underlying logic of the Soviet development.

In exploring the causes and precipitants of the Soviet collapse, scholars are confronted with two major analytic problems. First, there is the perennial problem of determining the nature of the Soviet system. As a result of the opening of Russian archives and vastly increased access to previously secret statistical material, an enormous volume of empirical data has recently become available for scholarly analysis and interpretation. By now it is beyond doubt that the Soviet system possessed a continuously recognizable identity, but a full-fledged theory of Soviet historical development has yet to be presented. Second, in examining the "grand failure"[4] of the Soviet Union, scholars simultaneously deal with two closely intertwined and interdependent but nonetheless distinct processes: the failure and eventual demise of the Soviet society as a particular type of socioeconomic and cultural system and the disintegration of the USSR as an autonomous political entity. Studies of the demise of the Soviet model[5] and of the collapse of the Soviet empire[6] often appear so disconnected as to address two totally different subjects. It is hardly a coincidence, however, that all multiethnic Soviet-type societies with distinct ethno-territorial structures collapsed almost simultaneously along ethno-territorial lines. The double problem of the collapse of the Soviet system and the disintegration of the Soviet empire calls for a thorough reassessment of the theoretical orientation of Soviet studies.

This discussion is based on the hypothesis that the exhaustion of the Soviet model in multiethnic societies manifests itself in their ethnoterritorial disintegration. To explain why the USSR collapsed at the time and in the way it did, I will briefly survey the Soviet system's distinctive features and developmental strategies and enumerate the particular structural problems that led to a general systemic crisis. My aim is to clarify why Soviet "military-industrial society" proved to be an unviable and unsustainable form of social organization. The Soviet party-state, operating in the particular ethnic environment of the former tsarist Russia, produced a nationality policy which was responsible for an intensive nation-building process and in the end maintained and reinforced the imperial character of the Soviet Union. Finally, I will focus on the inevitability of ethnoterritorial breakup of the Soviet empire as a consequence of Soviet systemic crisis.

The Nature of the Soviet System

Two basic conceptions or models have always dominated studies of Soviet society: the industrial-society model, which focuses on the features Soviet society had in common with other industrial societies, and the totalitarian-society model, which stresses those characteristics of Soviet society that distinguished it from the political systems of the West. The first emphasizes the advanced economic and technological progress achieved in the Soviet Union: continuous economic growth and industrialization, rapid urbanization, the extension of formal education to a large portion of the population, and the rise of modern communications were key features not only of Western industrial societies, but also of the Soviet one. The second concentrates on the striking differences between Soviet and Western industrial societies and attributes them to totalitarianism, a historically novel form of domination embodied in Stalin's and Hitler's regimes. Initially, the authors of this school often ignored its structural and global underpinnings, concentrating instead on the struggles and mutations of the political regime and the ruling party. But in the 1960s and early 1970s some scholars of Soviet society began to expand the scope of their inquiry beyond the political regime.[7] Having acknowledged that totalitarianism provided the Soviet system with a continuously recognizable identity, they examined the structural and cultural consequences of totalitarianism. In so doing, they suggested a useful synthesis of the industrial-society and totalitarian models for analyzing the Soviet experience, which was to understand it as a radical strategy of catch-up modernization.

Now, as the spectacular collapse of the Soviet Union prompts social scientists to advance new interpretations of Soviet history and legacy, a reexamination of the old debate between totalitarian and modernization theorists and a reassessment of the totalitarian model have taken hold of the scholarly agenda.[8] As Abbot Gleason has remarked, proponents of the totalitarian model now have "a whole new set of allies: Russian intellectuals and academics who themselves have come to feel that no term is as suggestive of their country's experience as totalitarianism."[9] The increasing use of the term in post-Soviet societies can hardly be explained as a manifestation of Russian and East European intellectual bewilderment or as an exculpatory tactic—the totalitarian nature of Soviet and Nazi German society has been debated among Russian intellectuals since the 1930s.[10] Far from perceiving totalitarianism as "the great mobilizing and unifying concept of the Cold War,"[11] those with firsthand experience of Soviet-type societies have viewed totalitarianism as a system which concentrates the overwhelming power over human beings and material resources in the supreme political authority of the party-state. The problem of defining the nature of systems, in which the enormous political power attained by the party-state was complemented by the concentration of all economic power and means of cultural control, remains an urgent task for social scientists trying to make sense of the twentieth century.

I do not see any compelling reason to reject totalitarianism as an ideal-type construction depicting a social system that found its fullest realization in Stalin's Soviet Union.[12] This concept has been accepted and elaborated upon by many analysts with firsthand experience of life in early totalitarian systems,[13] and millions of Soviets and East Europeans believe it to be a true reflection of their experiences under Stalinism. Those social scientists who reject totalitarianism as a value-charged concept are obliged to develop new concepts and categories with which to grapple with the Soviet system. It is true that neither the totalitarian model as presented in politological studies of the 1950s nor modernization theory as utilized in the 1960s are very helpful in "identifying the conceptual continuity of the Soviet regime."[14] Both totalitarian and modernization theorists of the 1950s and 1960s recognized the historically innovative and specific character of the Soviet system. In their approaches, however, they often reduced it to its political aspects and failed to provide a serious analysis of the central facet of Soviet society, its economic organization, and in so doing virtually ignored the pioneering works of such economists as Boris Brutzkus, Ludwig von Mises, and Friedrich von Hayek.

The major lesson to be drawn from decades of scholarly debate in the field of Soviet studies is that using an eclectic, multidisciplinary combination of paradigms from various social sciences provides a sound scientific approach for understanding the Soviet system as a novel form of social organization. The same eclectic approach is useful for articulating consistent theoretical accounts of continuity and change in that organization, beyond the well-known manifestations of totalitarianism as a political regime. It allows us to examine both the complex interconnections between the Soviet political order, and its economic, cultural and structural underpinnings, and the position of the Soviet state in the developing world system. On the one hand, the particular identity of the Soviet system was determined by both its essential, "genetic" features and its developmental characteristics that express the internal logic of the system's functioning.[15] On the other hand, this identity was forged in the process of interaction between the Soviet Union and its rapidly mutating international environment.

Following the Soviet disintegration, both Russian and Western scholars gained access to an enormous stock of information concerning the Soviet system's inner workings, as well as the plans and intentions of the Soviet leadership. As a result, reliable quantitative data on the true scope of the militarization of Soviet economy and society have been made available to stunned analysts.[16] These data not only represent a decisive contribution to a better understanding of Soviet reality, but also necessitate an elaboration of new models and paradigms related to the nature of the Soviet system. Inspired by Herbert Spenser's analysis of the contrasting organizational principles of industrialism and militarism and the distinction between the "externally oriented" and "internally oriented" states in the intellectual tradition of German historiography and political economy, Andrew Janos in his recent works justifiably insists that the paradigm of the externally-oriented garrison state and "militarized society" is indispensable for making sense of the Soviet experience.[17] There is no doubt that, in the light of newly available information, the notion of the Soviet syndrome based on an interdependent and mutually reinforcing single-party political regime and centrally planned economy has to be complemented by the military state paradigm. The specificity of Soviet modernization thus becomes the focal point of an analysis of the evolution and the subsequent devolution of the Soviet system.

The Stalinist revolution of the 1930s resulted in the formation of a "military-industrial society" that contradicts the conventional conception of industrial society as a form of social organization based on continuous technological progress and the growing productivity of labor. The one-party regime, armed with the Marxist-Leninist ideology and a blueprint for a socialist society, suppressed private property and the market. Central planning was introduced as the major mechanism of exchange, resource allocation, and social integration. The unquestionable dominance of central planning, in turn, reinforced and stabilized the one-party system. The result was a socioeconomic order characterized by a command economy and a fusion between political and economic management.[18] Under Stalin, the Soviet system was cemented by a growing militarization of the economy and society. This development delivered a final blow to the already weakened market relations in Soviet society, since the dominant military industry was largely immune to market considerations and economic rationality. Moreover, the military industry, largely exempt from cost-benefit analysis by definition, was the only branch of Soviet economy subject to direct and open competition with the West.

Central planning was instrumental in overcoming some aspects of Soviet economic underdevelopment at the early stage of industrialization by promoting the rapid exploration and development of the country's rich patrimony of natural resources and by mobilizing a large pool of underemployed labor. The party-state concentrated all societal resources on reaching parity with the advanced countries in selected branches of industry and sectors of the economy. This strategy prompted the Soviet state to pursue certain avenues of Western technological development. Massive investment in the education system and scientific research resulted in growing human capital. Central planning was especially useful for the priority development of heavy industry and specifically defense-related production. The substantive economic rationality of central planning meant that for a time the Soviet state managed an extremely efficient program of ideological and coercive mass mobilization. The state exploited fully the mobilizational potential of an ideology anticipating a socialist society vastly superior to the crisis-ridden capitalist world. At the same time, forced industrialization proved to be a perfect mechanism for creating and maintaining a state of permanent emergency, ideally suited for crash conversion to a war economy. A high rate of accumulation was combined with the drastic depression of living standards and with terror.

Given that the Soviet system was established within the life-span of a single generation, an enormous amount of coercion was inevitable. Mass terror was a precondition for both stability and relatively efficient party-state functioning, including central planning.[19] Terror as an indispensable mechanism of "revolutions from above" should always be seen as a complex unity of systemic functionality and dysfunctionality. In the Soviet case, while essential for securing the grip of the single party regime and for promoting radical change, the massive use of coercion under Stalin degenerated into a mounting spiral of terror that endangered the very survival of the system.

De-Stalinization did not signify a simple correction of Stalinist excesses, but rather a transition from a system-building to a system-maintenance phase. The Soviet system had reached maturity: a stable single party-state with a centrally planned economy dominated by a military-industrial complex had been established. Over subsequent decades, the coercive apparatus became less harsh and less visible, even though it remained a major instrument of intimidation "shaping people's perceptions of what could happen to them if they were to overstep the boundaries of acceptable behavior."[20] Terror and coercion were replaced by a system of incentives and rewards distributed through a state-engineered system of stratification. Unable and unwilling to rely on terror and extensive economic growth, the Soviet leadership had to divert a part of the economic surplus to social policy which guaranteed a high level of job security and artificially low prices for basic goods and housing. Thus, the coercive Soviet state turned into a redistributive one, without compromising the dominance of the military-industrial complex.

As the only employer and the dominant redistributive agency, the party-state created a hierarchical social structure in which power and privilege were determined largely by rank in the bureaucracy. Administrative barriers between various social groups were established together with rules, quotas, and limitations controlling intergroup transfer by administrative means. To maximize the social surplus and accomplish politically important tasks, the state treated certain social groups as strategically important by redistributing the surplus in their favor. Policies creating high priority branches of industry and industrial plants (the so-called closed enterprises) as well as privileged geographical locations (the so-called closed cities) are examples.[21] Soviet nationality policy based on a comprehensive system of ethnic stratification became an indispensable mechanism for maintaining social stability in a very complex multiethnic society.

This sketchy overview of the central institutional characteristics and developmental policies of the Soviet system should suffice to demonstrate the fundamental difference between Soviet and Western modernization. The following outcomes of Soviet modernization are especially relevant to the analysis of the causes of Soviet decline.

First, social groups with strong ties to the market—that is, those responsive to the market regulators of social activity such as merchants, entrepreneurs, and well-to-do peasants—were eliminated, often physically. This process contributed to a greater sociopsychological homogeneity of Soviet society, enhancing its "rural nexus."[22]

Second, modernization under Stalin was implemented by reactivating certain archaic, pre-capitalist patterns of social organization.[23] The twin policies of collectivization and forced industrialization generated huge masses of uprooted migrants, the new Soviet *Lumpenproletariat*.[24] No mass unemployment followed, however, since the centrally planned economy could absorb the additional labor, and the coercive apparatus could tie workers to their productive units. The Stalinist administration fought agrarian overpopulation by urbanization and industrialization, in the process transforming its population into state serfs.[25]

Third, once the foundation of technological society had been laid, emphasis shifted to military production,[26] both to achieve socialist victory on a global scale and out of security concerns. Until the USSR's collapse, the military-industrial complex enjoyed first priority in the Soviet economy, which Oskar Lange justifiably described as "a war economy sui generis."[27]

Fourth, Soviet urbanization differed considerably from its Western counterpart. In Stalin's time, mass migration from the countryside to the city occurred very quickly, even explosively. Cities were flooded with rural migrants escaping from collective farms, ready to work for subsistence wages provided by the burgeoning construction sites and industrial enterprises. This mass migration was not accompanied by a corresponding development of social infrastructure in the cities, since capital investment was directed to high rates of accumulation and skewed towards heavy, particularly military, industry. Consequently, the civilizing and individualizing effects of urban life did not fully materialize. Soviet cities, with exception of the major centers accorded a special status in the system of territorial stratification, were characterized by "a typically marginal, intermediary, 'barrack' subculture"[28] which combined partially preserved traditions of peasant community with the barely emerging values of urban civilization. Notwithstanding the traditional link between cities and markets, Soviet urban dwellers were also not exposed to market relations, but rather to state propaganda, indoctrination, bureaucratic administration, and rigid external controls. The Soviet party-state succeeded in creating a huge network of powerful socializing institution, while simultaneously avoiding the destabilizing effects that typically accompany the emergence of mass media in industrial societies. At least two generations of Soviet citizens were effectively cut off from the outside world by means of closed borders and a massive censorship program, including the jamming of foreign broadcasts and the ban on foreign press and books. Soviet education took the form of mass indoctrination, with complete uniformity achieved by a single set of teaching materials approved by the ministry of education. Finally, a huge army based on universal male conscription became a powerful agent of socialization and militarization.[29]

Fifth, the post-Stalinist years proved decisive to the formation of the basic personality type that became dominant in Soviet society. The "state-dependent worker"[30] was governed by a system of "organized consensus" that replaced Stalinist coercion, based on an implicit social contract between the regime and the populace. Having restored the right of workers to change their jobs at will, the Soviet leadership created a peculiar semi-free labor market in which job turnover, rather than higher productivity and better skills, became the major bargaining resource of industrial workers. The redistributive state molded the fundamental norms, attitudes, and expectations of the Soviet population. Total job security, price stability, and the guarantee of some basic benefits by the omnipotent state became inviolable norms of the Soviet way of life and necessary conditions for stable, consensual relations between the Soviet regime and the population.

Having reached maturity, the Soviet military-industrial society began manifesting tendencies that, taken together, pointed to a systemic crisis and testified to the system's growing inviability in a changing world. The role of the Soviet institutional framework in the economic decline can be summarized as follows. Initially, Soviet growth rates were impressive, but this was an input-driven growth. As Paul Krugman wrote, "If the Soviet economy had a special strength, it was its ability to mobilize resources, not its ability to use them efficiently."[31] The prevailing modes of production and the behavioral patterns they created encouraged both shortages and waste. The single-party regime and the centrally planned economy were unpropitious to innovation, except in the severely circumscribed sphere of military production and research. The predominance of the military-industrial complex magnified the system's wastefulness and ensured the backwardness of civilian industries. The hypertrophied growth of the military-industrial complex and increasing technological backwardness of civilian industry provoked industrial decay, general stagnation, and progressive exhaustion of the country's natural, social, and cultural resources.

The novelty of the Soviet experience is that its military-driven modernization endangered the foundations of long-term systemic reproduction and triggered the society's self-destructive dynamic. Since the crucial role of the military in modernizing a society and building a new state structure is well documented in both European and Russian history,[32] this outcome of the Soviet developmental strategy requires an explanation. The Soviet Union before the Second World War and the entire Soviet system that emerged in the postwar bipolar world have always been part of a larger and more inclusive sociocultural international system. Soviet development cannot be understood apart from the dominant trends in other technologically advanced societies. In other words, in analyzing the Soviet extinction one should not neglect the process of intersocietal selection.

The development of new military technologies and the concomitant logic of nuclear war, with its guiding principle of mutually assured destruction, made another world war infeasible, and this dealt a blow to a Soviet doctrine based on the inevitability of war between the socialist and capitalist camps. Even if Stalin himself held that atomic bombs were "intended for frightening those with weak nerves"[33] and gave no indication of ever "rethinking his approach to military affairs as a result of the new technology,"[34] his successors had to adapt their political designs to the realities of the nuclear age. Nonetheless, the Soviet military-industrial complex continued to receive an ever growing share of state investment which, in a period of prolonged peace, was justified by Soviet leaders on both domestic and international grounds. In the international arena, the Cold War with its concomitant arms race provided a *raison d'être* for continuous militarization. Domestically, the military-industrial complex played a preeminent role in maintaining the status quo. Due to its central place in the economy, the military sector attracted the best educated and skilled workers by guaranteeing extensive privileges. Skilled workers, engineers, and technical specialists who might have fallen in with a reform movement were instead thoroughly co-opted by the system: "This arrangement ensured that the social base for reform during the critical early stages of the economic crisis would be quite narrow, and that the chances for an authentic reformist leader to get to the top would be minimal."[35] As a result, the Soviet military-industrial complex delayed reaction to crisis tendencies.[36] Soviet militarization turned into militarization for its own sake, propelling the system into drawn-out self-destruction.

Causes and Manifestations of Soviet Counter-Modernization

The systemic decay of a military-industrial society is a phenomenon of counter-modernization—an abrupt reversal of the key developments that have characterized all industrial societies to date. This form of social degeneration was provoked in the Soviet case by the anti-innovative aspects of the economic system coupled with the self-destructive character of its military-driven modernization. The system's devolution can be factored into four interconnected processes: technological stagnation and declining productivity; decline in the complexity of social structure and the stagnation in the division of labor; the system's inability to develop new needs, beliefs, and values—all necessary for progress; and, finally, waste of resources and ever-spreading ecological damage.

The Soviet Union and Soviet-type societies of Eastern Europe began, in the 1960s, to experience a continuous, long-term decline in labor productivity and rates of economic growth. The declining productivity put a halt to extensive economic growth, leading to a shrinking economic surplus. The overall technological gap between Soviet-type and Western industrial societies has been growing since. Moreover, Soviet-type societies "were outperformed by a number of countries that in the mid-1960s were at a similar or lower level of economic development."[37] The Soviet Union became the first industrialized country to reverse the direction of the demographic transition, with an increase in infant mortality and a significant decrease in male life expectancy, accompanied in the southern periphery by a continued population explosion.

Soviet modernization produced a multi-tiered industrial social structure that included the working middle class, young professionals, highly-skilled workers, and intellectual and cultural elites, and to this extent resembled other advanced industrial societies.[38] But after the establishment of the "organized consensus" in the post-Stalinist period, the increasingly complex division of labor was arrested and the growing complexity of associations and communities characteristic of the West never fully materialized. The partial and selective diffusion of industrial technology and the generally anti-innovative character of Soviet modernization preserved huge numbers of unskilled laborers and generated a decline in the role and prestige of higher education.[39]

The prevalence of state dependence and bureaucratic redistribution minimized individual risk and guaranteed job availability, price stability, and an income policy that remained largely egalitarian irrespective of productivity. As a result, some social groups and individuals benefitted at the expense of others: the Soviet state valued blue-collar workers over white-collar professionals; employees in the top-priority heavy and military industries over those in the consumer-goods and service sector; mediocrity and obedience over skill, education, and entrepreneurial ability. Having fostered a specific social type of state-dependent worker as its major social base, the Soviet system created its own "grave-diggers": huge masses of people who loathed competition and craved stability, who were hostile to innovation or productive work, and who were thus especially receptive to the ideology of egalitarianism, redistribution, and "social justice." A resistance to change and the general lack of innovative spirit characterized behavior at all levels of the Soviet social structure.

The most salient aspect of the Soviet crisis can be seen in the USSR's relationship to both its ecological and international environment. In the international arena, the policy of the continuous confrontation with the West, in the form of the Cold War and constant peripheral wars by proxy states, with or without direct Soviet involvement, further exhausted national resources. As for managing the ecology, the destructive effects of Soviet technology were a telling indicator of socioeconomic decay. The increasing inviability of the Soviet system manifested itself most strikingly in the growing waste of natural resources and the spreading ecological crisis. As Murray Feshbach and Alfred Friendly put it, "When historians finally conduct an autopsy on the Soviet Union and Soviet Communism, they may reach the verdict of death by ecocide."[40] The inability to develop and introduce environmentally benign technology dictated a continuous reliance on obsolete energy-intensive and material-intensive production techniques that were both wasteful and damaging to the environment.

Soviet counter-modernization provides the first example in the modern industrial era of technological advance generating "negative" feedback that weakened and eventually extinguished the original developmental impulses. The Soviet crisis, therefore, cannot be attributed either to a transition from an extensive to an intensive growth stage or to a transition "from an industrial to a scientific-technological civilization,"[41] analogous to problems encountered earlier in Western industrial societies. Instead, the problems facing Soviet-type societies sprang from their specific structural and functional characteristics: they were byproducts of a particular socioeconomic system that suffocated incentive and slowed down technological innovation and development. The Soviet system proved inviable at the newest stage of scientific-technological revolution and social development. Decades of extensive growth fueled by wasteful backward technologies and aggravated by the priorities of the military-industrial complex, have resulted in a progressive depletion of resources and the ensuing loss of system's capacity for self-reproduction. Unable to reach this new stage of development because of economic irrationality in the management of its initially vast resources, Soviet society not only fell behind the industrialized West in levels of productivity and consumer satisfaction, but also degenerated into a self-destructive form of social organization, riddled with problems and ecological dangers.

Political Reforms and the Rise of Nationalism in the Soviet Union

The idea that Gorbachev's reforms were a major precipitant of Soviet disintegration should be evaluated in the context of Soviet counter-modernization and deepening systemic crisis. Intent on reversing the decline and saving the Soviet system, Gorbachev introduced the program of reforms known popularly as perestroika. Initially, this consisted of rapid but largely superficial improvements within the Soviet system, that left its major mechanisms and institutions intact.[42] During the first year of his rule, Gorbachev simply combined appeals for harder and more disciplined work with a clamp-down on the "second economy," a wide-scale anti-alcoholism campaign, and a number of administrative measures. Dissatisfied with the results, he then moved beyond this early disciplinarianism to introduce a vestigial program of economic reforms based on a policy of "growth acceleration." This involved a sharp increase in capital investment for machine-building, metal-working, and extractive industries at the expense of consumer-goods production. Not surprisingly, this reform reinforced the very same Stalinist policies that were primarily responsible for the Soviet decline by favoring the established interests of such monopolistic sectors of the economy as the military-industrial complex and certain branches of heavy industry which "had already brought other sectors of the economy to virtual technological bankruptcy."[43]

Disappointed with the results of these first reforms, Gorbachev's administration realized that economic reform was doomed unless popular participation in the decision-making process was increased, and that involved curtailing coercion and introducing limited democracy—most visibly, through competitive elections. Democratic reforms followed in rapid succession. The secret police and other forms of state-sponsored coercion were discredited, competitive elections were held, censorship was curtailed, and the party's monopoly on political power was formally repudiated. These reforms fundamentally changed the character of the Soviet political regime, with repercussions for the social atmosphere of the entire country and, indeed, the world.

Two most spectacular consequence of democratization was the astonishingly rapid collapse of the Soviet "external empire." Before Gorbachev, the East European single-party regimes and their antiquated centrally planned economies had been kept afloat by Soviet military force and economic assistance in the form of raw material and energy delivered at a fraction of the world price. In other words, the internal stability in the Soviet bloc had required the existence of a strong redistributive center with massive resources and an extensive military and coercive apparatus at its disposal. When these conditions no longer obtained, the opposition of millions of East Europeans to the externally imposed Sovietization, combined with Gorbachev's policy of democratic reforms and his eventual refusal to use force to prop up the besieged East European client regimes, created the necessary and sufficient conditions for the "velvet revolution" of 1989.

At home the effects of Gorbachev's reformist course were no less destructive for the Soviet system. The move towards democratization signified the weakening of coercion as a tool of the state. This development, combined with a further deterioration of the economy, a sharp drop in the living standards, massive shortages, and rationing of such staples as bread and sugar, unleashed dormant social forces and prompted the coalescing of popular discontent around groups and movements whose importance had obviously been underestimated by Gorbachev. This democratic social mobilization testified both to the success of Gorbachev's political reforms and to the unintended consequences of perestroika which the government could no longer control.

The profound transformation of major organizational principles of the Soviet system introduced by the reformist segment of the party created favorable conditions for mass political mobilization whose most potent base was ethnic rather than political. In the words of a Russian philosopher, "nationalities have turned into political parties" and powerful nationalist movements appeared in various Soviet republics. Thus, while the very nature of the uniquely Soviet military-industrial system led to its unarrestable decline, the forces of nationalism and separatism served as powerful precipitants of the USSR's actual disintegration. Moreover, the same nationalist and separatist impulses were responsible for the collapse of Yugoslavia and Czechoslovakia, testifying to a common logic underlying the disintegration of multiethnic societies built on the Soviet model. To grasp it, one should examine both the general factors responsible for the persistence and periodic resurgence of nationalism throughout the twentieth century, and the specifics of ethnicity and nationality policies in Soviet-type societies.

Soviet Empire and Its Nationality Policy

The breakup of the Soviet Union into fifteen different countries has generated a number of scholarly and eyewitness accounts.[44] As Ronald Suny has pointed out, "The Soviet Union, which a quarter century ago would have been described by most social scientists as a state and only occasionally, and usually by quite conservative analysts, as an empire, is almost universally described after its demise as an empire, since it now appears to have been an illegitimate, composite polity unable to contain the rising nations within it."[45]

The reluctance to recognize the Soviet Union as an empire had several explanations. Even though the Soviet Union incorporated into itself much of the territory of the earlier Russian empire, the origins of the Soviet empire are to be traced back not to the tsarist legacy but rather to the particular nationality policy and expansionism of the Stalinist regime. In the beginning, the Soviet regime was rather benevolent in its policy towards its nationals, emphasizing the right of national self-determination and resolutely opposing Great-Russian chauvinism. For decades Soviet propaganda with its ubiquitous anti-imperialist and anti-colonialist overtones[46] lived off these early attempts to support ethnic minorities. Soviet imperialism found its clearest manifestation in the annexation of the Baltic states, but in other areas the USSR's imperial impulse was less discernible, and varied at different stages of its development. Mark Beisinger justifiably stresses the importance of the subjective dimension of imperialism, but his insistence that the Soviet empire should not be treated as an "objective" structure and that the use of the term is itself "a claim and a stance"[47] requires serious qualification. Since the late 1930s, the Soviet Union was an empire in both an objective and a subjective sense of the term: the ethnoterritorial structure with boundaries between nationalities imposed and maintained by the state; the state-engineered system of ethnic stratification; and Soviet center-periphery relations in general—these represented the most salient imperial dimensions of the Soviet state. Even if the imperial character of the country was always a matter of degree, the Soviet system evolved in such a way as to strengthen its objective imperial characteristics, as well as the subjective perceptions of the ethnic political and cultural elites. The crystallization of this perception of the Soviet state as imperial was prompted by a gradual but inexorable decline of the Soviet economy and by the failure of the Bolshevik project of national integration based on a specific nationality policy.

Soviet policy was ostensibly committed to the goal of rapprochement and the merger of the various Soviet nationalities into a single state in some unspecified future. But in reality the Soviet leadership always gave precedence to the requirements of state over ideology. The basic goals of Soviet nationality policy were similar to those of any modern multiethnic state: it was designed to maintain USSR's territorial integrity and internal stability and strengthen the process of national integration. For a few decades this apparently pragmatic and relatively coherent policy successfully maintained internal stability. It resulted, however, in strengthening imperial qualities of the Soviet Union, promoting ethnic particularism, and fostering the process of nation-building.[48] A brief overview of the basic institutional arrangements and practices of the Soviet nationality policy may be helpful to account for such an outcome.[49]

Prior to Gorbachev, the ruthless suppression of nationalist and separatist movements was the centerpiece of Soviet nationality policy. Throughout Soviet history, the powerful coercive apparatus proved quite successful in destroying both real and imaginary ethnic oppositions, suppressing the activities of dissident nationality groups and punishing local leaders who tried to develop indigenous power bases. Still, the impressive internal stability, which began breaking down only during a few final years of Soviet existence, cannot be accounted for solely in terms of terror and repression.

Political and cultural, or civic and ethnic, understandings of nationhood as two alternative, even antagonistic principles of organizing citizenship and nationhood go back to the early nineteenth century. Marxist-Leninist ideology that barely tolerated nations and nationalism as a temporary, albeit unavoidable, evil obviously belonged to the tradition which understood nationhood as a political rather than an ethnocultural fact. The Bolshevik government, however, in trying to keep together the scattered parts of the former tsarist empire, was compelled to turn to the national principle as an expedient to secure the territorial and economic foundations of the emergent revolutionary state. The Soviet Union was built on the principle of nominal national-territorial autonomy with ethnoterritorial units as its basic structural elements. In Soviet society ethnicity was institutionalized on both group and individual levels. On the group level, major ethnic groups were assigned their officially recognized territories and organized into an elaborate administrative hierarchy of ethnic stratification, in which the fifteen Soviet republics represented the highest rank of statehood accessible to a Soviet nationality. Individually, the ethnic affiliation of all citizens was registered on their internal passports and treated as the person's ascriptive characteristic inherited at birth. The registration of nationality in passports both served as a determinant of individual identity and established rigid boundaries between nationalities.

The Soviet understanding of nationhood was firmly based on the Stalinist linkage between nationality, its territory, and its indigenous political elite which, in turn, was nominated and closely supervised from the center. National integration was to be achieved through the socioeconomic development of the republics by means of a policy of redistribution from more to less developed areas and preferential treatment to each nationality within its territories. All republics were granted identical state, bureaucratic, and educational structures, similar research and development establishments (including republican academies of sciences with comprehensive sets of research institutes), and similar organizations for the production and distribution of culture (from the state publishing houses and the ministries of culture and education to the creative unions of writers, artists, architects, and other cultural producers). This institutional isomorphism was complemented by the aforementioned policy of preferential treatment designed to co-opt the educated and ambitious members of each nationality into the ranks of their local political elite and educated middle class.

Control over higher education was another crucial aspect of nationality policy. For decades competition for university admission among applicants of various nationalities was regulated by a quota system which also favored the local nationality. Its members enjoyed privileged access to higher education and administrative and managerial jobs, leadership positions and high-ranking posts.[50] Since republican political elites were appointed and co-opted by the central party apparatuses, they remained loyal to the central authority rather than to their ethnic constituencies. The well-developed system of control and surveillance reserved some key leadership positions for the representatives of the center, who were overwhelmingly ethnic Russian, and this made the fostering of nationalist sentiments and aspirations on the part of local political elites both very risky and unlikely. The major accomplishment of this policy was to achieve a considerable degree of homogeneity in republican social structures. Even in the least developed republics the number of university-educated specialists grew to approach that of the Russian population. By protecting the educational and occupational interests of the indigenous elites and middle classes, Soviet nationality policy provided incentives for remaining loyal to the center. It was to be unusually successful in integrating these groups, receptive as they were to nationalist ideas and crucial to ethnic mobilization,[51] into the Soviet system.

Soviet investment was to a certain extent allocated according to a policy of transfer payments aimed at reducing differences in development among the republics. Its effectiveness should not be overestimated, however. Soviet militarist modernization always gave precedence to strategic considerations over redistributive goals and was unable to achieve equalized and comprehensive development of the non-Russian republics. The Soviet central ministries increasingly funded their own enterprises to the neglect of regional development, and centralized investment often went to ecologically harmful projects detrimental to the quality of life in the region. Over time, central planners increasingly turned to the "ratchet" principle of planning: they calculated investment and production targets "from the achieved level" by simply increasing those of the previous year by a certain percentage[52]—which penalized republics with below-average development and above-average birth rates. Soviet propaganda boasted of successes in narrowing economic disparities between the Soviet republics, and in the early 1970s Brezhnev announced that socioeconomic equality in the USSR had been "essentially" achieved. In practice, the economic ranking of the republics remained constant, with the Baltic republics ranking above the national average and all the Muslim republics left at the bottom. Differences in many indicators of regional development actually grew starting in the late 1950s, becoming particularly pronounced in the Brezhnev era.[53]

Center-periphery relations assumed a distinctly imperial character, both politically and economically.[54] The classic imperial differentiation of production in which high value-added production takes place at the center and low value-added production in the periphery was, however, successfully obfuscated by the operation of a marketless economy and the redistributive Soviet state. For a time the standards of living in the Russian center and in the ethnic periphery were inversely related to their respective levels of industrialization. Both Soviet and Western studies of regional inequalities in the 1970s yielded the somewhat paradoxical result that the standard of living in the Central Asian and Caucasian republics was higher than that of the industrially developed Russian center.[55] This apparent paradox was often interpreted by analysts as proof that considerable wealth was being transferred from the more prosperous to the poorer republics in the "southern belt."[56] Some scholars even saw in it a kind of "welfare colonialism"—"colonialism" because Central Asia produced abundant raw materials for processing in European USSR and because the shape and pace of the region's economic development were determined by Moscow, and "welfare" because the center subsidized the Central Asian standard of living.[57]

The notion of welfare colonialism rightly emphasized USSR's imperial qualities, but it postulated a massive subsidization of the periphery which in practice the central leadership was neither willing nor able to support. The paradox that living standards were often higher in the periphery than warranted by its level of development can be adequately explained without reference to welfare colonialism. The failure of the centrally planned economy was perhaps most evident in the permanent shortages of food and consumer goods. One consequence of those shortages was the development of the "second economy" and the free market for food and consumer goods that functioned in parallel to the Soviet economy. The ethnic periphery, because of its more favorable climatic conditions and especially lack of state control always had an easier time engaging in market activities. It was the existence of private agriculture and market operations, and not subsidies from the central state, that raised living standards. This fact did not change an objectively hierarchical differentiation of production between the center and the periphery characteristic of imperial organization. But the centrally planned economy and the redistributive central state operating in a society cut off from the global market temporarily dulled such consequences of imperialism as ethnic inequality and stratification.

Soviet nationality policy was pursued consistently, but produced contradictory results. It proved unusually successful in maintaining internal stability. By encouraging state dependency and protecting the educational and occupational interests of the local political elite and educated middle class, this policy blunted their aspirations to independent nationhood, neutralized their potentially destabilizing role and integrated them into the Soviet regime. On the other hand, it strengthened the imperial character of the Soviet Union by creating a hierarchical array of national societies, fostering differences between center and periphery, and exacerbating interethnic conflicts and center-periphery contradictions. Soviet nationality policy promoted a peculiar process of nation-building. The state erected practically impenetrable passport barriers between different ethnic groups, and administratively linked each ethnic community to its own territory and political leadership. Consequently, in the various republics there emerged such major preconditions for independent existence as their own administratively defined territories inhabited by the "titular" nationalities, their own political elites and educated middle classes, and continuous traditions of cultural production in their own languages. As one Soviet analyst put it, "the republics exhibit the full set of characteristics of independent states that have lost their independence."[58]

Soviet nationality policy, uniformly applied to very different ethnic groups at quite different stages of socioeconomic, cultural, and demographic development, preserved and often aggravated regional inequalities. The Soviet military-driven modernization and the Soviet nationality policy thus resulted in the USSR remaining an aggregate of both modern and traditional societies. These growing ethnoregional economic and cultural disparities were a source of grievance and political conflict that undermined the cohesion of the Soviet state. The policy also contributed to a reversal of a migration pattern that had characterized the Russian empire from the mid-nineteenth century through the first five decades of the Soviet Union's existence. By the end of the 1960s the direction of Russian migration from the center to the periphery had been reversed.[59] At the same time emigration of members of non-titular nationalities, especially ethnic Russians, from non-Russian republics accelerated as a result of exacerbated ethnic tensions. In sum, Soviet nationality policy, through its large-scale population transfers, fostered ethnic homogenization of the republics and set the stage for nationalist and separatist movements.

During the period of economic growth, when resources were abundant and coercion was effectively used as a method of social control, the Soviet Union was a relatively stable and viable imperial construction. By the 1980s, however, the resources needed to maintain growth had been depleted. The old social contract between the regime and the population ceased to be tenable because the regime could no longer afford the political and economic costs. In the absence of extensive economic growth it was no longer possible to protect the occupational interests of ethnic educated classes by co-opting them into swelling bureaucracies. The twin policies of passport nationality registration and preferential treatment of indigenous nationalities grew increasingly counterproductive, and resulted in the further decline of productivity. They also generated increasing dissatisfaction among minorities lacking territorial bases and among non-titular residents of the republics. In many cases they led to the emergence of a potentially explosive ethnic division of labor. The situation was particularly tense in those republics where the titular nationality had been changed into a numerical minority due to massive influxes of other nationalities—good examples being Kazakhstan and Yakutia where the first cases of ethnic unrest in Gorbachev's era were registered. The fear of the indigenous population for its traditional privileges and ethnic survival combined with an acute sense of injustice on the part of the new arrivals who felt themselves the targets of discrimination.

As the strength of the central state was eroded by declining productivity and depletion of resources, the state-engineered system of social stratification began to unravel. Under these conditions, institutionalized nationality—the only officially recognized distinction among Soviet citizens—gained significantly in social importance and became the principal base of social mobilization and collective action. An upsurge in a host of nationalist and separatist movements followed. In the Central Asian republics mobilization was directed against identifiable minorities and did not produce a viable nationalist movement. In the case of the Caucasus nationalists demanded sovereignty as nation-states as well as ethnic homogeneity and fought ethnic wars against neighboring republics or against ethnic minorities within their own territories. Finally, in the Baltic republics, Ukraine, and Moldavia secessionist movements were rooted in a sense of the injustice of their annexation by the Russian/Soviet empire. These movements were strongly anti-imperial, based on a quest for self-assertion and identity, on a group's concern with ethnic survival, and on a collective perception of economic self-interest, fueled by aspirations of joining the world market and the community of industrialized nations. The crisis of the Soviet economy and the redistributive center only strengthened their claim that the polity represented a fundamentally alien rule.

Separatist movements in the republics received unexpected support from the Russian center, where many were ready to get rid of the ethnic periphery and "secede from the Soviet Union to create the Russian national state."[60] The grievances of the Russian population centered on resource allocation and preferential treatment of territorially-bound titular nationalities. A drift towards isolationism and a separate Russian consciousness began with the advent of perestroika and intensified with the explosion of anti-Russian sentiments in the republics. Further fuel was provided by the deterioration of living standards which aggravated ethnic conflict over economic choices and policies and promoted ethnic politicization. A colossal project to divert the flow of Siberian rivers to Central Asia, which would have been ecologically harmful to Russian territory, provoked an open confrontation between the Russian and the Central Asian republics which in turn had a catalytic effect on the Russian nationalist movement.[61] Interethnic clashes in the army and Russian cities were growing in frequency and violence since, as a population explosion in the Muslim republics caused an influx of migrants and conscripts from the southern republics. As censorship weakened, the enormous investment required to contain unemployment and to implement large-scale irrigation projects in Central Asia became public knowledge, and leading Russian economists and demographers pointed out that, in view of the imminent secession of the Baltic republics, Russia would be the only source for this investment. Some Russian experts, asserting "the impossibility of further coexistence" of industrial and traditional societies within the same country, suggested that the only solution would be to abandon Central Asia.[62] These developments aggravated the schism in the ranks the Russian intelligentsia between those who espoused the imperial idea and those who espoused Russian separatism as the only way out of the economic and nationality crisis.[63] As the ethnic periphery rapidly turned into a liability, the hold of the imperial idea over the Russian population was attenuated.

That the sudden collapse of the Soviet empire, the largest state in the world, occurred without bloodshed can be explained by the confluence of strong secessionist movements in the ethnic periphery and the readiness of the center to drop out of the empire. The entire course of perestroika prepared the way for a transformation in the mentality of the Russian population from imperialist to isolationist. The Russians' isolationist nationalism was prompted by growing ethnoregional inequality following the collapse of the project of national integration. The hegemonic nation repudiated its own empire as the leadership of the former fought to arrest migration and avoid transfer payments to the impoverished periphery. After the secession of the Balts, the 1991 decision by Slavic republics to dissolve the Soviet Union imposed unwanted independence on the Central Asian republics. In Alexander Motyl's words, "Once the center had imploded and the dominant half of the imperial relationship had in fact ceased to exist, the subordinate part was left on its own and was virtually forced to take the path of national independence."[64]

The Soviet Union in its last years came much closer to an imperial structure than it had been at its inception or in the first decades of its existence. The temptation to explain its collapse by referring to the fate of other empires is therefore strong. A comparative analysis of the fate of the Soviet bloc in Eastern Europe and that of the Habsburg or the Russian empire may be illuminating for an understanding of some common circumstances of their collapse, but the analogy also has its limitations and should not be pushed too far. The comparison between the Habsburg or Ottoman empires and the Soviet Union, for example, may be legitimate as long as it is not allowed to obfuscate obvious structural dissimilarities between these historical entities. The Soviet Union was fundamentally different than other empires. While the center held power and political control and maintained a hierarchical distinction of production processes, the redistributive and non-market aspects of the party-state and of the planned economy did not have much in common with the classic imperial model. It was not an expression of the interests of the dominant nationality in exploiting subordinate ethnicities, and in fact it frequently worked against Russian national interests. It was also relatively successful in disseminating its supranational ideology among its population and even in developing a common Soviet identity.[65] A comparative analysis with nationality policies in contemporary multiethnic countries structured along ethnoterritorial lines, like Canada, Switzerland or Czechoslovakia, may be helpful for a better understanding of the Soviet dissolution. An effective comparison could also be made with those countries whose governments, confronted with glaring disparities between regions, relied for decades on redistributive policies of equalization and transfer payments from the more to the less prosperous regions. Italy, Czechoslovakia, and Yugoslavia are cases in point.

Conclusions

The collapse of the Soviet system and the disintegration of the USSR as a political entity represent two closely interconnected but distinct processes whose causes should not be confused. The forces of nationalism and regionalism were present throughout the entire existence of the Soviet Union. Nationalism obviously determined the form of USSR's dissolution as a political entity, even if the Soviet breakdown into fifteen independent states, according to the number of the union republics, was contingent. (One can easily imagine that, if it were not for a demotion of the Karelo-Finnish republic into the rank of an autonomous republic, we could have had sixteen independent states.) But the Soviet system devolved on its own and the forces of nationalism were not primarily responsible for the decay of this socioeconomic formation. The assertion that the collapse of Communist regimes must be viewed as having had its origin "in the dynamics of empire in general and of imperial decline in particular"[66] seems therefore invalid. An unanticipated consequence of such reasoning would seem to be the idea that if a Soviet-type society emerged in a nationally homogeneous environment it would have fared better and in the long run might have proven a viable form of social organization.

The Soviet military-industrial society gradually became unsustainable in a bipolar world in which the major adversaries could no longer engage in open warfare. After World War II nuclear arms advanced to the point where technology took precedence over ideology, stifling the aspirations of the Soviet ruling elite. The ever-growing military-industrial complex nonetheless remained the dominant sector of the Soviet economy, and the Soviet combination of an interdependent and mutually reinforcing single-party political regime, centrally planned economy, and massive militarization of economic and social life brought about the phenomenon of counter-modernization and exhausted the country's resources. As a result, the Soviet system lost its capacity for self-reproduction. At this new juncture, Soviet nationality policy, whose success had been inextricably linked to a strong central state pursuing a strategy of extensive economic development, became dysfunctional. Its rising costs added to the systemic crisis of Soviet society, and its nation-building provided the structural underpinnings for the emerging secessionist movements.

Gorbachev's attempt to preserve the Soviet Union's territorial integrity by democratizing the political regime and providing a market economy turned into a powerful precipitant for the Soviet Union's collapse. Gorbachev's revolution from above paralyzed the central state, loosening the reign on nationalist and separatist movements in some of the federation's most advanced republics. Though these movements triggered the disintegration of the Soviet empire, an inexorable decline of the Soviet economy, the debilitation of the central state, and the terminal crisis of the Soviet system as a whole paved the way. The collapse of the Soviet Union along ethnic lines complemented the political revolution from above and served as a structural equivalent of a military defeat that destroys the institutions and forces of the old system.

Notes

1. Ken Jowitt, *New World Disorder: The Leninist Extinction* (Berkeley: University of California Press, 1992).

2. Martin Malia, *The Soviet Tragedy: A History of Russian Socialism, 1917–1991* (New York: Free Press, 1994).

3. Ronald Suny, *The Revenge of the Past: Nationalism, Revolution and the Collapse of the Soviet Union* (Stanford, Calif.: Stanford University Press, 1993).

4. Zbigniew Brzezinski, *The Grand Failure: The Birth and Death of Communism in the Twentieth Century* (New York: Scribner, 1989).

5. Johann Arnason, *The Future that Failed: Origins and Destinies of the Soviet Model* (London: Routledge, 1993); Malia, *Soviet Tragedy*.

6. Miron Rezun, ed., *Nationalism and the Breakup of an Empire: Russia and Its Periphery* (Westport, Conn.: Praeger, 1992); Suny, *Revenge of the Past*.

7. John H. Kautsky, *Communism and the Politics of Development: Persistent Myths and Changing Behavior* (New York: John Wiley, 1968); T. H. Rigby, "Traditional, Market, and Organizational Societies and the USSR," *World Politics* 16, no. 4 (1964): 539–557; Alex Inkeles, "Models and Issues in the Analysis of Soviet Society," *Survey* 60 (1966): 3–17; idem, *Social Change in Soviet Russia* (Cambridge, Mass.: Harvard University Press, 1968); Juan Linz, "Totalitarian and Authoritarian Regimes," in ed. F. I. Greenstein and N. Polsby, *Macropolitical Theory* (Reading, Mass.: Addison-Wesley, 1975), 175–412; T. Anthony Jones, "Modernization Theory and Socialist Development," in ed. Mark G. Field, *Social Consequences of Modernization in Communist Societies* (Baltimore: The John Hopkins University Press).

8. See, for example, George Breslauer, "In Defense of Sovietology," *Journal of Post-Soviet Affairs* 8, no. 3 (1992): 197–238; Abbott Gleason, *Totalitarianism: The Inner History of the Cold War* (New York: Oxford University Press, 1995); Stephen Hanson, "Social Theory and the Post-Soviet Crisis: Sovietology and the Problem of Regime Identity," *Communist and Post-Communist Studies* 28, no. 1 (1995); Andrew Janos, "What Was Communism? A Retrospective in Comparative Analysis," *Communist and Post-Communist Studies* (forthcoming).

9. Abbott Gleason, "Totalitarianism and the Cold War: A Personal View," *NewsNet: The Newsletter of the AAASS* 35, no. 4 (1995): 3.

10. By necessity this debate was conducted orally. Memoirs and diaries of the period provide a glimpse into the scope and seriousness of the discussion. See, for example, Vladimir Vernadsky, "Dnevnik 1941 goda," *Novyi mir* 5 (1995): 179–215.

11. Gleason, *Totalitarianism and the Cold War*, p. 1.

12. A. H. Brown, *Soviet Politics and Political Science* (London: Macmillan, 1974), 36–41.

13. See, for example, Margarete Buber-Neumann, *Under Two Dictators* (New York: Dodd, Mead, 1950). Especially interesting are works by a group of Italian intellectuals in exile who in the first half of 1930s, in their journal *Quaderni* and *Giustizia e Libertá* published in Paris, analyzed origins and common characteristics of fascist Italy and the regimes of Hitler and Stalin.

14. Hanson, "Social Theory and the Post-Soviet Crisis," p. 126.

15. Jowitt, *New World Disorder*, pp. 10–49.

16. See, for example, William Broad, "Russian Says Soviet Atom Arsenal Was Larger Than West Estimated," *The New York Times*, September 26, 1993, p. 1. New data permitted Seymour Melman to calculate that the 1988 ratio of capital investments in military production to that in civilian production in the United States was 50:100; in Japan it was 4:100; in the Soviet Union it was minimally 122:100 and maximally 370:100, with a true figure closer to the maximum. See S. Melman, "Rossiya—ne Weimar," *Vsemirnoe slovo* 8 (1995): 79–80.

17. Andrew Janos, "Social Science, Communism, and the Dynamics of Political Change," *World Politics* 44, no. 1 (1991): 81–112; idem, "What Was Communism?"

18. T. H. Rigby, *The Changing Soviet System: Mono-organizational Socialism from Its Origins to Gorbachev's Restructuring* (Aldershot: Edward Elgar, 1990); Alec Nove, "Socialism, Planning, and the One-Party State," in ed. T. H. Rigby, Archie Brown, and Peter Reddaway, *Authority, Power, and Policy in the USSR: Essays Dedicated to Leonard Shapiro* (New York: St. Martin's, 1980), 77–97; Walter Connor, *Socialism's Dilemmas: State and Society in the Soviet Bloc* (New York: Columbia University Press, 1988), 5–28.

19. Alex Dallin and George Breslauer, *Political Terror in Communist Systems* (Stanford, Calif.: Stanford University Press, 1970).

20. Donna Bahry, Brian Silver, "Intimidation and the Symbolic Uses of Terror in the USSR," *American Political Science Review* 81, no. 4 (1987): 1067.

21. Victor Zaslavsky, *The Neo-Stalinist State: Class, Ethnicity and Consensus in Soviet Society*, 2nd ed. (Armonk: Sharpe, 1994).

22. Moshe Lewin, "Russia/USSR in Historical Motion: An Essay in Interpretation," *The Russian Review* 50, no. 3 (1991): 254–261.

23. Zbigniew Brzezinski, "Soviet Politics: From the Future to the Past?," in ed. Paul Cocks, Robert Daniels, and Nancy Whittier Heer, *The Dynamics of Soviet Politics* (Cambridge: Harvard University Press, 1976), 337–51; Moshe Lewin, *The Making of the Soviet System: Essays in the Social Theory of Interwar Russia* (New York: Pantheon Books, 1985), 43.

24. V. G. Khoros, "Istoricheskij perekrestok sotsializma," in ed. V. P. Kiselev and I. M. Klyamkin, *Sotsializm: protivorechiya sistemy* (Moscow: IEMSS, 1989), 100–101.

25. I. M. Klyamkin, "Pochemu pobezhdayut utopii," in Kiselev and Klyamkin, *Sotsializm*, pp. 226–228.

26. Holland Hunter and Janusz Szyrmer, *Faulty Foundations: Soviet Economic Policies, 1928–1940* (Princeton: Princeton University Press, 1992), 136–143.

27. Quoted in Alec Nove, *The Soviet System in Retrospect: An Obituary Notice*, The Fourth Annual W. Averell Harriman Lecture (New York: Harriman Institute, 1993), 25.

28. E. N. Starikov, "Marginaly," in ed. A. Vishnevsky, *V chelovecheskom izmerenii* (Moscow: Progress, 1989), 184.

29. Mark von Hagen, *Soldiers in the Proletarian Dictatorship: The Red Army and the Soviet Socialist State, 1917–1930* (Ithaca: Cornell University Press, 1990), 271–325.

30. Yurij Levada, ed., *Sovetskij prostoj chelovek. Opyt sotsialnogo portreta na rubezhe 90-kh godov* (Moscow: VTsIOM, 1993); Piotr Sztompka, "Civilizational Incompetence: The Trap of Post-Communist Societies," *Zeitschrift für Soziologie* 22, no. 2 (1993): 85–95; Leonid Kosals, *Why Doesn't Russian Industry Work?* (London: I. B. Tauris, 1994); V. Zaslavsky, "Contemporary Russian Society and Its Soviet Legacy: The Problem of State-Dependent Workers," in ed. B. Grancelli, *Social Change and Modernization: Lessons from Eastern Europe* (New York-Berlin: De Gruyter, 1995), 45–62.

31. Paul Krugman, "The Myth of Asia's Miracle," *Foreign Affairs* 73, no. 6 (1994): 69.

32. Von Hagen, *Soldiers in the Proletarian Dictatorship*, pp. 326–343; David Holloway, *Stalin and the Bomb: The Soviet Union and Atomic Energy 1939–1956* (New Haven, Conn.: Yale University Press, 1994); Michael Howard, *The Causes of Wars* (London: Temple Smith, 1983); Otto Hinze, *The Historical Essays of Otto Hintze*, in ed. Felix Gilbert (New York: Oxford University Press, 1975), 180–215.

33. *Pravda*, September 25, 1946, p. 1.

34. William Curti Wohlforth, *The Elusive Balance* (Ithaca: Cornell University Press, 1993), 109.

35. Victor Zaslavsky, "From Redistribution to Marketization: Social and Attitudinal Change in Post-Soviet Russia," in ed. G. Lapidus, *The New Russia: Troubled Transformation* (Boulder, Colo.: Westview Press, 1994), 128.

36. John A. Hall, *Powers and Liberties: The Causes and Consequences of the Rise of the West* (Berkeley: University of California Press, 1985), 23.

37. Bartlomej Kaminski, "Pathologies of Central Planning," *Problems of Communism* 36 (1987): 88.

38. Blair Ruble, "The Social Dimensions of Perestroyka," *Soviet Economy* 3, no. 2 (1987): 171–183.

39. For an excellent analysis of this process, see N. V. Korovitsyna, *Agoniya sotsmodernizatsii: Sud'ba dvukh pokolenij dvukh evropejskikh natsij* (Moscow: Nauka, 1993).

40. M. Feshbach and A. Friendly, *Ecocide in the USSR: Health and Nature Under Siege* (New York: BasicBooks, 1992), 1.

41. Ivan Szelenyi, "Eastern Europe in an Epoch of Transition: Toward a Socialist Mixed Economy?" in ed. Victor Nee and David Stark, *Remaking the Economic Institutions of Socialism: China and Eastern Europe* (Stanford, Calif.: Stanford University Press, 1989), 213–216.

42. V. A. Mau, *Ekonomika i vlast': Politicheskaya istoriya ekonomicheckoj reformy v Rossii 1985–1994* (Moscow: Delo, 1995), 3–15.

43. V. Yaremenko, "Ekonomika khanzhestva," *Pravda*, September 1, 1990, p. 1.

44. Peter Reddaway, "The End of the Empire," *The New York Review of Books*, November 7, 1991, pp. 53–59; Jack Matlock, Jr., *Autopsy on an Empire: The American Ambassador's Account of the Collapse of the Soviet Union* (New York: Random House, 1995).

45. R. G. Suny, "Ambiguous Categories: States, Empires and Nations," *Post-Soviet Affairs* 11, no. 2 (1995): 187.

46. Waldemar Gurian, ed., *Soviet Imperialism: Its Origins and Tactics* (Notre Dame, Indiana: University of Notre Dame Press, 1953), 9–10.

47. Mark Beissinger, "The Persisting Ambiguity of Empire," *Post-Soviet Affairs* 11, no. 2 (1995): 155.

48. Yuri Slezkine, "The USSR as a Communal Apartment, or How a Socialist State Promoted Ethnic Particularism," *Slavic Studies* 53, no. 2 (1994): 414–452.

49. In analyzing Soviet nationality policy I rely on my previously published works: V. Zaslavsky, *Das russische Imperium unter Gorbatschow: seine ethnische Struktur und ihre Zukunft* (Berlin: Wagenbach, 1991); and idem, "Nationalism and Democratic Transition in Postcommunist Societies," *Daedalus* 121, no. 2 (1992).

50. Seweryn Bialer, *Stalin's Successors: Leadership, Stability, and Change in the Soviet Union* (Cambridge: Cambridge University Press, 1980), 214–216; L. L. Rybakovskij and N. V. Tarasova, "Migratsionnye protsessy v SSSR: Novye yavleniya," *Sotsiologicheskie issledovaniya* 7 (1990): 40.

51. Miroslav Hroch, "How Much Does Nation Formation Depend on Nationalism?" *East European Politics and Societies* 4, no. 1 (1990): 115.

52. Igor Birman, "From the Achieved Level," *Soviet Studies* 30, no. 2 (1978): 153–171; Joseph Berliner, *Soviet Industry from Stalin to Gorbachev* (Ithaca: Cornell University Press, 1988), 287–288.

53. Alistair McAuley, *Economic Welfare in the Soviet Union: Poverty, Living Standards, and Inequality* (Madison: University of Wisconsin Press, 1979); Gertrud Schroeder, "Regional Living Standards," in ed. I. S. Koropeckyj and G. E. Schroeder, *Economics of Soviet Regions* (New York: Praeger, 1981); Leslie Dienes, "Regional Economic Development," in ed. A. Bergson and H. Levine, *The Soviet Economy: Toward the Year 2000* (London: Allen and Unwin, 1983).

54. For an analysis of center-periphery relations of centralized empires, see S. N. Eisenstadt, *The Political Systems of Empires* (New Brunswick, N.J.: Transaction, 1992).

55. Alistair McAuley, *Economic Welfare in the Soviet Union: Poverty, Living Standards, and Inequality* (Madison: University of Wisconsin Press, 1979); B. S. Khorev, *Territorialnaya organizatsiya obshchestva: aktualnye problemy regionalnogo upravleniya i planirovaniya v SSSR* (Moscow: Mysl, 1981).

56. John Gillula, "The Economic Interdependence of Soviet Republics," in *Soviet Economy in a Time of Change* (Washington, D.C.: Government Printing Office, 1979), 652; Jan Dellebrant, *The Soviet Regional Dilemma: Planning, People, and Natural Resources* (Armonk, N.Y.: Sharpe, 1986), 52.

57. Martin Spechler, "Regional Development in the USSR, 1958–1978," in *Soviet Economy in a Time of Change.*

58. Boris Strugatsky, "Zhit' interesnee chem pisat'," *Literaturnaya gazeta*, April 10, 1991, p. 9.

59. A. S. Bruk, V. M. Kabuzan, *Migratsionnye protsessy v Rossii i SSSR* (Moscow: INION, 1991), 108–110; Yu. V. Arutyunyan, ed., *Russkie: Etnosotsiologicheskie ocherki* (Moscow: Nauka, 1992), 17–87.

60. Mikhail Shirokij, "Perestrojka, natsionalnaya problema v SSSR i russkoe patrioticheskoe dvizhenie," *Vestnik Russkogo Khristianskogo Dvizheniya* 153 (1988): 192. See also Vladimir Balakhonov, "Sokhranenie imperii ili samosokhranenie na puti natsionalnogo suvereniteta—glavnaya natsionalnaya problema russkogo naroda segodnya," *Russkaya mysl*, June 23, 1989, p. 7.

61. N. N. Petro, "'The Project of the Century': A Study of Russian National Dissent," *Studies in Comparative Communism* 20 (1987); J. Dunlop, "Russian Nationalists Reach Out to the Masses," *Working Papers in International Studies* (Stanford, Calif.: Hoover Institution, 1990).

62. Sergej Polyakov, "Ostavit Srednyuyu Aziyu v pokoe," *Strana i mir* 4 (1990): 128.

63. Roman Szporluk, "Dilemmas of Russian Nationalism," *Problems of Communism* 38 (1989).

64. Alexander Motyl, "From Imperial Decay to Imperial Collapse: The Fall of the Soviet Empire in Comparative Perspective," in ed. Richard Rudolph and David Good, *Nationalism and Empire: The Habsburg Empire and the Soviet Union* (New York: St. Martin's Press, 1992), 37.

65. Yu. Levada, ed., *Sovetskij prostoj chelovek. Opyt sotsialnogo portreta na rubezhe 90-kh* (Moscow: VtsIOM, 1993).

66. Motyl, "From Imperial Decay to Imperial Collapse," p. 16.

PART TWO

Collapse of Empires: Consequences

8

THINKING ABOUT CONSEQUENCES
OF EMPIRE

KAREN BARKEY

Sparked by the fall of the Soviet "empire," the study of empires has again caught fire, but much of the new literature that has resulted has focused on the causes of imperial decline; there has been little systematic study of its consequences aside from blaming it for the interethnic conflict of the twentieth century. Many scholars are quick to identify ethnic warfare as the major consequence of the decline of empires, arguing that imperial suppression had constrained (while it manipulated) ethnic hatreds. When an empire is no more, constraint disappears and ethnic warfare erupts. This simple argument, however, ignores the multifarious effects of empire—ideological, economic and political—on the multitude of states that emerge from it. Ethnic warfare is not always the consequence of imperial decline: it has taken various forms, and it has occurred where no empire existed.

Discussions of imperial decline tend to center on two key debates—whether the development of nationalism caused the breakup of the empires, and what role international forces, war, and socio-economic decline have played. There has been no comparable debate on the consequences of empire: ethnic conflict has acted as a "catch-all" for a variety of consequences. As a result, the contributors to this section of the conference found little in the way of common ground; each chose instead to emphasize one particular consequence over others: Serif Mardin, for example, dealt with the intricate continuities and changes in the relationship between the imperial core domain and states that break up from it, and Rogers Brubaker focused on the migrations and "unmixing of peoples" in post-imperial settings.

Here I will replace this overemphasis on ethnic conflict with an examination of emergent national states: What are the overall characteristics of nation-building in post-imperial times? How do they compare with the patterns of earlier western European nation-building? How do people define their nationhood? What are the differences between nations that emerge from the core and those that emerge from the periphery of an empire? What do emergent nation-states carry over from empire to nation? Do aspects of imperial structure and political culture endure beyond imperial decline, and if they do how do they affect the development of the nascent state?

Today with the fall of the Soviet Union and the break-up of the Yugoslav state (which itself was the result of the break-up of empires), many new national states are trying to define their nationhood and shape appropriate policies. In many respects they are comparable to nation formation in the aftermath of the Ottoman, Habsburg and Romanov empires, but markedly different from western European nation-state formation most of which lacked direct imperial legacies. Moreover, western European cases had the advantage of long centuries to build their national unity.

Theories developed from the western European experience discard ethnicity as irrelevant to the process of modernization and nation-building. As citizens of the nation learned to communicate in the same language, analysts assumed ethnic differences would tend to disappear and a homogeneous nation would emerge.[1] This did not happen completely even in Europe, where there are still many ethnoregional movements, but it was even more demonstrably wrong in the case of nationalisms outside western Europe. Ethnicity did not disappear. On the contrary, ethnic differences survived and flourished amidst economic and political development.

Theories developed from the western European experience also identify differences in forms of nationhood—a civic and an ethnic one—each deriving from distinct patterns of nation-building. The civic form is attributed to western Europe, where nation-building proceeded to incorporate all citizens, overtime giving them individual, political and social rights. The ethnic form is attributed to Germany, Eastern Europe and the rest of the "late comers" to nationalism.[2] It has been described as a form of exclusive nationhood, defining the nation and providing the rights of its citizens based on cultural and ethnic criteria. There has been no serious explanation for these differences in forms of nationhood. Mostly, explanations have focused on the active resentment and competition that Germany and Eastern European countries have felt for western Europe, prompting them to concentrate and glorify their peculiarities, their nation, culture and language.

The established theoretical models are unsuitable on three counts: first, ethnicity continues to persist as an identity marker and second, ethnic and civic forms of nationhood coexist in Eastern Europe. Third, the theoretical models do not take into account imperial legacies since western European cases were different in this aspect. The Western-based theoretical framework for modern nation-building has to be rethought. The process of post-imperial nation-building provides us an excellent opportunity to do so. We attempt this by focusing on the traditional contiguous empires—the Ottoman, Habsburg, Russian and on the Soviet Union—and only tangentially comparing them with overseas colonial empires such as the British and the French empires.

Legacies of the Imperial Past

The collapse of an empire leaves several legacies for the political entities that develop in its aftermath. Among these are social and economic structures, state institutions of a certain nature and strength, a particular set of elites, demographics, and an overall political cultural legacy. Unless an empire is destroyed through revolution, much of its social structure is reproduced in the post-imperial context. Two of the empires studied in this book, the Ottoman and Habsburg, provide excellent examples of this continuity.

The Ottoman empire through centuries of control managed to establish a more or less uniform (at least for the Balkans and Anatolia) agrarian social structure, based on an independent and strong peasantry living on the family farm unit.[3] The implications of this social structure for the post-imperial politics of many countries go beyond the persistence of a strong peasantry, for the lack of a landed aristocracy (except in Romania) makes the dynamics of nation-state building quite different. Maria Todorova has recently argued that a strong peasantry is not really "a living legacy" in the Balkans since none of the politicians in the post-imperial period championed peasant rights.[4] The issue, however, is larger than whether politicians had to contend with the peasantry or not; what the Ottoman empire left behind was a production system rooted in agriculture by the peasant for the peasant. This had implications (together with other factors such as urban development) for the progress of capitalism.

The Habsburg empire offers us a useful comparison. Here, the structural legacy was different and more varied. Not only was an independent peasantry not the rule, but a powerful aristocracy with strong economic and political control over the peasantry was widespread. In fact, in the Habsburg lands servile labor requirements were formally abolished in 1848, providing nearly everywhere for a weak rural social class, dominated by the nobility and, in rare cases, burgeoning industrialists and capitalists. In a country such as Hungary there is no doubt that the way the aristocracy dominated politics was partly a consequence of the imperial social structure. In Bohemia, industrialization was the result of textile production, which—located as it was in the countryside—was promoted by an aristocracy eager to increase its resources. Although the Bohemian lands provided different opportunities for modern development, here too, the importance of a strong landed nobility cannot be ignored. Overall, despite differences in intensity, most of the successor states to the Habsburg and Ottoman empires shared the legacy of large peasantries (although of different strengths and degrees of independence) and underdeveloped towns, which hindered economic development.[5] As Fischer-Galati points out, the peasantry was important in all of Eastern Europe because one of the key socioeconomic issues that the successor states had to contend with was land and its redistribution.[6]

One of the oldest topics in Ottoman historiography has been the legacy of a strong and bureaucratic state. While most Ottomanists see this as one of the stronger legacies of the empire, Balkan and Arab historians have complained of the largely ineffectual bureaucratic tradition that they inherited. Echoing many others, Ozbudun speaks of "strong and centralized state, reasonably effective by standards of the day, highly autonomous of societal forces, and occupying a central and highly valued place in Ottoman political culture."[7] On the one hand, the long tradition of a strong central state devoid of representative institutions has hindered the development of democracy in many post-Ottoman nations. On the other hand, the Ottoman empire left behind a complicated political cultural legacy, as seen in the complex relationship between Islam and the state. The Ottoman empire was an Islamic empire, yet it allowed for a certain separation between state and religion; as Serif Mardin explains, "Ottomans introduced Islam for administrative purposes," thereby providing for the daily amalgam of religion and secularism.[8] This aspect of political culture contributed to the formation of a strongly secular Turkey that has only recently been challenged by Islamic movements.

The political legacy of the Habsburg empire cannot be the same since it never acquired a centralized bureaucratic state comparable in strength to that of the Ottomans. Closer to the Western European pattern, the Habsburg dynasty shared and fought for power with the forces of feudalism. Even later when a more absolutist regime was established, a form of decentralization became institutionalized after 1867 when three governments were in effect.[9] As a result, we can see a more tame statist tradition in the successors to the Habsburg empire. But the absence of a strong state did not lead to more instances of democracy among the successor states because the larger political culture of the Habsburgs "had its roots in ecclesiastical and monarchical paternalism."[10]

In order to study the political legacy of empires, we need to look carefully at the institutions of administration and control that survive in successor states. But we also need to trace the existence and continuity of imperial elites. The institutional arrangements of indirect rule between center and periphery determined the type and prominence of elites that would carry out the transition to modern national states. While the social structure of the empire helps identify the resourceful groups, the political arrangements help us locate the powerful leaders. It is in the particular nature of indirect imperial rule that every empire leaves a legacy of elite groups.

On another level, empires transmit a marked demographic and ethnic legacy. Whether they carried out policies of 'demographic surgery' or not, ethnic mixing occurred during the tenure of all four of the empires studied. Therefore, a frequent consequence of breakup was the discovery of "unhappy" ethnic mixings;

the ethnic mosaics which were the pride of empires became liabilities. As Brubaker demonstrates, a process of ethnic "unmixing" then occurred through population exchanges, forced migrations, and land transfers (often negotiated by a third international power)—all with an eye to homogenizing previously commingled populations. This type of homogenization, for example, was used to nationalize the states of Greece and Turkey. Where such "unmixing" did not occur, a core ethnic group tended to dominate the others, and in such a situation, the conflict between the core and the minority groups reproduced itself.

The standard anti-imperialist line has been that empires, through the manipulation of ethnic groups, caused ethnic hatreds which rose to become full-fledged conflicts after imperial collapse. Most such arguments claim that empires lay the foundations for conflict by manipulating ethnic groups, by relocating them, and by creating ethnically mixed enclaves.[11] Given the different occupational skills of groups, some level of manipulation of ethnic differences did occur. Moreover, the demographic and territorial aims of empires led them to repopulate areas or move groups around, therefore changing the original balance and ethnic mix.

There is, however, little sense in looking at these ancient manipulations for answers to modern ethnic hatreds.[12] Despite such policies, empires, especially the Habsburg and Ottoman, remained free of violent inter-communal conflict during most of their existence. In fact, for long centuries empires were political systems where ethnicity, language and religion did not have much national content. This began to change with respect to language and ethnicity only at the end of the eighteenth century. Before this time, people switched between languages and interacted across communities with relative ease.[13]

It follows from this that looking at imperial ethnic diversity to explain modern ethnic conflict will not do. Rather, we need to examine the policies of the new nationalizing states in the context of imperial legacies. And, as Chirot convincingly argues, we also need to pay attention to the timing of nation-building, and the cultural unity necessary for the enterprise. In his analysis, only a relatively small number of Western European and East-Asian nation-states were successful at nation-building. All of these had had long periods of cultural unity, at least at the elite level, prior to the creation of modern states.[14]

Whatever their historic background and the length of imperial domination, all of the newly emerging nation-states were intent on nationalization. Their priority was to define a nation inside (or outside) their territorial boundaries, and to impose a compelling notion of nationhood on its members. Nationhood is the most important project of the new state. History matters little. The "invention of tradition" and myths of nationhood do not necessarily respect history.[15] When needed, elites simply go to pre-imperial history and forge their national symbols and legends in whatever way they can. We need, then, to focus on the ways in which nation-builders define their nation, the tools they employ, and the policies they adopt.

From Empire to Nation

The most obvious consequence of the end of an empire in the twentieth century has been the physical and political division of a large multiethnic, multilinguistic conglomerate of core and peripheries into a multitude of smaller countries aspiring to become national states. In structural terms, this amounts to the disintegration of one imperial state and the formation of many non-imperial states.

These national states bring to their development different aspects of their imperial legacy. First, these national states have different imperial legacies depending on where they were located in the empire. If the national state breaks off from the core imperial domain—a rump state—it will have a different legacy than a national state that breaks off from the periphery. Second, national states are governed by an elite which has reached the helm of the state through different routes, with different programs and different appeals to various constituencies. Third, their elites have to contend with inherited imperial institutions of varying strength and efficiency: they might or might not have a "state apparatus." Fourth, they have to grapple with uneven levels of economic development and industrialization. Finally, enveloping all these structural legacies of empire, they have a political culture that has evolved over centuries. How much of this legacy continues in the national state is difficult to measure, but it needs to be taken into account.

For rump states, the continuity between empire and nation is in the state apparatus. In such cases as Turkey and Austria, those who control the state have an easier time defining the politics of nationhood than in many other national states emerging from the periphery of empires. As Keyder shows elsewhere in this volume, centralizing elites have a better chance at controlling the state apparatus. To the degree that they are sustained by a strong ideology, they can mobilize support and move toward the construction of a new national state.

The nationalizing states of the periphery do not necessarily end up with a strong state apparatus or a set of well-defined institutions as their imperial legacy. Still, the role of elites, their various capacities and their mobilizational action defines the route for nationhood. The rump state remains more confident and united by imperial legacy than the periphery, gaining its strength from its previous imperial domination; it has better developed institutions and state apparatus. Peripheries, with no such clearly established institutions and often with a legacy of having been dominated, are apt to turn to ethnic nationalism as their best tool for unification and solidarity.

Continuity and Crisis for the Rump States

In the traditional contiguous empires which are the topic of this book, both core and periphery were transformed when they broke up. By contrast, as Eric

Hobsbawm argues, colonial overseas empires did not undergo the same drastic changes in their cores that traditional empires do. He agrees that traditional empires have less distinct divisions between core and periphery, as well as a "more or less coherent web of internal relations" that bonded core with periphery. In the case of colonial empires, the distances involved also mattered: in colonial empires the formal separation between core and periphery was much clearer and the core was an organic, self-contained unity with its own identity. In the case of the British empire, by the contrast drawn between "us" and "them" the colonies helped define the English.[16] There was little confusion over to whom the English "we" referred.

In traditional empires the multiplicity of overlapping forms of control and sovereignty, the variously embedded forms of intermediary structures between core and contiguous periphery, made distinctions less clear cut. With such intricate forms of control, multiple identities also developed in the traditional empires, each working alongside the others, and rising to the fore only under special conditions: religious, national, class, and regional identities all coexisted. While it is comparatively simple to talk of a core and a colonial identity in colonial empires, traditional empires did not lend themselves to such clear distinctions. Therefore, when the empire broke apart, the results were disruptive and complicated for both core and periphery.

After collapse, the Ottomans, Habsburgs and the Soviet Union, quickly became rump states with shrunken territory, possessing imperial ideologies that no longer made sense, and economies in retreat. In addition to structural discontinuities, the cores of these traditional empires confronted "identity crises" (to use current terminology) during the course of decay and collapse. The crisis each confronted was dealt with in different ways. The Ottoman–Turkish center quickly gave up its imperial identity, the Russian core replaced one imperial ideology by another. There was continuity between the Czarist and the Soviet empire, both the product of Russian cores. Between 1918 and 1920, the former Habsburg core of Austria tried to merge with Germany.

Elite politics set the stage for the rump ideology and policy. For example, late nineteenth century Ottoman elites were well aware that the empire had to undergo major structural transformations, but they differed on what these various possible changes should be. Caglar Keyder has shown that the winning strategy of the Young Turks altered the political landscape of the empire (and the state to follow) once and for all. Had the Liberals won instead, with their platform of economic and political liberalism and administrative decentralization, the course of Turkish politics would have been quite different. A centralist Committee on Union and Progress not only attracted a nationalist constituency, but also shaped a resolutely unitary state.

That Russia remains at a turning point is clearly demonstrated by the Chechen war and the elections in 1995–1996. Whether it will become a multinational, democratic country or return to the old Soviet boundaries are issues continually debated by Russian elites. Democracy, communism, market economics, and excessive ethnic rhetoric are all part of this search for a stable and reliable identity.

An interesting question is what makes for variations in imperial rhetoric and the presence or absence of aggressive behavior on the part of rump states? Can we argue that the faster the empire collapses, the greater the likelihood of militancy on the part of the center?[17] While this explanation fits the Soviet and Ottoman cases, it cannot be generalized. To the degree that imperial centers find alternative forms of identity and loyalty, they adapt. The Ottoman state molded a fresh identity from its Turkish historical capital; the Austrian rump state looked over the border to identify with a strong German entity.

The separation of center and periphery also often involves an uneven distribution of resources. Traditional empires built a coherent web of internal relations over time, that precluded the need for an equitable distribution of resources. Core areas developed by extracting the resources of the periphery, much of which had been incorporated previously to supply specific agricultural, mineral, or other needs. Empires therefore developed unevenly. Some peripheral areas were industrialized (such as Bohemia under the Habsburgs), others were strong trading outposts (such as Greece under the Ottomans). In the Russian case, the differences in relative development during the eighteenth and nineteenth centuries forced the center to view the German elites of the Baltic states as examples to be emulated. Today, after the breakup of the Soviet Union, this same type of asymmetric interdependence is playing itself out in the lopsided relations between the old imperial center and the peripheries. New peripheral states remain dependent on Russia for basic services, and are often compelled to supply Russia with their primary exports as payment. The Minsk Automotive Factory is an example of such interdependence since every component part of the heavy-duty trucks manufactured there came from a region now outside of Russia. After the collapse of the empire and the formation of the fifteen independent republics, to procure such goods from so many countries became practically impossible, paralyzing the industrial process. Such problems have led and will continue to lead to inter-state rivalries, competition, and conflict.

Despite the diverse sources of conflict, nationalizing states that have grown out of the center of empires have demonstrated stronger tendencies towards civic forms of politics than the states of the periphery. There is no doubt that an ethnic discourse existed and played a significant role in national politics. But, overall, a strong state-led civic, assimilationist and in some cases liberal, federalist discourse has been promoted. This was certainly true for both Austria and Turkey. In Turkey, by the end of the War of Liberation, the strong etatist elites had adopted French-style, state-driven programs of national incorporation and assimilation. They were helped in this endeavor by the absence of significant minorities in rump Turkey. After the World War and the War of Independence, Armenians and Greeks had been eliminated, and the opposition among the

Kurds quickly quashed. A similar state-led civic assimilationist project was carried out by the Hungarians who, unlike the Turks had to confront a much more heterogeneous population. While Hungary after Trianon might have become 90 percent Magyar, it was not so during the early years of nation-building. The Hungarian elites were at the helm of a solid state, a legacy of centuries of the special status the Hungarian aristocracy enjoyed even before the Dual Monarchy; they enforced Magyarization as a policy of assimilation into the Hungarian state. While Magyarization, like Turkification, might have worked in areas where it happened in conjunction with economic development, it also involved some serious conflicts.

Overall, the nationalizing states that emerged out of the center of these traditional empires were well organized and endowed with working institutions and elites, even though they were now constrained geographically. Despite the availability of ethnic nationalist repertoires, they were more likely to adopt an assimilationist, inclusive vision of nationhood.

The Formation of National States in the Imperial Periphery

In the periphery, the new nations initially claimed liberation and higher moral grounding than the core. Given that they were left with minorities within their territory, they replicated the imperial relationship of domination between a core ethnic group and minorities. Yet, they confidently declared themselves to be *national* states in pursuit of democracy and self-determination. The rhetoric of these new national states remained strongly nationalizing, lingering on from their anti-imperial struggle and from the economic difficulties that confronted them. As Brubaker describes them, "nationalism becomes an 'aspect' of politics—embracing both formal policies and informal practices, and existing both within and outside the state—rather than a discrete movement."[18] Furthermore, ethnicity also becomes an aspect of politics, used to consolidate the still fragile nation-state.

The rhetoric of liberation from empire served the purpose of uniting the nation, and bringing states and their populations together around the goal of nation-building. Opposition to empire provided the ideological fuel for the offshoots from the Habsburg and the Ottoman empires. The rhetoric included a glorious past in history (most often as defenders of the faith), a shared ethnic and linguistic heritage, and other markers of distinct peoplehood. Nationhood was perceived and articulated in ethnic terms and policies were the result of ethnic consolidation.

The view that ethnic forms of nation-building dominated the peripheries has to be modified in two ways. First, peripheral states also demonstrate evidence of both ethnic and civic understandings of nationhood. Embodied by different sets of elites, and different political positions and platforms, they easily coexisted. In Greece, for example, there was serious contention between civic and ethnic leaders. The civic component of Greek politics was represented by the old guard of Greek Independence, the merchants and statesmen. The ethnic component, represented by the low-level clergy and common folk emphasized community, and distinctiveness from the Turkish invader. These different factions engaged in battles for the definition of Greek nationhood, which helped engender the Greek irredentist political principle of *Megali Idea*, the dream of Greater Greece.

Second, there was no uniformity of nationhood and nationalizing policies in these new states; variations existed in both conceptions of national self and in the nationalizing policies in the periphery of these two empires. Some of these states clearly tended toward more inclusive definitions of the nation and the polity; others remained firmly grounded in their cultural, linguistic and religious markers. Czechoslovakia was among the most civically-oriented states; Romania, among the most ethnic. Bulgaria steered an essentially civic course, Greece vacillated between the two. The easiest way to discern the differences between these countries in terms of their conceptions and policies is to look at citizenship laws. All of the successor states of the Habsburg and Ottoman empires adopted citizenship legislation, ranging from the most inclusive to the most exclusive. These countries also differed in the degree of ethnic unmixing that they carried out. But more subtle differences can also be detected in the language policies of these states, their economic development programs, their land reform programs, and other ways politics shapes nationhood.[19] These differences are even clearer in the post-Soviet context, where the states of the ex-Soviet periphery have adopted widely divergent definitions of nationhood and have proceeded on different courses of development. Latvia and Estonia are extreme cases of ethnic definition of a citizenry; Ukraine, Lithuania, and Kazakhstan are molded on civic models.[20]

The old "ethnic east" and "civic west" dichotomy does not hold; both political cultures had civic and ethnic components. Overall, western European cases tend toward civic outcomes; post-imperial states have shifted between the two, with many finally adopting ethnic definitions of nationhood. How do we explain the more unstable political culture of the post-imperial cases?

In the past, one answer was based on the ethnic politics of empires. The argument went that since empires governed by manipulating religious or ethnic differences between communities, the post-imperial states applied a similar mode of politics to their new nation. But not all cases of nationhood out of empire have been ethnically based. In addition, the politicians of the post-imperial era were very much aware of democratic and civic options in politics, and some even pursued them despite trying circumstances. For example, among the Hungarian leaders, Lajos Kossuth (1802–1894) was not only aware of the European discourse, but eager to apply it to Hungary, which had clearly espoused a French model of nation-state building with strong state control. Other politicians embraced such politics only superficially, when it was necessary to pander to western Europe. It is therefore unreasonable to think that the ethnic option was the only one.

Elites and institutional development provide another answer, albeit partial. These variables seem to work in the past cases, they are less useful to explain post-Soviet nation-building. In the post-imperial era, some states gained sovereignty as a result of strong elite-led independence movements; some others had relatively weak elites and no independence movement to speak of. Where strong elites and well-developed political institutions coincided, nation-building proceeded in the French style under the aegis of a strong unitary state. Weaker elites acquired independence as the result of imperial breakup, but lacked the capacity to carry out the demands of nation-state building. New countries with the weaker type of political elites, more often than not encourage ethnic mobilization as a method of nation-state building. In the absence of a strong state apparatus and an adequate institutional legacy, elites have very little to rely on to mobilize a sense of nationhood other than ethnic differences and perceived injustices. Gellner has also argued that nationalism of this sort emerges in cases of complete institutional vacuum.[21] Politics in institutional terms cannot function; therefore ethnic politics become a tool for mobilization. This then occurs when the structural legacy of empire is minimal, but since the institutional legacy of the Soviet empire is far from minimal, it is difficult to understand the ethnic politics of many successor states. Cases of ethnic mobilization in Estonia and Latvia, where the political and institutional legacy is strong, are troublesome.

The exigencies of economic development also lead nationalizing elites in the direction of ethnic politics. When elites are expected to bring about socio-economic change rapidly they often resort to ethnic forms of mobilization as diversion.[22] The need to demonstrate rapid economic progress is a pressure shared by all elites with or without strong institutional frameworks. Economic downturns can consequently have a significant impact on the route politics will take, and can favor appeals to ethnicity.[23]

Institutions, Elites, and Associations

Discussions of levels of institution-building or economic development attained do not provide us with a sufficient explanatory framework of post-imperial nation-building, because we can find cases with strong institutions that demonstrate civic tendencies and cases with similarly strong institutions that demonstrate ethnic policies. The level of economic development shows similar variation. We need to formulate a better integrated and more concrete framework for analysis of nationhood.

At this task, we start with Brubaker's conceptualization of the nation as "institutionalized form, practical category, contingent event."[24] Nationhood develops over time, but also crystallizes suddenly when certain forms and definitions become more important than others, only to undergo subsequent changes further. As it emerges from within the discourse of state and society nationhood is fluid, but it can become quite fixed and unyielding when it becomes codified in laws and policies. Three different legacies of empire have to be analyzed to understand the crystallization of nationhood: institutional, elite, and associational. The institutional legacy of the empire sets the stage for the formation of national states. Mostly, strong state institutions are more complementary with civic politics.

Local, regional participatory associations and civil associations in society encourage participation from their members and promote the development of civic nationhood. As Margaret Somers has argued, "Quasi-democratic citizenship rights can emerge only in certain institution-specific relational settings and only in the context of particular social practices, namely practices that support popular public spheres."[25] Robert Putnam has recently argued for the "vibrancy of associational life" when describing the civic politics of northern Italy.[26]

In many parts of the Habsburg empire, incipient forms of associations, and various networks of commercial interests and other forms existed. Similarly, in most of the port cities of the Ottoman empire economic and social associations functioned as if they were part of a broader civil society.[27] While these associations are now being studied, their impact on different forms of nationhood has not been assessed. Not only the strength of state institutions, but also the strength of associational life help determine the likelihood that civic politics will take hold.

Most explanations of nationhood we have considered have elite action in common. The arguments run: if there are institutions, elites will implement more civic policies, and if economic development is lagging elites will implement ethnic strategies. One way to get away from these more case-based arguments is to focus directly on elites. Empires leave behind institutions and elites struggling to make them work. Elites are the main agents to take advantage of available institutions. They shape and reshape the political spectrum of the new nation through their actions. Yet, they have been trained, socialized and politicized in the context of empire and have become elites through functioning within the empire. They therefore bring different institutional and cultural frameworks of action to the new states. When we think of them as strong or weak elites, we do so in institutional terms: elites are strong if they are at the helm of a more or less well-fashioned state apparatus; they are weak elites when they have little institutional backing.

Strong elites hold influential positions in their community and share high levels of political, cultural and economic capital. When strong institutions and elites and developed local and regional associations are the legacy of empire, the likelihood of civic nationhood is high. The Czech elites that emerged out of the Habsburg empire combined political, cultural and economic capital. Bohemia, for example, the industrial center of the Habsburg empire, had well-developed industrial production and a burgeoning middle class. Significantly tied to embourgeoisement, the Czechs also had a strong cultural renaissance whose intellectuals were at the forefront of defining and redefining Czech culture and language. Many middle-class Czechs also assumed local political positions, which were the training ground for future governance. In many ways, then, the Czechs elites were best endowed with all three forms of capital. The development of elites with different forms of capital also helped incipient associational life, drawing the public into a cultural, economic, and social network of associations. These three factors combined to make it possible for the Czech national state to flourish along civic lines. Again, this does not mean that Czech political discourse entirely eliminated ethnic politics; the treatment of German minorities in the 1920s and the ethnic conflicts with Slovaks show that even the most democratic and civic among the new national states, could be wanting in its policies.

Romania, where ethnic politics and virulent nationalism culminated in the rise of fascism, had very different origins than Bohemia. It also had a different combination of institutions, elites and associations. Although privileged under most of Ottoman rule (as semi-independent, tribute-paying principalities of Moldavia and Wallachia), Romania by the eighteenth century had fallen under the rule of Greek Phanariots, developing no real nationalist movement and strong elite. It was the later Russian occupation that modernized Romania; by the end of the nineteenth century they had acquired a constitution, and in 1878 with the Congress of Berlin they became a nation-state. Romanian elites only gradually, following the Russian occupation, started to develop a sense of nationhood, building the necessary institutions for the diffusion of Romanian nationalism. Unlike the Czechs, Romanians lacked indigenous elites, a strong state and the associational life that comes from the development of commerce and towns.

While this combination of variables provides for different paths of internal national development, international competition and conflict can play havoc with national policies. When ethnic groups perceive territories to have been assigned unjustly, boundaries decided by administrative fiat, or manipulated by foreign powers, and when groups perceive that they have not been awarded what they lawfully should possess and enjoy, ethnic struggles will emerge. Nation-building then has to be embedded into an international context. Many of the conflicts in Eastern Europe between the wars were in part the result of the treaties of Paris. When the victorious Allies drew the modern borders of the region, they sought to apply principles of "self-determination," but partly out of self-interest and partly because of the complex intermix of ethnicities, these borders exacerbated old and produced new tensions.

The Allies strongly endorsed the principles of "self-determination," yet also often violated them. They made plans and secret deals among themselves, and

extended promises to potential allies that played havoc with such principles. They
played favorites, letting the Czechs get away with territories they should not have
acquired, while forcing millions of Hungarians to live under foreign rule. They also
interfered in the internal politics of the new states, and established minority protection deals with their elites. If during the tenure of empires ethnicity was used for
political ends, the European states certainly continued the practice.

Most of the borders drawn by European powers in the Middle East also caused
conflict and war in the following decades. The Arab-Israeli, the Iran-Iraq and the
recent Iraq-Kuwait struggles can all be traced back to the post-Ottoman settlements. In Eastern Europe, Versailles, St. Germain, Neuilly, and Trianon all created minority problems and fueled serious irredentism in the area, mainly by detach-
ing populations from their homelands, such as was the case for the multitude of
Hungarians who found themselves living in Romania and Czechoslovakia (now in
Slovakia), or the Germans in Poland. Therefore, in order to understand much of
the immediate post-imperial conflict we also need to look at the various peace settlements imposed upon the disintegrated empires.

Here I have tried to provide a framework for studying nation-building in post-
imperial situations. I set the stage for such an analysis first with an overview of
imperial legacies. Having then identified at least two definitions of nationhood,
civic and ethnic, I argued for the existence of a much more mixed repertoire of
post-imperial cases. In contrast to traditional understandings, I have found both
civic and ethnic definitions of the nation to be available to state and nation-
builders. I have also presented a causal and contingent framework for understanding the development of post-imperial nation-building. A trio of causal tightly
interrelated variables—institutions, elites and associations—determine the road
down which nations travel, with international contingencies providing roadblocks
along the road.

Notes

1. This explanation was espoused by a generation of Marxist scholars as well as mod-
ernization theorists, the most vocal of whom were scholars such as Stein Rokkan and Karl
Deutsch. See esp. Deutsch, *Nationalism and Social Communication*, 2nd ed. (Cambridge,
Mass., MIT Press, 1966).

2. Hans Kohn, *The Idea of Nationalism* (New York: Macmillan, 1945), 18–20, 329–331;
Liah Greenfeld, *Nationalism: Five Roads to Modernity* (Cambridge, Mass.: Harvard Uni-
versity Press, 1992), esp. 7–9, 14–17; John Plamenatz, "Two Types of Nationalism," in ed.
Eugene Kamenka, *Nationalism: The Nature and Evolution of an Idea* (New York: St Martin's
Press, 1976). Plamenatz offers a slight variation on the argument by viewing the German
and Italian versions of nationalism as western as well. His argument, however, holds for
Eastern Europe and the rest of the non-West.

3. Halil Inalcik, "The Meaning of Legacy: The Ottoman Case," in ed. L. Carl Brown,
Imperial Legacy: The Ottoman Imprint on the Balkans and the Middle East (New York:

Columbia University Press, 1996); Fikret Adanir, "Tradition and Rural Change in South-eastern Europe During Ottoman Rule," in ed. Daniel Chirot, *The Origins of Backwardness in Eastern Europe: Economics and Politics from the Middle Ages Until the Early Twentieth Century* (Berkeley: University of California Press, 1989).

4. Maria Todorova, "The Ottoman Legacy in the Balkans," in ed. L. Carl Brown, *Imperial Legacy*, p. 61.

5. See Daniel Chirot, ed., *The Origins of Backwardness*. This book contains many articles on the economics of Eastern Europe, and some specifically explore the relationship between agrarian systems, the rise of towns and economic development; see especially the chapters by Peter Gunst and Fikret Adanir. For the Habsburg empire, also see John Komlos, ed., *Economic Development in the Habsburg Monarchy in the Nineteenth Century: Essays* (New York: Columbia University Press, 1983).

6. Stephen Fischer-Galati, "Eastern Europe in the Twentieth Century: 'Old Wine in New Bottles,'" in ed. Joseph Held, *The Columbia History of Eastern Europe in the Twentieth Century* (New York: Columbia University Press, 1992), 4.

7. See Ergun Ozbudun, "The Ottoman Legacy and the Middle East State Tradition," in ed. L. Carl Brown, *Imperial Legacy*, p. 133. See also Carter Findley, "The Ottoman Administrative Legacy and the Modern Middle East," in ed. L. Carl Brown, *Imperial Legacy*; idem, *Bureaucratic Reform in the Ottoman Empire: The Sublime Porte, 1789–1922* (Princeton: Princeton University Press, 1980); Engin D. Akarli, "The State as a Socio-Cultural Phenomenon and Political Participation in Turkey," in ed. Akarli and Gabriel Ben-Dor, *Political Participation in Turkey: Historical Background and Present Problems* (Istanbul: Bogazici University Publications, 1975), 135–138; and Halil Inalcik, "The Nature of Traditional Society: Turkey," in ed. Robert E. Ward and Dankwart A. Rustow, *Political Modernization in Japan and Turkey* (Princeton: Princeton University Press, 1964).

8. Personal communication. See also Serif Mardin, "Power, Civil Society and Culture in the Ottoman Empire," *Comparative Studies in Society and History* 11 (1969); Halil Inalcik, "The Meaning of Legacy: The Ottoman Case," in ed. L. Carl Brown, *Imperial Legacy*, p. 21.

9. As Barbara Jelavich explains with the Ausgleich, at the top there was a joint Austro-Hungarian administration and two separate governments for Austria and Hungary, all united by the person of Franz Joseph. See Barbara Jelavich, *History of the Balkans*, 2 vols. (Cambridge: Cambridge University Press, 1983) vol. 2, p. 51.

10. Fischer-Galati, "Eastern Europe in the Twentieth Century," p. 3.

11. One recent example of this kind of "legacy" argument can be found in Mark N. Katz, "The Legacy of Empire in International Relations," *Comparative Strategy* 12 (1993): 365–383. See also Ted R. Gurr and Barbara Harff, *Ethnic Conflict in World Politics* (Boulder: Westview Press, 1994).

12. Dennison Rusinow, who writes on Yugoslavia's disintegration, similarly argues that while the Ottoman past contributed to the ethnic diversity, it cannot be blamed for the brutal conflict today. See Dennison Rusinow, "Yugoslavia's Disintegration and the Ottoman Past," in ed. L. Carl Brown, *Imperial Legacy*.

13. For an interesting analysis of this for the Ottoman empire see Aron Rodrigue, "Difference and Tolerance in the Ottoman Empire," *Stanford Humanities Review* 5, no. 1 (1995). Another example of this multilinguistic, multicultural life under empires is pro-

vided by Daniel Chirot in his personal account of life in Vilna; see idem, "Herder's Multicultural Theory of Nationalism and Its Consequences," *East European Politics and Societies* 10, no. 1 (1996).

14. Daniel Chirot, "Nationalist Liberations and Nationalist Nightmares: The Consequences of the End of Empires in the Twentieth Century," in ed. Beverly Crawford, *Markets, States, and Democracy: The Political Economy of Post-Communist Transformation* (Boulder, Colo.: Westview Press, 1995).

15. Eric Hobsbawm and Terence Ranger, eds., *The Invention of Tradition* (Cambridge: Cambridge University Press, 1983).

16. Linda Colley, *The Britons: Forging British Identity, 1707–1837* (New Haven, Conn.: Yale University Press, 1992).

17. Alexander J. Motyl certainly seems to argue this in his unpublished paper, "After Empire: Competing Discourses and Interstate Conflict in Postimperial Eastern Europe." As an extension of his distinction between sudden collapse and decay, he makes the point that empires that collapse suddenly have a tendency toward imperial and militant politics.

18. Rogers Brubaker, "Nationalizing States in the Old 'New Europe'—and the New," *Ethnic and Racial Studies* (forthcoming): 10.

19. Brubaker, "Nationalizing States." Brubaker provides an excellent summary of the different nationalizing policies of these new states.

20. Again, many variations exist in actual policies. But it is very difficult to do the cases justice in an overview.

21. Ernest Gellner, "Nationalism in the Vacuum," in ed. Alexander J. Motyl, *Thinking Theoretically About Soviet Nationalities* (New York, Columbia University Press, 1992).

22. Chirot, "National Liberations and Nationalist Nightmares"; and idem, *Modern Tyrants: The Power and Prevalence of Evil in Our Age* (New York: Free Press, 1994).

23. Joseph Rothschild, *East Central Europe Between the Two World Wars* (Seattle: Washington University Press, 1974).

24. Rogers Brubaker, "Rethinking Nationhood: Nation as Institutionalized Form, Practical Category, Contingent Event," *Contention* 4, no. 1 (1994): 3–14.

25. Margaret Somers, "Citizenship and the Place of the Public Sphere: Law, Community, and Political Culture in the Transition to Democracy," *American Sociological Review* 58 (1993): 589.

26. Robert Putnam, *Making Democracy Work: Civic Traditions in Modern Italy* (Princeton: Princeton University Press, 1993).

27. Caglar Keyder, Eyup Ozveren, and Donald Quatert, eds., "Port-Cities in the Eastern Mediterranean," Special Issue of *Review* 16, no. 4 (1993).

9

THE OTTOMAN EMPIRE

SERIF MARDIN

The transition of Turkey from empire to nation between 1918 and 1922 can, in its most visible form, be summarized as loss of territory: the Balkans had been lost during the earlier Balkan wars (1912–1913), and were now irrecuperable; the Levantine provinces were bent on establishing their own national identity; and finally, the Ottoman Hijaz, the locus of the most sacred Islamic places, emerged as the center of an Arab uprising engineered by no other than the Turcophobe infidel, "Lavrens." Anti-Ottoman Arab "treason" was to be the source of a long-lasting Turkish *Dolchstosslegende*, which explains some of the cautiousness of the foreign policy of the later Turkish Republic. That Ottoman loss of territory had a deeper, structural dimension can be gathered from the reminiscences of a Turkish journalist who had witnessed the last stages of the empire's military debacle from the Mount of Olives.

> In olden times when we spoke of the nation (*millet*) we would understand the Turkish population of Rumelia. The boundaries of the *millet* would perhaps go as far as the city of Bursa or Eskisehir. Anatolia [i.e. Asia Minor] did not give us a feeling of "wholeness." The regional dialects were so different from one another as to make it difficult for people to understand each other. The people of Trabzon, Konya and Bitlis would not be in tune as was the case for the population of Turks from Saloni-ka, Skopje or Maonastir. Anatolia would be remembered only when people had to be exiled from Istanbul or when another ten thousand men would be sent to their death in Albania or Yemen. Since the Arabs had now taken sides [with others], for Turks, Anatolia was the last fatherland.[1]

But even below this layer of shock mixed with nostalgia existed other unresolved Ottoman problems that also needed attention. One of these was the project of "Ottomanism" which by the end of the World War had to be definitively buried.[2] This was an undertaking that had run parallel to the nineteenth century Ottoman reform movement, known as the Tanzimat (1839–1876).[3] Contradictory though the conservative and liberal versions of reform had been, they shared the hope of a consociation of the various religious and ethnic groups found in the empire to be achieved under an umbrella where members of these groups would gather as Ottoman citizens. The hope of such a synthesis had now vanished for good. A much more subterranean, but potent, *mythomoteur*, that of the Ottoman state as the torchbearer of Islam, had also been crushed by the visible impotence and defeat of Turkey.[4] But not quite, for the person who was in the process of resurrecting Turkey, Mustafa Kemal Pasha, was himself known as a Gazi, i.e. a fighter *ad dei gloriam*. Mustafa Kemal (later Atatürk) had taken pains during his struggle against the Allies' partition of Anatolia which followed the defeat of the empire to appear as the champion of Ottoman-Islamic "patriotism." His role as a fighter for the faith had been recognized by Anatolian notables and, in most unequivocal terms, by Indian Muslims in the way in which they dug deeply into their pockets to support him.

This Islamic-patriotic stance, which Mustafa Kemal underlined during his leadership of the Turkish national resistance movement of 1919–1922, has often been seen as the conscious exploitation of the ambiguity of the term "millet." Originally the word had been used to characterize Ottoman religious groups, but beginning in the nineteenth century it was increasingly used to translate the French *nation*.[5] It was then used *against* the Ottomans to promote the rights of nationality of the empire's constituent parts, but, in a further development, was taken over by more radical Ottoman thinkers of the late nineteenth century to promote the notion of a Turkish nation.[6] To gather and energize a population materially and morally depleted by the Turkish involvement in the "Great War," Mustafa Kemal was appealing to the Muslim identity of some and to the Turkish patriotism of others by defining his goal as the salvation of the millet. Kemal's stand, which should have involved the promotion of an Islamic or pan-Islamic ideology, was belied by his subsequent involvement in building up a Turkish nationalism which in its extreme form (1932) smacked of racism, and in that respect, was alien to Turks of both Muslim and nationalist-Turkic inclinations. Barring the kernel of truth in this accusation, Mustafa Kemal's genuine patriotism and, in particular, the origin of his conviction, expostulated throughout his life, of the superior qualities of the Turks, still have to be explained. These were qualities, which in his view, would allow Turks to lift themselves by their bootstraps and go on to establish themselves as leaders of civilizations.

Mustafa Kemal's certitude was expressed as the viability of a project of recuperating the qualities found in the folk, an idea that no doubt had its roots in the theories of the Turkish sociologist Ziya Gökalp (1860–1923), but originally trickled down from Herderian romanticism. One of the most striking expression of such pride, however, antedates even Ziya Gökalp. It can be found in the works of the nineteenth century Ottoman patriot and bard of liberty Namik Kemal (1840–1888), who was clearly inspired in his faith by his belief in Ottoman (which turn out to be Turkish) achievements as state-builders.[7] But the story is more complicated than this straight-lined filiation would suggest. During the short period between the Young Turk revolution of 1908 and 1918, Ottoman intellectuals had experienced a number of transformations of Ottoman patriotism, with roots that went far back. This patriotism was a sentiment among Turkish-speaking Ottoman Muslims that was anchored in the much earlier, traditional fidelity to the Ottoman state (*devlet*). *Devlet* was a primary focus of legitimacy. Mustafa Kemal shared in the transformations of this ur-patriotism through the medium of a series of changes which took place at the time of the Balkan wars (1912–13). While we have little information as to what impact this process had on him, we can follow it in an autobiography of his contemporary, Şevket Süreyya Aydemir. Here, the transition from Ottoman state patriot to pan-Turkic idealist and to disillusionment with this very ideal is described in detail. Mustafa Kemal did not take the further step of Aydemir, which was Marxism, but a whole generation of Turks went through the first three stages of Aydemir's ideological journey, an ideology which for Aydemir began in the structuring aspects of everyday life in a frontier town but was further nurtured in Ottoman military schools. In the first stage of the boy's world view it was the might of Ottomans as empire builders that was underscored.

[W]hen I first registered in military [secondary] school [I] easily slid into its ranks without any feeling of estrangement. Soon thereafter I too began to see myself as someone who would become part of a great army, who would rush from border to border, who would defend the existence of a great empire with his sword. . . .

On the maps which hung on the walls of this school the lands of this wide empire were shown in sugary pink. These lands seemed to me as wide as the world itself, . . . but I still found them too narrow.

In Africa they extended to Tripoli-Bengaze and the Sahara desert in the middle of Africa, then to Egypt and the Sudan up to the borders of Ethiopia. Even the Beylicate of Tunisia was bordered in a pink line which meant, in fact, a protectorate. And then the lands all the way to the Indian Ocean, Yemen, and Arabia were ours. Iraq, Syria to the Sinai, and finally Anatolia up to the borders of Russia and Iran were ours. Crete, Cyprus, the Aegean all of Thrace, all of the provinces of Rumeli [i.e. the Balkans] were ours. So even Bulgaria with its status of a protectorate could be counted as ours. Beyond Macedonia and Albania, Bosnia Herzegovina, itself pink, would extend the boundaries of the empire to the Sava and Dalmatia.

During recess, we the children would gather in front of the maps, we would look at the frontiers of our state. We would say for the land framed by these boundaries, "Our Land," and we would repeat joyfully, "Our land, our state." While pronouncing these words we would feel that something in us would sing, swell up, and that these feelings made me grow in stature, gave me a feeling of pride. . . .

I now knew that the fatherland was everywhere the boundaries of the state would reach. Wherever our boundaries stretched was our fatherland, and these boundaries were the places our army could reach.[8]

Following the Balkan defeats these dreams of Aydemir tumbled.

However, in the midst of all this confusion a new understanding emerged in the minds of some people. This was a new conception of a fatherland and a nation. In this new understanding the fatherland was no longer the place where the army was in control. We began to think that the real, the profoundest truth was the *people* not the fatherland. . . . Before [these events] we had also been Turks, but it was thought that the word Turk, reminiscent as it was of the hegemony of one people over others, in an empire which brought together many people, would be wounding. And yet the other races living in the empire would all speak of themselves with the name of the nation to which they belonged. In the military school . . . privileged scions of families from Yemen and Kurdistan, the youth who came from Cherkess villages because they had relatives in the palace, would all sing the praises of their nation and would look down upon us. But we Turks would never bring our racial connections to the fore. We would deny that link, and whenever the name of our nation had to be mentioned we would simply calls ourselves "Ottomans."[9]

The Committee of Union and Progress, the original Young Turk organization which took the step of becoming a political party in 1913, had to shoulder the consequences of these ideological developments, promote a new identity of Turkishness, *tout court*, and, at the same time, maintain a pretense of a united Ottoman empire until the end of World War I. The missions that Young Turk leaders sent to Central Asia after their flight and exile (1918) to establish links with Muslim leaders in the interregnum following the Russian Revolution[10] were among the signs of this new search for a foundation of Turkishness. The forays of Turkish generals in the Caucasus were another aspect of this not very well thought-out policy.[11] The need to discover the nation had led Şevket Süreyya to an extension of Turkishness, i.e. pan-Turkism. Mustafa Kemal stopped at Turkish nationalism.

Turkish nationalism was not a strictly local product. It was "imagined" in the sense of being a view of Turkic-Central Asian history that came from the West. At a second reading its origins may also be traced to ideas of imperial Russian Muslims in their attempt at self-government (1904–1920), but it was not "imagined" in the simplistic sense that comes out of B. Anderson's studies. It was *constitutive* of society in the sense of stemming from a felt need to reach a wider Turkish audience, a process begun in the nineteenth century. In this process "Print Capitalism" does not have the centrality Anderson attributes to it; language as such was much more at the center of the stage and was to become the focus of the reworking of an identity during the 1930s.

The "Ottoman" language, the language used by the Ottoman literati, was a mixture of Arab, Persian, and Turkic. Ottoman sophisticates considered this elite elaboration, which had become more convoluted with time, to be a success that had enabled them to build an instrument with a conceptual sophistication above the "rough" Turkish of the poorer classes and Turkmen tribes. In the 1860s the Ottoman liberal-constitutionalist group decided that to appeal to the Turkish-speaking population—a choice in itself instructive—they would have to abandon this linguistic sophistication and engineer a middle of the road language understandable to the wider audience that had grown up as a result of the increase in literacy and the new readership of newspapers. Debates concerning the simplification of the alphabet also appeared at this time.[12] In retrospect, these stirrings appear as the earliest propellants of modern Turkish nationalism. The consciously promoted support of the vernacular was very early transformed into what may be described as the "project" of national literature, the aim of creating a fund of Turkish writing that would unite readers rather than simply propagandize ethnic roots. The trend was invigorated and energized as an intellectual current around the 1890s when a fierce debate in the press opposed those who believed the Turkish language to be the foundation of "Ottoman" identity to a group promoting Arab culture as foundational.[13] To retrieve ethnic Turkish origins was another tack encouraged by Turkish *littérateurs* both in the 1890s and after 1908. Ottoman Muslim conservatives proposed Islam as another alternative which took the shape of an Islamic renaissance between 1910 and 1918.[14] All of Mustafa Kemal's speeches indicate that he, as well as the founding fathers of the republic, believed that Ottomanism, Islamism, and pan-Turkism had failed as ideological frames for the promotion of new principles of citizenship. Turkish nationalism was his own answer, but the prior development of this idea in the nineteenth century is essential to understanding the layers it subsumed.

In the 1930s, Turkish nationalism assumed an increasing starkness with the notion of Turkish race and theories about the Central Asian Turks as the fountainhead of all civilization.[15] This was one of the major weaknesses of Kemalist nationalism. An earlier, milder synthesis, promoted by the sociologist Ziya Gökalp,[16] was couched as an attempt to recuperate the soul of the folk; it survived to become one of the constituents of Turkish nationalism today. Its most recent avatar is the so-called Turkish-Islamic synthesis which distances itself from the Jacobin secularism of Kemal's republic and has become a force in current Turkish politics.[17] In the end, the creation of national identity was the item of Kemalism which was grafted on the rump of the empire with the greatest success. Its present further elaboration as anti-Kurdish chauvinism is, however, another story.

Republicanism

One of the consequences of the demise of the empire was the founding of the Turkish Republic in 1923. From monarchic empire to republic was no mean change and one which radically transformed Ottoman political structure. It therefore constitutes a primary focus for our attention in questions regarding "consequences."

Research on the nineteenth century Ottoman empire has demonstrated that during the Tanzimat political power was held by high officials of the Porte, causing much frustration in the palace. Between 1877 and 1908, Sultan Abdul-hamid took power into his own hands, but once more research has shown that he was habitually the supreme bureaucrat and only randomly the oriental despot.[18] In any case, the constitution of 1876 which he had put to rest continued to appear at the head of state almanacs during his reign. Reestablished in 1908, following the Young Turk revolution, the Ottoman constitution was further amended in 1909 to increase the powers of the legislative branch.

At the end of World War I the defeated Ottomans were soon split into two contending parties: the sultan's government in Istanbul versus the movement of resistance to the Allies' intention of dividing up the empire, located in Ankara. The Allies' promotion of the invasion of Anatolia by Greek forces in 1919 had uncovered their wider policy: the forces of resistance had a clear Anatolian-Turkish (and at the beginning of the process partly Kurdish) focus; the leaders of the Arab populations having opted out of the empire were not part of the movement. Anatolia, the setting in which the resistance movement crystallized, provided a unified platform for a group that deep down exhibited the already existing split of Young Turk politics between secularists and moderate-to-radical Islamists. This was also partly a dividing line between a Western-oriented bureaucratic elite and provincial notables. Their difference had already appeared in a heated sociopolitical debate between 1908 and 1918. The fulcrum of this discussion was not so much the desirability of democracy per se, since even Muslim conservative intellectuals of the period had supported the principle of the sultan's responsibility towards his subjects.[19] The contentious point was the foundation of such a democracy, i.e., would it rest on the law of God or on the will of the people?

At the time the proposal was that the laws passed in parliament be made to conform to Islamic *fiqh*; a second concern of Muslim conservatives was about the paramount position of the sultan as the Caliph of all Muslims. The Young Turks, establishing their own *diktat* after 1913, had left this issue unsettled, although they had shown their own inclination before and during the World War by secularizing some of the laws of the realm. On April 23, 1920, the resistance movement had gathered a National Assembly in the provincial capital of Ankara. On January 20, 1921, the assembly promulgated a constitution for the new Turkey, the first article of which stated, "Sovereignty resides in the people and this without limitation." So the issue of the source of legitimacy was—in theory—settled for good.

On November 1, 1922, the assembly voted to separate the caliphate from the sultanate; on October 29, 1923, the republic was proclaimed; on March 3, 1924, the caliphate itself was abolished. The final settlement of the dichotomy between secularists and Islamists through a number of secularizing reforms of the new regime between 1923 and the early 1930s is, in itself, fascinating and the ends achieved truly momentous; the details of this change are widely available in texts on Turkish history.[20] But a point that is less in evidence in these texts and that has to be underlined is that this basic shift was made possible by the greater organizational and ideological cohesion of a minority in the National Assembly, a minority which, in the following decade, went on to establish one-party rule in Turkey. The basic propellant of this transformation merits some attention.

What we see is that the Kemalist founding fathers were clearly the intellectual heirs of their Young Turk predecessors. The latter had been exposed, during their years of opposition to Sultan Abdulhamid II in Europe (1895–1908), to a diffuse form of disillusionment with parliamentary government and political parties prevalent at the end of the nineteenth century in Europe. These were the currents expressed in the works of Ostrogorski and Michels as well as in Lenin's "democratic centralism." The key issue in the activist version of these theories was no longer how to legitimate government through popular participation, but how to get the masses to move in order to change the world, an emphasis that is fundamental to the ideology of the Turkish Republic and eventually made up an underlying premise of the ideology labeled "Kemalism."

Sorel was typical of the more philosophically inclined of these European theoreticians in his denunciation of the theory of natural rights, his view of myths as historical forces, and his cult of energy. The trickle of these speculations that reached the Young Turks was an activism that included in its extreme form what newspapers in Paris around 1905 labeled *la politique par le fait*, i.e., arguments supported by violence. Such general activist views had worked well to energize the Young Turk officers in Macedonia around 1902–1908: they adopted the tactics of their Bulgarian terrorist enemies, bringing to life a view of political action promoted by the Macedonian revolutionary organization, the "Black Hand," a tactic known in Turkey as *komitecilik*, i.e., "committee action." Kemalism had therefore an ambivalent stand with regard to the role of a political vanguard in the sense in which it had to be both activist (ruthless) and democratic.[21]

While the Europe that Mustafa Kemal's generation knew was pre-Fascist, it received these ideas together with earlier Western paeans to constitutionalism, liberty, and representation. The specific experience of the Ottoman parliament after 1908, with its ethnic/ideological gridlock, confirmed among Kemalists a suspicion that a multi-party system was unworkable. What remained of all these influences and experiences by the end of World War I was a plan to mobilize the masses for an ultimate project of democracy which they would earn through apprenticeship in formally democratic but in fact authoritarian institutions, an apprenticeship of indefinite duration. In practice, this somewhat vague ideal promoted a continued ambivalence between democracy, the promotion of individual rights, and a system navigating at the command of a vanguard party and its leaders. The revival of the *Führerprinzip* in the Europe of the 1930s reinforced this tendency. The Second World War once more froze whatever democratic ideals the republic had embodied at its foundation. The single party tightened, but this was the beginning of the end for the single party.

The Tanzimat had already taken what could be of use in the old system into this venue through its extensive bureaucratization of the state. It lacked the mobilizational element, but that was added by the republic. This mobilizational project set around nationalism was not completely successful. In the long run it would be hampered by the unanticipated outcome of the republican project of modernity itself which was of wider scope than nationalism. That wider project generated demands for resources to build up both personal and social identity, demands that were brought to center stage by the very success of some of the policies of modernization that had been promoted between 1923 and 1950. On the other hand, the extraordinarily powerful means at the disposal of Islamic discourse for satisfying both these demands and the consequences of the politicization and globalization of the world on daily life, in the long run, reinforced, rather than weakened, Islam. The point to be emphasized (in contradiction to the somewhat superficial venue of Turkish Marxists) is that modern Turkish history suggests that religion is *constitutive* of society and thus not merely a superstitious, manipulative drug. The one-party system of Kemalism lost the battle for the souls of its citizens by overextending the boundaries of its own rhetoric without providing a deeper rationale.

From the 1930s on, the single-party state was in control, even though the state seems to have overtaken the single party in the long run. But what was most important in this development was not that the state-run party was a powerful instrument of control, but that it had to operate on the basis of a new language of sociopolitical relations in which "republic," "national sovereignty," "law," and "the nation" were elements of a set that made up the sociopolitical formula that was being copied from the West. Each one of these elements had to be given a meaning for a population which had used a different set of integrating concepts in its daily life and was now drawn into the new life of the republic. Not only were the meanings new, but their valences were being rapidly transformed in the age of dictatorships. All of this was confusing and extremely difficult for leaders as well as followers to keep under control within the frame of the new political formula.

Education

For Kemalism, science was "the surest guide in life." By "science" was meant Western "positive" science and its methods. That education could shape a country anew was also part of an earlier Ottoman understanding that collectivities could be molded by the political center: population resettlement and continuous administrative restructuring were part of the traditional Ottoman bent for "social engineering." Sultan Abdulhamid's use of Islam for mobilizational purposes had been the latest version of this tradition.

The military schools of the Tanzimat were from the beginning centers of modernization which some observers even saw as centers of "materialism."[22] Through its promotion of normal schools, the educational reforms of the Tanzimat created the type of teacher who belonged to a species far removed from that of the "master." Pedagogy, or the attempt to provide a uniform view of the modern world, replaced the older type of master-apprentice relation with its idiosyncratic "oriental" features of an enchanted world.

One result of the rise of the republic was an ever-increasing importance given to public education. The schoolmaster became an icon of Kemalism and the carrier of Kemalist ideology. A second generation of ideologue schoolteachers emerged in the 1930s who did not have the cosmopolitan experience of the republic's first-generation founding fathers, nurtured as they had been in the ancien régime. This second generation promoted a less tolerant version of Kemalism that began to rankle the better-educated third generation of university graduates in the late 1940s. But even more important was that the ideological position that the schoolmasters had to adopt was itself contradictory and destabilizing. On the one hand, they had to praise the West; on the other, they had to be good nationalists and "pure Turk"—a new popular notion after the 1930s. These internal contradictions contributed to the strong criticism that eventually began to be directed against Kemalism in the 1940s.

A second bifurcation, related to the increased stock of information the West introduced in the Ottoman empire, went beyond that received on school benches. Printing (1729) had brought with it the newspaper and, in the later nineteenth century, the magazine. In both cases the fare offered was a potpourri which one could label encyclopedism: the uses of steam, geology, the animal kingdom, the distance to the stars, but also at a less exalted level, the material culture of the West and Western fashions in clothes, furniture and style of life. As can be seen from the report of the first Ottoman ambassador to the West (1720), Ottomans could be as impressed by the glitter of Versailles and its *douceur de vivre* as by its military achievements. Turning a Muslim hadith around in his interpretation the ambassador commented: "The world is the prison of the believer and the paradise of the infidel."[23] The imitation of the West continued during the Tanzimat, creating, in the Ottoman literature of the third quarter of the nineteenth century, a recurring type of the superficially-Westernized foppish Ottoman.[24] The desire for the amenities of everyday life bringing with it a concomitant Western aestheticism continued in the early twentieth century. Turkish *littérateurs* looked upon French symbolism as an inspiration and attempted to feel the closeness with classical Greek culture that they found in J. M. de Heredia. In the time of Young Turk rule, when Turks were still wearing fezzes, one famous educator went around snipping off fez tassels to show how ridiculous he believed this headgear to be. At the time when family names did not yet exist, the only effect this had was to identify him by the nickname of "tassel-snipper." Mustafa Kemal felt the ridiculousness of Ottoman appearance so acutely that he totally proscribed the fez.

Mustafa Kemal's renunciation of his military position and his change to civilian clothes underlines an aspect of Republican ideology which is often treated cursorily but which reveals a profound change of political formula from that of the Ottoman state. In his writings, civilian life is further highlighted in a number of guises. The first of these is in the condemnation of the Ottoman *mythometeur* of conquest and empire-building,[25] conjoined with praise for the "scientific and administrative" achievements of the West.[26] A constant theme in his writings is that of the "civil laws" of Europe as an enviable achievement. The same theme also appears in his contrast between the valuation of military valor and the secondary role crafts played in the Ottoman empire.[27] The conditions for "true victory," according to him, were laid down by the victories of the Turkish army in its struggle against the Greek invaders, but could only come into their own through a victory of the teachers.[28] This clear yearning for a "civilian" society was the consequence of making the military a counter-foil in the elaboration of his political program. This was not an entirely new element: the civilian officialdom of the Tanzimat was similarly inclined, but it was new in the sense of being promoted by a victorious general. In fact, the growing institutional components of the Turkish Republic brought about so many "civil" activities that citizens were gradually let to organize their life around them. This process had already advanced remarkably by 1918. But it was the stark contrast between its demands and the bureaucracy of Kemalism that eventually led to the building of an opposition that destroyed the one-party state. The linkage here also involved one of the carriers of the new "civil" and "civilian" social system, the jurists.

The strongest push for the rethinking of Kemalism in the 1960s came from the ranks of a new, specialized group of men of law. Kemalist Turkey did not have a principle of judicial review. Nevertheless, it developed an institution, first seen during the Tanzimat, which underlined the accountability of the state under administrative law. Within the one-party state this was obviously the most open field for contesting actions of the state. It was an area where semi-constitutional and political questions were raised in a tangential manner. While civil and criminal law also consisting of translations of Western codes did not need philosophical foundations, decisions of the supreme administrative court, the Council of State, often had to refer to more abstract principles regarding political philosophy. These foundations were discovered in the ideas of what has been called the French "institutional" school of law.[29] It was consequently among the practitioners of administrative law that the foundations of Kemalism came to be questioned. The resulting ideological destabilization was latent, rather than something written about openly; nevertheless, it constituted the theoretical/legal dimension of the opposition to Kemalism in the late 1940s which emerged out of its own ranks.

Religion

Arab Muslims have always looked on Turkish Muslims as latitudinarians; the proofs are adduced from the "Mongol" political and social institutions which the Turks brought into the Islamic fold. Although Muslim Turks hated Mongols for what they remembered as their oppressive rule in Anatolia in the thirteenth century, the Arab accusation has a kernel of truth. The Ottomans, while they believed themselves to be torchbearers of Islam, did indeed institutionalize secular state practices which separated the demands of administration from those of religion, and they did so much more systematically than earlier Muslim empires.[30] Doctors of Islamic Law and the very pious balked at some of these "heathen" practices. A succession of sultans strove to maintain a balance by augmenting and diminishing secularism of this type as circumstances changed.

In retrospect one sees that the contribution of Ottoman Hanafi Islam was stronger in terms of religio-administrative innovations than in terms of theological speculation. Paradoxically, this secularist stance allowed the men of religion to invoke religious principles when they considered that the state went too far in its takeover of matters which should have been regulated by "civil" Muslim law. Because of its potential weight against central authority this venue into contestation has had a revival whenever contestation has become an issue of politics; it achieved a new relevance when democracy became an operative ideal.

In a number of papers I have proposed that it was the element of secularism in Ottoman political culture that facilitated growth of an increasingly powerful bureaucracy beginning with the end of the eighteenth century.[31] These were the men who led the reform movement of the Tanzimat and its secularization of education, of the judicial, and of professions such as medicine. Yet already by the 1860s the foes of these bureaucrats, the Young Ottoman constitutionalists, sought allies among Islamic clerics who found themselves pushed to the outer boundaries of the system of the Tanzimat. At a more sophisticated level of opposition, the famous statesman Cevdet Paşa, a "defrocked" doctor of Islamic law, protested when an attempt was made to install the Code Napoleon as the Ottoman civil law (1868), stating that the cultural essence of Ottomanism, Islam, was being taken out of central areas of society.[32]

Later, the Young Turks in opposition (1889–1908) to Sultan Abdulhamid were primarily positivists. They saw religion in the Comtean perspective of an important element of social cohesion, the influence of which was nevertheless bound to disappear with time.[33] Unexpectedly, the revolution they carried out in 1908 liberated a flood of Muslim speculation in print. Islam, in this press, bending to its requisites, became more populistic, disregarding the fine differences that doctors of Islamic law could appreciate, and took on an ideological

cast. But it also brought to the fore a set of highly educated Muslim intellectuals who initiated a debate over the place of Islam in Ottoman society.[34] They
recognized the stagnation of Islam brought about by the displacing of religious
discourse during the Tanzimat and underlined the interpenetration of the economic backwardness and poverty of Turkey with this stagnation, even though
they believed Islam to be the core of Ottoman civilization. These socioreligious
considerations were expressed with particular poignancy by the poet Mehmed
Akif, who later wrote the national anthem of the republic, and whose religious
conservatism eventually drove him into voluntary exile.[35]

The Young Turks tried their best to use this tendency, as they did pan-Turkism. Their sociologist of mark, Ziya Gökalp, took a more serious view of the
problem. He nourished a strong conviction about the reasons for the stagnation
of Islam which had been able to promote a brilliant initial thrust: according to
him such rigidity was due to the fact that Islam had not allowed the local cultures on which it fastened to develop their specific character.[36] This was, according to him, what had happened with the Ottoman Turks. There existed a means
of turning the trend around by recasting Islam so that it would be integrated
with the local culture of the modern Turks. Mustafa Kemal took exception to
Gökalp's stance in the sense of letting such an Islamic-Turkic synthesis take
place at the level of the religious faith of individuals rather than promoting an
ideological project of Islamic reform on the Gökalp model. Years later, in the
1940s, Gökalp's proposal found its echo in Turkey in the form of the so-called
Turk-Islamic synthesis.[37]

A major error Mustafa Kemal seems to have committed in this respect is to
have believed that secular education as a resource and nationalism as an ideology could together be a substitute for Islam and that these two foundations of the
Turkish Republic would fill in for all the functions of Islam. In reality the new
set, education and nationalism, could not bring together the resources of narrative background, of construction for personal identity and *mysterium*, that Islam
had provided. Mustafa Kemal also underestimated the way in which religion
functioned as a communication network in peasant/provincial society. Two elements allowed religion to emerge as a datum in the multiparty politics of Turkey
in the 1950s. The first was the solidity, through time, of earlier Islamic communication networks ready to be used by a modern political party that would exploit
them. Second, the potential for protest of Islam, already in place, was made an
integral part of political protest against one-party rule, a rule which lasted from
1924 to 1950. But once again, the consequences of modernity, i.e., the republic,
appeared at a number of contradictory levels. An increasingly well-educated population had an increasing number of quandaries to resolve at the level of personal or social identity, the level Kemal had neglected. Integrated into a new division
of labor—a success of the republic—Turks were increasingly demanding equali-
tarian values that this first step in economic development did not by itself provide. Neither did the ideology of Kemalism provide them with any answers other

than that their values lay in the "scientific attitude." Since the Turks of the 1950s and 1960s had graduated from the Kemalist modern secular educational establishment their questions, even though more concrete, were set to a deeper level and were more insistent than those of the founding fathers. Islam was an answer to this perplexity, but it was among Islamist graduates of Kemalist universities that these questions were debated with a new sophistication with no comparable scope in the Islamic world.

Notes

1. Falih Rifki Atay, *Batış* Yillari *(Istanbul, 1963), 73.*
2. On "Ottomanism," see Niyazi Berkes, *The Development of Secularism in Turkey* (Montreal: McGill University Press, 1964), 221; and my *Genesis of Young Ottoman Thought* (Princeton: Princeton University Press, 1962), 331.
3. For the Tanzimat see Berkes, *Development of Secularism*, pp. 143–204; Mardin, *Genesis*, pp. 107–132.
4. For the concept of a *mythomoteur*, see John A. Armstrong, *Nations Before Nationalism* (Chapel Hill: University of North Carolina Press, 1982), 129.
5. See Berkes, *Development of Secularism*, p. 96.
6. See Mardin, *Genesis*, p. 274; David Kushner, *The Rise of Turkish Nationalism, 1876–1908* (London: Frank Cass, 1977), 28. The term *millet* had been used with the same ambiguous connotation by the Muslim revivalist Jamal ad-Din al-Afghani; see Nikki R. Keddie, *Sayyid Jamal ad-Din "al-Afghani": A Political Biography* (Berkeley: University of California Press, 1972), 135–136.
7. Mardin, *Genesis*, pp. 328–329.
8. Şevket Süreyya Aydemir, *Suyu Arayan Adam* (Istanbul: Remzi, 1967), 44–45.
9. Ibid., pp. 59–60.
10. See Zeki Velidi Togan, *Hâtıralar* (Istanbul, 1969), 324–325.
11. Audrey L. Alstadt, *The Azerbaijani Turks* (Stanford, Calif.: Hoover Institution Press, 1992), 90–91.
12. Mardin, *Genesis*, p. 240, n. 188.
13. Kushner, *Rise of Turkish Nationalism*, pp. 81ff.
14. See Ismail Kara, *Türkiye 'de Islâmcılık Düşüncesi (Istanbul: Risale, 1989).*
15. Büşra Ersanli Behar, *Iktidar ve Tarih* (Istanbul: Afa, 1992), especially Dr. Reşit Galip (1932), 145–146.
16. See Ziya Gökalp, *Turkish Nationalism and Western Civilization: Selected Essays of Ziya Gökalp* (London: George Allen and Unwin, 1959), 79.
17. Tanil Bora and Kemal Can, *Devlet, Ocak, Dergâh*, 3rd ed. (Istanbul: Iletişim, 1994).
18. See Stanford Shaw and Ezel Kuran Shaw, *A History of the Ottoman Empire and Modern Turkey*, 2 vols. (Cambridge: Cambridge University Press, 1977), vol. 2.
19. Ismail Kara, *Islâmcilarin Siyasî Görüşleri (Istanbul: Iz Yayincilik, 1994).*
20. See Erich J. Zürcher, *Turkey: A Modern History* (New York: I. B. Tauris, 1993).
21. A seldom understood element of Kemalism; see Mete Tuncay, *Türkiye Cumhuriyetinde Tek-Parti Yönetimi'nin Kurulmasi (1923–1931)* (Istanbul: Yurt Yayinlari, 1981), 313, n. 20.
22. Berkes, *Development of Secularism*.

23. Gilles Veinstein, "Introduction" to Yirmisekiz Mehmet Çelebi, *Le Paradis des Infideles*, trans. Julien-Claude Galland (Paris: Maspero, 1981).

24. See my "Super-Westernization in the Ottoman Empire."

25. *Atatürk'ün Kültür ve Medeniyet Konusundaki Sözleri*, ed. Aydin Sayili (Ankara, 1990).

26. Ibid., p. 12.

27. Ibid., pp. 20–21.

28. Ibid., p. 29.

29. Albert Broderick, ed., *The French Institutionalists*, trans. Mary Welling (Cambridge, Mass.: Harvard University Press, 1970).

30. See Halil Inalcik, *The Ottoman Empire: The Classical Age, 1300–1600* (New York: Weidenfeld and Nicolson, 1973).

31. See my *Genesis*, pp. 147 and passim.

32. Berkes, *Development of Secularism*, p. 168.

33. See my *Jön Tüklerin Siyasî Fikirleri*, 3rd ed. (Istanbul: Iletişim, 1989), 43, 136.

34. Kara, ed., *Turkiye'de Islamcılık*, passim.

35. Ibid., pp. 309–406.

36. Gökalp, *Turkish Nationalism and Western Civilization*, p. 265.

37. Bora and Can, Devlet, p. 294.

10

THE HABSBURG EMPIRE

ISTVÁN DEÁK

In October of 1918 the political leaders of Austria-Hungary's many ethnic groups dissolved the monarchy. The decision was wrenching, for throughout the war, they had all pledged their loyalty to the ancient Habsburg realm, but the reasons for the dissolution were compelling: the Central Powers were about to lose the Great War, and the Entente Powers had made clear in their declarations that the peoples of the monarchy, whether Czechs, Slovaks, Poles, Ukrainians, Slovenes, Croats, Serbs, Bosnians, Romanians, Italians, Hungarians, or German-speaking Austrians would do best to desert their monarch. Undoubtedly the time had come, the ethnic politicians reasoned, to create their own independent states or, in the case of the Serbs, Romanians, Italians, and the German-speakers, to join the neighboring state where their co-nationals lived. The process of dissolution took only a few days, and it brought immediate benefits, at least to those who had engineered the process.[1] The long-term consequences of the dissolution of Austria-Hungary were less clear: the rest of the twentieth century would bring nothing but misery and bloodshed to Central Europe. It is fair to add, however, that in no case would the old supranational empire have been able to maintain itself in an age of heightened nationalism. Because of the stubbornness of the monarchy's ethnic politicians, the only other conceivable alternative to dissolution was federalization, and it never had a chance to move beyond the planning stage.

The spoils of dissolution were impressive: to the new states fell, among other things, the Dual Monarchy's extensive transportation network, including a dense and modern railroad system constructed between the 1840s and 1914. Further, the successor states took over a number of imposing wrought-iron railroad stations, soaring viaducts and suspension bridges, municipal parks, eclectic theater buildings, grandiose opera houses, splendid museums, baroque churches, Mauresque synagogues, ostentatious parliament buildings, neo-Gothic or neo-Classical city halls, spacious military barracks, hospitals, and the red-brick buildings of thousands upon thousands of state schools. Added to these was the extensive network of well-constructed administrative buildings, most of which are still in use today, painted and repainted in the traditional "Habsburg yellow" of Empress Maria Theresa's summer palace at Schönbrunn. The most valuable legacy of the Dual Monarchy, however, were the many well-trained administrators, judges, officers, members of the free professions, businessmen, shopkeepers, and skilled workers. The honesty, efficiency, and work ethic of these groups compared well with those of their counterparts in the West; certainly, they ranked above their peers to the south and the east of Austria-Hungary.[2]

As one moved east within the monarchy, from Passau on the German border or Bregenz on the Swiss border, all the way to what is today western Ukraine or central Romania, one did, it is true, inevitably meet with less and less prosperity, education, and efficiency. Yet even in such backwater regions as eastern Galicia, Dalmatia, or Bosnia-Herzegovina, evidence of the Habsburg Monarchy's successful modernizing efforts is still visible today—aside, of course, from places such as Sarajevo where Habsburg era public buildings have been reduced to rubble by Serbian artillery. All those accomplishments owed much, to be sure, to the dedication, hard work, and talent of the local inhabitants; yet it is also fair to say that their achievements would have been far less spectacular without the Pax Austriaca imposed more or less successfully by the ancient House of Austria over several centuries.

It is amazing how quickly such a venerable state was replaced. The various National Committees, created by imperial order on October 16, 1918, succeeded in assuming ultimate power, with only token resistance from the old regime. Nationalist propaganda later presented these takeovers as risky and heroic affairs, but in reality imperial power had disappeared as if by magic as the more astute members of the ancien regime quickly embraced the flag of their new state.[3] How else to explain that the collapse of the old order and the birth of the new in Prague consisted of not much more than noisy street celebrations, the tearing down of some Habsburg-era statues, and the replacement of the black and yellow colors of the House of Austria with the tricolor of the new Czechoslovak state? Most Bohemian administrators remained at their desks and continued to run things as if nothing had happened. Not even the numbering of the files diligently produced by this all powerful bureaucracy was altered to honor the dawn of a new era. The partial purge of the German-speakers from among the Bohemian officials would occur only later—to be followed, after 1938, by the partial purge of the Czechs and, in 1945, by the expulsion of all Bohemian Germans.[4]

The pillars of the old order crumbled under the impact of military defeat and the bloodless national revolutions. The cosmopolitan Habsburg aristocracy and the Catholic high clergy hastened to proclaim their loyalty to the new nation states, and Emperor-King Charles was abandoned even by his splendidly caparisoned Arcieren, Trabanten, and Hungarian noble body guards, for whom this would have been the first genuine opportunity in history to defend their ruler. During the last days of the empire, teenaged artillery cadets mounted guard at Schönbrunn Palace to protect Charles from the threatening Vienna mob.[5]

The revolutionary takeover in Vienna consisted mainly of some venerable Social Democratic and Christian Social politicians proclaiming both the birth of "German Austria" and the new state's determination to fuse with democratic Germany.[6] In Zagreb the new South Slav state was created primarily by Croatian-speaking officers of the Austro-Hungarian army; they too had met no resistance from the representatives of the old order. Trouble did come, but not until a short time later when newly independent Croatia and freshly created Slovenia were asked to merge with the Kingdom of Serbia, a former enemy state, and the leaders of victorious Serbia made clear to all that Yugoslavia was to be run primarily for and by the Serbs.[7]

Only Hungary had experienced something resembling a genuine revolution at the end of October 1918 when democrats, bourgeois radicals, and Social Democrats seized power and promised not only national independence but also fundamental internal reform. But not even in Budapest did the military and the police of the old regime put up more than a token resistance. A few months later, Hungary changed to a Communist Republic of Soviets, but by November 1919 it had reverted to the rule of the old elite, who then hunted down the revolutionaries. The differences between Hungary's prewar regime and Habsburg Admiral Miklós Horthy's new regime were mainly in tone and tactics. Traumatized by military defeat, the truncation of Hungary, and the democratic as well as the Bolshevik takeovers, members of the old elite shed those among them who were unwilling to be ruthless. Those who remained, mouthed radical nationalist and racist slogans and cracked down hard on Jews, potential dissenters, and the restless agrarian proletariat.[8]

What made the process of dissolution so ominous for the future was that the end of the war and the collapse of the monarchy were celebrated everywhere with nearly the same enthusiasm as the beginning of the war had been four and a half years earlier. Liberation from the Habsburg yoke, it was commonly felt, would mark the dawn of a new era, the start of social reform and of a glorious national future. In this respect, there was barely a difference between Czechoslovakia, the new South Slav state, and emerging Greater Romania, on the one hand, and German Austria and Hungary, on the other hand. Yet according to the peculiar logic of the Entente Powers, the first-named three states and their peoples counted among those who had won the war, whereas the latter two countries were among the losers, to be punished severely for their evil deeds. Never mind that Czechs, Slovaks, Croats, Slovenes, Bosnians, and even Transylvanian Romanians had fought roughly in the same proportion as the Hungarians and Germans in the armies of the Habsburg Monarchy, and that only a fraction of the Czechs and South Slavs in the prisoner-of-war camps had joined the anti-Habsburg legions organized by the Russians and Italians! During the last days of the war, after the Hungarian government had recalled its regiments from the front, and after the German-Austrians had largely gone home, the advancing Italians were held up by troops composed chiefly of Slavic soldiers. Note also that Croats, Slovenes, and Bosnians were counted among the most reliable soldiers of the Habsburg army![9]

One of the immediate benefits of the collapse of the monarchy was that political jobs multiplied, a process that had actually begun back in 1867 when in the so-called Compromise Agreement, Austria and Hungary became separate states under the crown. From that time on, this "Dual Monarchy" had not one but two prime ministers, two cabinets, and two parliaments, and to serve them, two rather inflated state bureaucracies. Moreover, in the three ministries that handled the so-called common affairs—foreign relations, war, and the financing of the first two ministries—there was often a duplication of positions so as to accommodate both Hungarian and non-Hungarian job seekers. Now, after 1918, there were suddenly still more prime ministers, cabinets, diplomatic corps, armies, parliaments, and bureaucracies—all juicy plums for the anti-Habsburg political parties that were now in charge. Note that state and municipal employment had always enjoyed greater prestige in the region than, for instance, business which was customarily left to foreigners.

Not every nationalist politician had reason to celebrate. The post–World War I arrangements failed to fulfill the political ambitions of Slovak, Croatian, Bosnian, and Ukrainian nationalists. Their day would come during World War II, but only so long as their protector, Nazi Germany, reigned supreme in the region. Recently, these peoples have come into their own again, the result being a dazzling multiplication of states and bureaucracies. Where as late as 1848 there were three empires, the Ottoman, the Romanov, and the Habsburg, there are today some twenty sovereign states.

The end of the Great War did not bring peace to Habsburg realm: new wars flared up even before the armistice was signed, fought by armed civilians and scattered units of what had once been a single army. Between the end of 1918 and the early 1920s, armed clashes erupted in Galicia among Poles, Ukrainians, and "White" as well as Soviet Russians; in the Bukovina between Romanians and Ukrainians; and in Hungary between Reds and Whites. Meanwhile, the Hungarian Red Army fought the hastily collected Habsburg regulars of the new Czechoslovak Republic as well as the Romanian and Serbian armies. The war between Romania and the Hungarian Soviet republic ended only after Romanian troops had occupied Budapest in August 1919. A short time later, Hungarian irregulars entered into a bloody conflict with the gendarmes of the Austrian Republic over the possession of Burgenland. Previously, Slovene and Austrian free corps troops battled each other in the Austrian Alps; the French occupation forces in the Banat barely prevented the Romanian and South Slav armies from clashing in the region; Czechs and Poles fought over the possession of the Principality of Teschen, and Czech troops gunned down such Sudeten German civilians who had publicly declared their desire to join Austria rather than to become a minority in the new Czechoslovak Republic.[10]

The generalized Central European civil war of the immediate postwar years was followed by the barely controlled enmities of the interwar period, especially between Hungary and its Czechoslovak, Romanian, and Yugoslav neighbors. The bone of contention was the three powers' rule over two-thirds of Hungary's prewar territory and of more than three million ethnic Hungarians. In order to contain what they perceived to be Hungary's aggressive revisionism, Czechoslovakia, Romania, and Yugoslavia formed a diplomatic alliance called the Little Entente. Never mind that Hungary could only oppose an ill-armed volunteer force of 35,000 to their conscript armies numbering well over a million men! The mindless preoccupation of the Little Entente with the Hungarian danger caused these states largely to ignore the real threat of Nazi Germany. But there existed nearly similar hostility and suspicion in the interwar years between Italy and Yugoslavia as well as between Poland and Czechoslovakia.[11]

The Peace Treaty of St. Germain concluded with Austria in September 1919, and that of Trianon concluded with Hungary in June 1920 substantially confirmed the territorial status quo created by the postwar conflicts. Although officially based on the principle of ethnic self-determination, the final borders took into consideration ethnicity only when it favored the pro-Entente Central European states. In other places strategic or commercial interests prevailed over nationality.[12] As a result, Poland emerged from the peace treaties with a minority population of nearly one third; the Czechoslovak "nation state" with only 50 percent Czechs, and Romania with minorities amounting to about 28 percent. Yugoslavia was no less a people's mosaic than the Habsburg and Ottoman empires had been, despite the Yugoslav government's spurious claim that Serbs, Slovenes, Croats, Muslims, and Macedonians were in reality one and the same nation.

To make matters worse, both Horthy's Hungary and the democratic Austrian Republic had to share in responsibility for having started the war and to promise to pay heavy war reparations. They were also forbidden to re-arm themselves. The victorious Central European powers were not entirely happy either, because, among other things, they had to promise in the peace treaties to respect the rights of their ethnic and religious minorities. This humane and well-meaning measure backfired, as did unfortunately so many other measures adopted after the war. The insecure and aggressive new regimes considered the minority treaties a blatant interference in their internal affairs. Romania and Poland especially tried to make life difficult for the minorities, particularly the Jewish minority, though the oppressive measures taken in the interwar period were child's play compared to what would come during and after World War II.

German Austria officially proclaimed its unwillingness to exist, but in the peace treaty it was forbidden to join Germany and was even obliged to change its name to Republic of Austria. Among the many unfortunate consequences of the collapse of the Habsburg empire, this was perhaps the most unfortunate. It was the Anschluss of 1938 and the delirious reception the Austrian public gave the invading German troops that shook the faith of the Western powers in the justness of their own cause, opening the way to further German annexations and to World War II.[13]

The poverty of the new states meant that the magnificent material and technical infrastructure that the monarchy had left behind soon fell into disrepair. The transportation system suffered particularly, because the many new borders impeded traffic and necessitated the construction of new, uneconomical highways and railroad lines. But did not the monarchy's legacy include things more spiritual and humane than highways and railroads, such as mutual toleration and the fostering of multinational coexistence? It certainly should have, yet proofs of such a legacy are difficult to find, or at least they are difficult to demonstrate. Would things have been even worse without the collective memory of the empire's supranational political practices and its policy of absolute religious toleration? Perhaps so. To give only one example, Regent Horthy often took a lenient and moderate stand when reminded of his happy days as aide-de-camp to Emperor Francis Joseph, but he tended to adopt brutal measures when in the company of his White counter-revolutionary cronies.[14]

The only genuinely all monarchial institution maintained to the end of the Habsburg state was the so-called Common Army. It says something about the failure of the monarchy to create a lasting sense of Central European identity and citizenship that the Common Army transmitted no tradition of friendly cooperation to the armies of the successor states. There was widespread nostalgia among former officers for the army of old, and they liked to boast that the officer corps once constituted a happy family irrespective of race, religion, and ethnicity. Indeed, in the prewar officer corps, ethnic conflicts were at a minimum. Yet once the symbol of unity, the Emperor, was gone, former career officers eagerly joined the armies of the mutually hostile new states. Professionalism and the need to earn a living explain much but not the entire phenomenon. During World War II, former Habsburg officers serving either in the Polish or the German armies, became unhesitating enemies. Following the Anschluss of Austria in 1938, only a handful of former Habsburg officers refused to serve Nazi Germany, despite Hitler's well-known hatred for the Habsburgs and his contempt for the multinational Austro-Hungarian army. In fact, more than 300 former Habsburg career officers reached the rank of general in the Wehrmacht or the Waffen SS. Moreover, whereas religious discrimination was strictly forbidden and was indeed barely, if at all, practiced in the old army, former Habsburg officers of the new Hungarian national army led the drive to purge not only the Jewish officers but also the baptized Jews and half-Jews.[15]

The occasional cooperation between former Habsburg officers now serving in different armies that did exist was of a kind unlikely to have pleased Francis

Joseph: during World War II, former Austro-Hungarian soldiers in Hungarian uniform eagerly cooperated with their former comrades in Wehrmacht and SS uniforms in Nazifying Hungary. Not much more edifying was the cooperation between officers of the independent Croatian state and German officers in establishing a regime of terror in Yugoslavia. By preference, Hitler sent former Habsburg officers, experienced in Balkan warfare, to that area because they could be trusted to adopt harsh measures in areas infested with Chetniks and Partisans.[16]

Undoubtedly, the interwar years brought social change to the region, although it is far from clear whether these changes resulted from the dissolution of the monarchy. Similar changes would, no doubt, have occurred under Habsburg rule as well. At the beginning, it looked as if the collapse of the monarchy and the redrawing of the political frontiers had failed to alter social and economic relationships in any meaningful way. The British historian Francis L. Carsten went so far as to argue that, because in the countries that once formed the Habsburg Monarchy the government machinery, the civil service, and the police continued to function in 1918, and because the masses desired above all to return to peaceful and orderly conditions, the revolutions quickly petered out, and things continued within society very much as before the war.[17] Yet social transformation was inevitable in the Danube basin, and if it did not come faster than it did, this was mainly because nationalism, cleverly manipulated by the politicians, came into conflict with socialist drives. There were a few concrete steps in the direction of social reform, principally the distribution of many large estates in Czechoslovakia, in Romania, and in the South Slav Kingdom, but even these measures had strong nationalistic overtones. Most of those who lost their estates were not Czechs, Slovaks, Romanians, or South Slavs.

In the interwar period the state came to assume an increasingly important role in industrialization, a role that had begun during the war. Simultaneously, all Central European countries made great strides in the direction of becoming welfare states. More important, from a social point of view, was the political removal of entire nationalities, such as the Germans in Moravia and the Hungarians in Transylvania. As the Moravian German aristocrat and the Transylvanian Magyar civil servant disappeared from the scene, their places were taken by men who were often of peasant origin. Even in Hungary, the most traditionalist of all the Central European states, there was a drastic social change in the interwar years. At first it looked as if nothing had changed: political power was in the hands of a bureaucracy of gentry origin, and economic power in the hands of Jewish and German capitalists. But the trauma caused by the war and the collapse of the monarchy influenced social relations in Hungary also. The power of the gentry no longer rested on consensus but on violence, and the power of the Jewish capitalists was in reality severely undermined by anti-Semitism. Following the Great Depression, the nobility lost the remnants of their political influence, and their places too were taken by new men who sported gentry attitudes but were in reality commoners.

True, in the old Habsburg Monarchy there had been an ever-increasing number of commoners in high military, administrative, and political positions, but they had upheld the moral values of the aristocracy. The commoners who pushed ahead in the 1930s were, despite all their talk about tradition and history, essentially vulgar men with policies and ambitions that fitted the fascist age. Captain Gyula Gömbös, the pro-Axis prime minister of Hungary in the 1930s, was indeed a pale imitation of such great aristocrats of old as the two Andrássys, the two Tiszas, or Count István Bethlen. The introduction of anti-Semitic legislation in Hungary in the late 1930s brought a changing of the guard in the economy. Finally, when the fascist Arrow Cross formed a government in October 1944, it firmly established the rule of the upstart commoners over the old elites and marked the beginning of a social revolution that accelerated with Hungary's liberation in 1945, and assumed dizzying speed when the Communists seized power in 1948.

Whether a similar social transformation began in Austria and Czechoslovakia after 1918 is difficult to determine. As the bourgeoisie in these countries had wielded influence over the economy and politics even before the Great War, social change in the interwar period was less spectacular than in semi-feudal Hungary. Yet mass politics and compulsory education brought their inevitable results in Austria and Czechoslovakia also, in terms of the democratization of politics and the increasing number of lower-class elements in the army, the bureaucracy, the economy, and the professions.

The most profound consequence of the dissolution of the Habsburg Monarchy, especially in terms of social change, was what we now call ethnic cleansing. Because it has resulted in the gradual emergence of truly monoethnic nation states, today it carries the promise of the end of ethnic conflicts and of the oppression of ethnic minorities. But the process is not yet over, and the price in blood has been horrifying. Consider that during the nineteenth and early twentieth centuries, only a handful of people were killed because of their religion or nationality! The only notable exception to this was the revolutionary period of 1848–1849 when, especially in southern Hungary and Transylvania, people were slaughtered for the first time in history, not because they were landowning nobles, priests, serfs, guild masters, Protestants, or Jews, but because they were of the wrong nationality. However, the Habsburg army managed to restore order within a year, hanging no more than a few hundred Hungarian, Polish, and German rebels.[18]

We do not know how many people have been killed in the region since 1918 for ethnic or religious reasons, but they must number in the millions. Add to this the many millions of deportees and refugees, and it becomes clear that the twentieth century produced the most extensive ethnic cleansing and the greatest migration of peoples in all history. Those who were not killed or expelled moved, spontaneously and consistently, from east to west throughout the century, bringing about an ethnic revolution of still unfathomable proportions. Consider that in towns and entire regions once inhabited solely by Germans and Jews, there now live Poles, Czechs, Slovaks, Hungarians, and Romanians! Where there were once Poles, to give another example, there are today Ukrainians and Belorussians, as well as people hailing from much farther to the east. While the inhabitants of the cities in the eastern half of the monarchy once spoke mainly German or Yiddish and lived by their own laws, in today's East Central Europe former peasants from neighboring communities have become the dominant urban element.[19]

The ultimate victims of the dissolution of the Habsburg Monarchy have undoubtedly been the Jews. Whereas in the nineteenth century, the Habsburgs were able to overcome their traditional Catholic distrust of the Jews to become their staunch protectors, the post-Habsburg regimes almost invariably turned against them. Needless to say, nineteenth-century anti-clerical liberalism played an even greater role than the dynasty in the emancipation and integration of the Jews, while the decline of liberalism at the end of the nineteenth century powerfully contributed everywhere to the rise of anti-Jewish feelings. Still, the progressive role of the dynasty, especially under Francis Joseph, in this respect is undeniable; he set a good example by punishing even the most minor manifestation of intolerance in his army and administration.

The Emperor had good reason to be philo-Semitic: the Jews (and the Armenians) were without a national homeland in the Monarchy, and no neighboring nation exercised an irredentist pull upon them. The Jews were immensely grateful to the monarchial authorities for their emancipation. Consequently, they became the preeminent *Staatsvolk*, the group most likely to be loyal to the dynasty and the Austrian *Staatsidee*. Only where Jewish assimilation had become a reality, as in Hungary, did many Jews embrace local nationalism. But even there, unlike the non-Jewish Hungarians, Jews confidently expected to be able to combine Hungarian nationalism with loyalty to the ruling house.

World War I marked the apogee of Jewish participation in the life of Central Europeans. In the delirious enthusiasm of August 1914, Jews were among the greatest enthusiasts. They endorsed war, in part because the enemy was the anti-Semitic Russian empire, in part because the outcome of the conflict promised to bring their final and complete acceptance. About 300,000 Jews served in the Austro-Hungarian army during World War I, among them 25,000 Jewish officers, a figure far above the proportional representation of other confessional groups in the officer corps. The reason was the great number of Jews in the wealthy and educated classes.[20]

All this changed after World War I. The prewar popular anti-Jewish resentment and especially the economy-driven anti-Semitism of the Christian middle classes now erupted. The situation was aggravated both by the high proportion of Jews in the Bolshevik and other leftist movements and regimes at the end of the war, and even more by the fact that, in Central Europe, nationalism and anti-Semitism were often interwoven ideologies. As a result, except for democratic Czechoslovakia, popularly supported governmental measures were sooner or later taken everywhere against the Jews. When the German Nazis arrived, the local administrative machinery and much of the public were ready to assist in their deportation. From this general rule neither war-time Slovakia nor the Czech Protectorate can be exempted. The post–World War II return of Jewish survivors and the eager participation of many Jews in the Stalinist East European regimes further widened the emotional gap between Jews and non-Jews that nineteenth-century liberalism had almost managed to close. Today, Jewish presence in East Central European affairs is as much of an exception as is the presence and participation of ethnic Germans. Under the Habsburgs the ethnic German minorities were an economically and socially crucial element in Hungary, Transylvania, Bohemia, and the Bukovina; today the Germans are either gone from the region or have been absorbed by the majority nationality. Let us remember that, after World War II, tens of thousands of ethnic Germans perished or were killed outright in Czechoslovakia and Yugoslavia and millions of other Germans were expelled from countries that had once been part of the Habsburg dominions.[21]

The Central and Eastern European horrors of World War II and their Stalinist aftermath would surely have been mitigated had any of the successor states been able to cooperate against Nazi and Soviet imperialism. But there was never any question of political synchronization; the remembrance of the post–World War I border conflicts and of the injustices and follies of the Paris peace treaties was much too vivid for people and governments to develop an internationalist policy. Thus it happened that in 1938–1939 Poland and Hungary rushed to profit from the dismemberment of Czechoslovakia; that in 1939 Poland fought unaided against the German and Soviet invasions; that in 1940 Hungary and Romania almost went to war over Transylvania with Germany acting as an honest broker; that in April 1941 Hungary and Bulgaria joined the Germans in invading Yugoslavia; that in June 1941 Hungary entered the anti-Soviet military "crusade" in a race for German favor against already committed Romania; that in 1943–1944 the Hungarian surrender to the Allies was prevented, in part, by the threat of a Romanian, Slovakian, and Croatian invasion of the country. One could go on for a long time; here it should be sufficient to remind the reader of the threat of a Romanian and Czechoslovak invasion of Hungary in 1956, and the actual Hungarian, Polish, etc., invasion of Czechoslovakia in 1968.

Regional cooperation does not seem to be a realistic possibility today. Individual Central European countries are competing with one another for entry into NATO and the European Union. Wherever ethnic minorities are left, this fact alone suffices to cause bad relations between neighboring countries. The secret of the Habsburg Monarchy was that an ethnically disinterested person—neither German, nor Hungarian, nor Slav—ruled over the twelve nationalities of the state. As early as 1867, the Hungarians acquired their "nation state" within which, in fact, they constituted a minority. Francis Joseph as King of Hungary played a vastly different role from Francis Joseph, Emperor of Austria. Still, the monarchy endured. Not until the peoples of the region agree on an ethnically disinterested superior authority—perhaps in the form of the European Union—is there any hope for genuine reconciliation.

Notes

1. The dissolution of the Habsburg Monarchy boasts a substantial literature, such as Arthur J. May, *The Passing of the Hapsburg Monarchy, 1914–1918*, 2 vols. (Philadelphia: University of Pennsylvania Press, 1966); Richard G. Plaschka, Horst Haselsteiner, and Arnold Suppan, *Innere Front: Militärassistenz, Widerstand und Umsturz in der Donaumonarchie 1918*, 2 vols. (Munich: R. Oldenburg, 1974); Richard Georg Plaschka and Karlheinz Mack, eds., *Die Auflösung des Habsburgerrreiches: Zusammenbruch und Neuorientierung im Donauraum* (Vienna: Verlag für Geschichte und Politik, 1970); Manfried Rauchensteiner, *Der Tod des Doppeladlers: Österreich-Ungarn und der Erste Weltkrieg* (Graz: Styria Verlag, 1993); Leo Valiani, *The End of Austria-Hungary* (New York: Knopf, 1973); and Z. A. B. Zeman, *The Break-Up of the Habsburg Empire* (London: Oxford University Press, 1961).

2. Among the best histories of the Habsburg Monarchy, in English, are: Oscar Jaszi, *The Dissolution of the Habsburg Monarchy* (Chicago: University of Chicago Press, 1961); Barbara Jelavich, *The Habsburg Empire in European Affairs, 1814–1918* (New York: Rand McNally, 1975); Robert A. Kann, *A History of the Habsburg Empire, 1526–1918* (Berkeley: University of California Press, 1974); C. A. Macartney, *The Habsburg Empire, 1790–1918* (London: Weidenfeld and Nicholson, 1968); Alan Sked, *The Decline and Fall of the Habsburg Empire* (New York: Longman, 1989); and Victor L. Tapié, *The Rise and Fall of the Habsburg Monarchy*, trans. Stephen Hardman (New York: Praeger, 1971). On the Habsburg dynasty, see Adam Wandruszka, *The House of Austria: Six Hundred Years of a European Dynasty*, trans. Cathleen and Hans Epstein (Garden City, N.Y.: Doubleday, 1964); and Dorothy G. McGuigan, *The Habsburgs* (New York: Doubleday, 1966). Economic developments in the Monarchy are described in, among others, David Good, *The Economic Rise of the Habsburg Empire, 1750–1914* (Berkeley: University of California Press, 1984). The material infrastructure and administration of the late Dual Monarchy is well described and documented in Alexander Sixtus von Reden, *Österreich-Ungarn: Die Donaumonarchie in historischen Dokumenten* (Salzburg: Druckhaus Nonntal Bücherdienst, 1984).

3. For a general discussion of the Central European revolutions, both national and socialist, see Francis L. Carsten, *Revolution in Central Europe, 1918–1919* (Berkeley: University of California Press, 1972). The best book on the history of the region in the interwar years is Joseph Rothschild, *East Central Europe Between the Two World Wars* (Seattle: University of Washington Press, 1974). See also R. J. Crampton, *Eastern Europe in the Twentieth Century* (New York: Routledge, 1994); and Joseph Held, ed., *The Columbia History of East Central Europe in the Twentieth Century* (New York: Columbia University Press, 1992).

4. On the creation of Czechoslovakia, see Todd Huebner, "The Multinational 'Nation-State': The Origins and the Paradox of Czechoslovakia, 1914–1920," Ph.D. diss., Columbia University, 1993; and Victor J. Mamatey and Radomir Luza, eds., *A History of the Czechoslovak Republic, 1918–1948* (Princeton: Princeton University Press, 1973).

5. On the collapse of imperial power, see, among others, István Deák, *Beyond Nationalism: A Social and Political History of the Habsburg Officer Corps, 1848–1918* (New York: Oxford University Press, 1990), ch. 11.

6. On interwar Austria, see especially Charles Gulick, *Austria from Habsburg to Hitler*, 2 vols. (Berkeley: University of California Press, 1948); and K. R. Stadler, *The Birth of the Austrian Republic, 1918–1921* (Leyden: A. W. Sijthoff, 1966).

7. Some of the best books on Yugoslavia are Ivo Banac, *The National Question in Yugoslavia* (Cornell: Cornell University Press, 1984); Aleksa Djilas, *The Contested Country: Yugoslav Unity and Communist Revolutions, 1919–1953* (Cambridge, Mass.: Harvard University Press, 1991); and Fred Singleton, *A Short History of the Yugoslav People* (New York: Cambridge University Press, 1985).

8. On the post–World War I Hungarian revolutions and the counter-revolution, see Andrew C. Janos, *The Politics of Backwardness in Hungary, 1825–1945* (Princeton: Princeton University Press, 1982), chs. 5 and 6; Oscar Jászi, *Revolution and Counter-Revolution in Hungary* (London: P. S. King and Son, 1924); Peter Pastor, *Hungary Between Wilson and Lenin: The Hungarian Revolution of 1918–1919 and the Big Three*, East European Monographs, no. 20 (New York: Columbia University Press, 1976); Peter Pastor, ed., *Revolutions and Interventions in Hungary and Its Neighbor States, 1918–1919*, East European Monographs, no. 260 (New York: Columbia University Press, 1988); Rudolf Tokes, *Béla Kun and the Hungarian Soviet Republic* (New York: Praeger, 1967); and Ivan Völgyes, ed., *Hungary in Revolution, 1918–19: Nine Essays* (Lincoln: Nebraska University Press, 1971).

9. On the Habsburg army in general, see Deák, *Beyond Nationalism*, and Gunther Rothenberg, *The Army of Francis Joseph* (West Lafayette, Ind.: Purdue University Press, 1976). The ethnic situation in the Austro-Hungarian armed forces is described in Robert Nowak, "Die Klammer des Reichs: Das Verhalten der elf Nationalitäten Österreich-Ungarns in der k.u.k. Wehrmacht 1914–1918," 4 vols., unpubl. manuscript, Kriegsarchiv, Vienna, B/726, no. 1; Plaschka, Haselsteiner, and Suppan, *Innere Front*; Plaschka and Mack, *Die Auflösung des Habsburgerreiches*; and Richard G. Plaschka, *Cattaro-Prag: Revolte und Revolution* (Graz: H. Böhlau, 1963). On the prisoner-of-war camps in Russia and Italy and the Czechoslovak as well Yugoslav legions formed in them, see Samuel R. Williamson, Jr., and Peter Pastor, eds., *Essays on World War I: Origin and Prisoners of War*, East European Monographs, no. 126 (New York: Columbia University Press, 1983).

10. To the best of my knowledge, there exists no systematic analysis of the post–World War I military conflicts in Central Europe. The reader is referred to Rothschild, *East Central Europe Between the Two World Wars*.

11. See Robert Machray, *The Little Entente* (New York: H. Fertig, 1970); and Magda Adam, *The Little Entente and Europe (1920–1929)* (Budapest: Akadémiai Kiadó, 1993).

12. The peace treaty with Hungary is discussed in Francis Deak, *Hungary at the Paris Peace Conference* (New York: Columbia University Press, 1942); and C. A. Macartney, *Hungary and Her Successors: The Treaty of Trianon and Its Consequences, 1919–1937* (London: Oxford University Press, 1937). There are no similar works on the peace treaty with Austria.

13. On the Anschluss of Austria in 1938, see, among others, Jurgen Gehl, *Austria, Germany, and the Anschluss, 1931–1938* (London: Oxford University Press, 1963).

14. There is, at last, a good biography of Miklós Horthy by Thomas Sakmyster, *Hungary's Admiral on Horseback: Miklós Horthy, 1918–1944*, East European Monographs, no. 396 (New York: Columbia University Press, 1994). See also, Admiral Nicholas Horthy,

Memoirs, with an introduction by Nicholas Roosevelt (New York: Speller, 1957); and Miklós Szinai and László Szücs, eds., *The Confidential Papers of Admiral Horthy* (Budapest: Corvina Press, 1965). The ideology and practices of the Horthy regime are best described in C. A. Macartney, *A History of Hungary, 1929–1945*, 2 vols. (New York: Praeger, 1956–1957).

15. The lot of Habsburg officers after 1918 is described in Deák, *Beyond Nationalism*, Epilogue. The mistreatment of Jewish officers in Horthy Hungary is discussed in Randolph L. Braham, *The Politics of Genocide: The Holocaust in Hungary*, 2 vols., 2nd ed. (New York: Columbia University Press, 1994), vol. 1, ch. 10, et passim. On Austrian soldiers in the service of the Third Reich, see Johann Christoph Allmayer-Beck, "Die Österreicher im Zweiten Weltkrieg," in ed. Herbert St. Fürlinger and Ludwig Jedlicka, *Unser Heer: 300 Jahre österreichisches Soldatentum in Krieg und Frieden* (Vienna: Fürlinger, 1963), 342–375. The statistical data on the Austrian generals are on p. 359.

16. On the role of Austrian officers in the Balkan campaigns of the Wehrmacht and the Waffen SS in World War II, see Peter Broucek, ed., *Ein General im Zwielicht: Die Erinnerungen Edmund Glaises von Horstenau*, 3 vols. (Vienna: Böhlau Verlag, 1980–1987), vol. 2; and Christopher R. Browning, *Fateful Months: Essays on the Emergence of the Final Solution*, rev. ed. (New York: Holmes and Meier, 1991).

17. Carsten, *Revolution in Central Europe*, pp. 18–19.

18. On ethnic cleansing in the Central European revolutions of 1848–49, see István Deák, *The Lawful Revolution: Louis Kossuth and the Hungarians, 1848–1849* (New York: Columbia University Press, 1979), 140–141 et passim.

19. Ethnic cleansing in the twentieth century, the fate of refugees, and the westward migration of the East European peoples are best described in Michael Marrus, *The Unwanted: European Refugees in the Twentieth Century* (New York: Oxford University Press, 1985); and Raymond Pearson, *National Minorities in Eastern Europe, 1848–1945* (New York: St. Martin's Press, 1983).

20. Data on Jewish soldiers and officers in World War I are in Deák, *Beyond Nationalism*, pp. 195–197.

21. The best work on the Jewish Holocaust is still Raul Hilberg, *The Destruction of the European Jews*, 3 vols., rev. ed. (New York: Holmes and Meier, 1985). On the murder, flight, and expulsion of thirteen million German civilians from Eastern and Central Europe, see Alfred M. de Zayas, *A Terrible Revenge: The Ethnic Cleansing of the East Europan Germans, 1944–1950* (New York: St. Martin's Press, 1994).

11

THE RUSSIAN EMPIRE

RONALD G. SUNY

Even under the assault of the post-modernists, the discipline of history remains wary of the uncertain and the speculative, and often indifferent to paths not taken. Russian and Soviet historians, however, have been more wistful than their colleagues in other historical fields about alternatives, whether by thinking about the trajectory of imperial Russia's last reforms had there been no world war, or musing about the revolution's chances for a democratic outcome had not the Bolsheviks willfully interfered, or elaborating a variety of opinions on the end of NEP and the "necessity" of Stalin. Consequences are at one and the same time deceptively easy to map out and difficult to get underneath, to weigh deep determination and contingency.

Through its centuries of expansion and internal consolidation, tsarist Russia succeeded in building a bureaucratic absolutist state and an multinational empire of vast dimensions, but it failed to create a "Russian nation" within that empire. While Muscovy and imperial Russia were successful in integrating the core regions of its empire, often referred to as the *vnutrennie guberniia*, into a single nationality, diverse administrative practices, as well as the compactness of the local ethnicities and the effects of settlement policies, maintained and intensified differences between the Russian core and the non-Russian peripheries. After relatively successfully conquering and assimilating the Orthodox population of central Russia (Vladimir, Novgorod, other appanage states), Muscovy set out to "recover" lands with non-Orthodox populations, like Kazan. Russia followed the logic of empire-building; after acquiring territory, usually by conquest, often by expanding settlement, the agents of the tsar co-opted local elites into the service of the empire.[1] But in many peripheries, like Transcaucasia and Central Asia, integration succeeded only with the elites (and only partially), not with the basic peasant or nomadic populations which retained their tribal, ethnic, and religious identities. Some elites, like the Tatar and Ukrainian nobles, dissolved into the

Russian *dvoriantsvo*, but others, like the German barons of the Baltic or the Swedish aristocrats of Finland, retained privileges and separate identities. In some areas the tsarist regime managed to create loyal subjects through the transformation of cultural identities, but its policies were inconsistent and varied enormously. It did not succeed (or even try very hard) in an ethnic nation-making project even among Russians. There was no program, as in France, to educate and affiliate millions of people around an idea of the nation. As Roman Szporluk said tellingly at a recent conference on empire, the tsarist government failed to turn peasants into Russians. Russia's experience was one of incomplete nation-making, and in the final crisis of the empire the dynasty had no national legitimating formula to defend it against the claims of its opponents.

The end of the tsarist empire was at the same time the end of a state, the displacement (though not complete eradication) of a political/religious ideology, and a social somersault that brought the mighty low and raised up the lowly. A powerful new state was formed in revolution and civil war, which in time would become an empire in its own right, and a number of smaller states were formed that managed, for a time, to remain independent, though never completely free of the centripetal pull of the new Soviet state. Unlike the Ottoman and Austro-Hungarian cases, the end of empire in Russia did not result simply in fragments that became states but in a reconstructed multinational state, the Soviet Union. The states that managed to resist the first wave of Soviet reintegration—Estonia, Latvia, Lithuania, Finland, and Poland—were all located along the Baltic Sea, accessible from Europe, and had indeed been assisted in the founding moments of their independence by Western European powers. All constructed their new state and national identities after Western models of nation-states, and faced by the ever-present danger of the former imperial power, their foreign policies (and domestic policies toward the Communist left) tended for the next twenty years to be hostile to the USSR. Both in self-representation and in European eyes the new Baltic states were part of a *cordon sanitaire* against the spread of Bolshevism. Thus, the replacement of one state by several also marked the boundary between two antagonistic social and political developments—one aimed at recreating liberal parliamentary polities in capitalist economies and in the context of nationalist legitimation, the other dedicated to a grand social experiment to build a non-capitalist society and a post-liberal political system in the context of an international revolutionary program.

The Revolution of 1917 and the civil war that followed fit almost any conventional definition of revolutionary transformation. A deep rupture with the structures and practices of tsarism, the revolution ended both a political regime and a social order. The years 1917–1921 are usefully understood as a series of overlapping revolutions. The first was the workers' rebellion (actually initiated by women), followed by the soldiers' mutiny, that ended with the establishment of two centers of authority. The revolutionary lower classes, or *demokratiia* as they were styled by the socialists, elected their own organs of power, the soviets, while the middle and upper classes, the military officers, much of the state bureau-cracy and educated society identified with the Provisional Government self-selected by leading members of the Duma. Much of the period from early March until October 1917 can be seen as a second or "liberal" revolution, led by middle-class politicians and part of the intelligentsia that attempted to create a constitu-tional order. In October the workers' revolution was renewed, in the establish-ment of Soviet power, but this time intellectuals and party activists governed in the name of the workers, gradually displacing the class they purported to repre-sent. Simultaneous, and gaining momentum, was the peasant revolution that cul-minated in the seizure of land, the expropriation of the nobility, and the leveling of landholding in 1918. Finally, the multiple revolt of the non-Russian peoples of the empire splintered the unitary empire and gave rise to the establishment of nation-states along the peripheries of Russia.

The political revolution of February-March 1917 ended the monarchy and the half-a-millennial evolution of imperial autocracy. Tsarism in its failure to defend the empire during the First World War and its steady alienation from ever more numerous groups in the population had squandered its support, even among aris-tocratic elites, by the time of its demise. During the civil war interest in monar-chy revived among some White leaders, but in general the sympathy for the imperial family and its right to rule had dissipated as rapidly as the institutions that supported them. The liberal political transfer of power from the tsarist elite to the cluster of Duma politicians in the Provisional Government led rapidly to the undermining of the old aristocratic order. The February Revolution under-mined the justifications for privilege based on birth. First ideologically, then juridically, and finally economically and physically, the aristocracy lost its power and privilege. The final blow given to the old *soslovie* order came only initially from the legislation of the Provisional Government and subsequently from the direct actions of hundreds of thousands of peasants who through 1917–1918 expropriated the land, homes, and wealth of the landed nobility. To date the monarchy has not been restored, and the nobility, like its first noble, has not been reconstituted. Nineteen seventeen in the first instance obliterated the last "rem-nants of feudalism," to use a somewhat overworked Soviet phrase, and once the civil war had run its course, a range of alternative regimes based on blood, the old army, and ruling elites had been eliminated once and for all.

The political revolution that destroyed the old elites was imbedded in and expanded by a broad social revolution, which brought to the fore the lower classes, first, of the cities and, later, of the countryside. February was made by women, workers, and soldiers. Though they allowed the formal prerogatives of power to be taken by the Provisional Government, made up of politicians and intellectuals from the middle and upper classes, the workers and soldiers simul-taneously organized their own "class" organs of power, the soviets, factory and soldiers' committees, to check on the government, factory owners, and officers, and ultimately to limit their prerogatives and power. The social revolution was contained for the first eight months of the revolution within the bounds set by moderate socialists and liberal politicians, but it seethed underneath as the economic crisis driven by the war gave credence to the Bolsheviks' reading of the revolution. Day by day the real power of workers in factories and soldiers in the ranks grew at the expense of managers, owners, and officers. Russia was run (or ruined, some would have said) by committees and councils.

After October 1917 and the Bolshevik call to the peasants to take matters into their own hands, rural Russia responded by dismantling all landlord and state authority outside the towns and taking full power into the hands of peasants, their communes, soviets, and committees. By late 1918 Russia had experienced an extraordinary "democratic" revolution, in the immediate sense of the *demos* taking matters into its own hands. The power of the center dissipated, while the power of localities grew, at least for a time. The Bolshevik state, for much of the civil war, and in some ways right up through collectivization and the Great Terror, fought to reverse the radical democratization and decentralization of actual power and to reassert the state authority of the center. The extraordinary mobility and mobilization of the population and the weakness of the Soviet state together contributed to the regime's repeated turn toward repression and terror.

The Russian Revolution and civil war may have been a "proletarian" revolution in the cities (plebeian, following Michael Reiman,[2] might be a better term), but for the great bulk of the people of post-revolutionary Russia (and the non-Russian Soviet republics), the peasants, it was a "petty bourgeois" revolution. Ordinary working peasants took control of their villages, land, and lives after the October Revolution, and even though they were battered by food detachments and Red Army recruiters they managed to thwart the full intervention of state authority into their villages. The success of the Communists in the civil war depended on their ability to win over or at least neutralize the peasantry. As a party largely based in the cities and towns, they had few contacts with peasants before 1918. Moreover, the policy of forced requisitioning of grain that they initiated that year antagonized the peasants. Yet by the end of the war the peasants, fearing the return of the old landlord behind the armies of the White generals, opted for the Communists as the lesser of two evils.[3]

Encouraged by Bolshevik policy and the chaos in the countryside, peasants all over Russia seized the land and expropriated the landlords. In many ways the peasants confirmed the workers' revolution and made impossible a restoration of the old regime. They destroyed the whole structure of governance in the countryside, replacing the old local administrations with ad hoc peasant committees and, later, soviets. Like the workers and the soldiers, the peasants became more active in running their own lives as a result of the revolution. As a result of the Bolshevik land reform and the peasant revolution in the countryside, two important political benefits fell to the Soviets: the economic base of the opposition to Bolshevism was destroyed; and active and passive support among the peasants for the new government had been established (however temporarily).

In the first six months of Soviet rule, peasants simply ran their own economy and social life. But once the food shortage in the cities became acute, the Bolsheviks intensified efforts to gain some control over the countryside. They forcibly requisitioned grain to feed the towns and the army, alienating much of the peasantry. Returning peasant soldiers, sympathetic to the Bolsheviks, were active in establishing the power of the soviets in the villages, viewing themselves as leaders of the revolution in the countryside and challenging the traditional hierarchies. The peasants were ultimately pacified, but Soviet power remained weak in the countryside from the revolution until Stalin's collectivization of the early 1930s. The New Economic Policy (NEP) established a kind of truce between peasants and the state, which left the countryside and its grain largely under the control of the peasants. Only with collectivization and the crushing of the villagers, the elimination of their communes, and the institutionalization of forced requisitioning of peasant output did the state break the back of the independent peasantry, end the popular revolution in the countryside, and impose its bureaucratic rule over the vast breadth of the Soviet Union. The cost of that imposition was the ruination of agriculture and the creation of an apparatus of terror that a few years later was directed against the party and the army, the very instruments that Stalin had used against the rural population.

The new political elites that emerged after the two revolutions of 1917 were themselves far more popular in sociological makeup than the ones that had ruled Russia before February or even between the two revolutions. They were made up of radical intellectuals, "specialists" from the old intelligentsia and officer corps, and tens of thousands of workers and peasants. The new Soviet order eliminated from the *pays legal* all members of the propertied classes and the clergy; only "toilers" were eligible to vote in the soviets, and the disenfranchisement of *tsentsovoe obshchestvo* (propertied society), as well as people who hired labor, kulaks, priests, and officers in the White armies, was enshrined in the first Soviet constitution in 1918. Sheila Fitzpatrick has most convincingly demonstrated the upward mobility of millions as a result of the Russian Revolution, as well as the "downward mobility" of millions more as they lost social status and, in the late 1930s, their lives as well.[4] But the radical democratization of the ruling elites and the state apparatus and the influx of popular elements into the ruling elites was tempered by Lenin and Trotsky's policy of inviting military and "bourgeois specialists" to work with the regime to counterbalance the inexperience of many of the workers and peasants recruited into positions of responsibility and authority.

Early Soviet history was a battlefront on which egalitarian tendencies were checked by demands for expertise, higher productivity, and discipline. Many leading Bolsheviks believed that decentralization and democratization were too costly and experimental for a backward country at war. From the other side the more authoritarian and hierarchical trends were challenged by voices of opposition, from the Left Communists, the Democratic Centralists, the Military

Opposition, and the Workers' Opposition. Both trends continued—ordinary people flowed into management and administration, the officer corps and the party, while at the same time elites imposed their own vision without reference to their constituents; dissenting voices were silenced; and checks from below were replaced steadily by bureaucratic pressures from above.

The Russian Revolution thus was "democratic" in a sociological or demographic sense but not in the conventional political sense of representative government formalized and institutionalized in periodic elections, constitutional limits on executive authority, and protection of the rights for citizens against the claims of the state. However democratic the politics of 1917, with frequent elections to soviets and factory committees, during the civil war the attacks of the ruling party on the effervescent political pluralism of the grassroots, the repression of other political parties (even other socialist, indeed Marxist parties, like the Mensheviks who had abjured armed struggle against the regime), and the growing habits of command and the exercise of violence against enemies destroyed the buds of political democratic practice. The Bolsheviks' own ideological aversion to parliamentarianism and a free press (which they considered to be a weapon in the hands of the bourgeoisie), as well as their escalation of political rhetoric into a Manichaean us versus them (He who is not with us is against us), rendered the give and take of normal politics impossible. The Bolsheviks spoke of superseding politics altogether (for example in Lenin's *State and Revolution*; see the critique by A. Polan[5]), but they never seriously considered giving up state power once they had seized it. A minority party basing its power on an evaporating and politically unreliable working class, the Bolsheviks faced the stark choice of allowing democratic elections, as in the November 1917 elections to the Constituent Assembly and losing them to the peasant majority or holding on to power at all costs—in desperate anticipation of the expected international proletarian revolution that never came—and building an authoritarian (in their words, bureaucratic) regime. For the Bolsheviks there was no way democratic politics would allow them to exercise power.

The Russian Revolution was a prolonged agony. Its origins lie both in the prewar social crisis that polarized Russian society between a lower urban class growing more radical and a middle and upper class also pulling away from the autocracy and in the devastation visited upon the country (and particularly the army) by the First World War. The economy began to collapse even before February and continued its disintegration long after October. As William G. Rosenberg has shown most convincingly, capitalism was no longer a functioning economic system by early 1918.[6] Despite the efforts of Lenin's government to restore some kind of "state capitalism" in the first six months after October, the exigencies of backwardness, economic chaos, and civil war gave them little alternative but to have the state take over what was left of the urban economy. Capitalism of the free-market variety was never restored during the Soviet period, though in the NEP a highly regulated market-state capitalism flourished for about seven years.

With the Stalin revolution, capitalism was buried for sixty years with the enormous consequences that Yeltsin's Russia and the other Soviet successor states face today. Russia, the least "bourgeois" of the large states of Europe, never had its "bourgeois revolution," never went through a fundamental capitalist transformation of the economy and society, and never experienced the remaking of "human nature" that took place in the developed West. The virtues of hard work, delayed gratification, careful calculations of the use of time, sobriety, honesty in business dealings, the drive toward accumulation of material wealth did not become deeply ingrained in the broad masses of the population. And intellectual elites, whether prerevolutionary socialist or conservative or postrevolutionary Bolsheviks, ridiculed and scorned the bourgeoisie, either for its materialism, lack of culture, or identification with the West.

The revolutions of 1917–1918 moved rapidly from liberal to democratic, urban to rural, Russian to multinational. Out of a single Russian-ruled empire emerged a host of new states, some of them nation-states. Those states that ended up independent—Finland, Poland, and the Baltic republics—were aided by foreigners and had the advantage of being more easily accessible from Europe. Ukraine and Belorussia were somewhat artificial states at the time, backed by the Germans. The Belorussian national movement was notoriously weak, and Belorussian statehood was almost completely the work of German intervention. Ukraine was fragmented regionally, ethnically, and socially, with many Russians favoring Soviet power, most cities divided ethnically, peasants identifying themselves more with local leaders and interests, nationalists being isolated in towns and among intellectuals, and local Bolsheviks demonstrating an intransigence that drew the Moscow leadership back into Ukraine repeatedly. In Transcaucasia Azerbaijan was a republic propped up by Turkey (later Britain), initiated by a small nationalist elite, with little popular sympathy, and unable to digest the militant working-class center, Baku, its designated capital. Armenia, led by a popular nationalist party, the Dashnaktsutiun, was a land of refugees and peasants, absolutely dependent on outside support for its survival. Caught between nationalist Turks and the Red Army, Armenia capitulated to the Soviets for its own survival. Like Poland and Finland, Georgia was a relatively coherent nation-state, with a recognized and popular national (but only moderately nationalist) leadership (the Georgian Social Democrats). It would have survived as an independent state had local Bolsheviks, like Orjonikidze, and their patrons in the center, most importantly Stalin, not acted against Lenin's instructions and invaded the republic.

Nationalism was a relatively weak political force in 1917, largely confined to urban intellectuals, with some popular following among Armenians, Estonians, Finns, Georgians, Poles, and Ukrainians. Wherever it was a force to be reckoned with, nationalism was allied with some form of populism or socialism. During the civil war and the brief period of independence, nationalist sentiments grew in much of the periphery, but their potency has yet to be adequately assessed by scholars. Many historians have followed the estimates of nationalists and argued either that nationalism is a natural, primordial response and needs no elaborate explanation or that the views expressed by intellectuals and activists reflected in an unmediated way the more general sentiments of the people. Whatever the degree of ethnic identification of millions of peasants, that sense of ethnic community should not be collapsed into support of the program of the nation as imagined by intellectuals.

While Bolsheviks interpreted the civil war as a struggle of class against class, worker against peasant and bourgeois, nationalists saw it as a national war of Russians against minorities, the center against the peripheries. They viewed the experiences of the borderlands as unique events that fulfilled and justified the natural historical evolution to national independence. Yet nowhere in the non-Russian regions of the fallen empire was the conflict free of social as well as ethnic elements. Indeed the combination of cultural and class cleavages rendered the fighting particularly ferocious. In the national peripheries even when the conflict took on aspects of national wars, the social struggles between workers and industrialists, *tsentsovoe obshchestvo* (propertied society) and *demokratiia* (the lower classes), city and countryside were powerfully present. Almost everywhere, the nationalist movements were either strengthened or fatally weakened by the nature of their class base. Because ethnic solidarity, activism, Russophilia, or Russophobia were very often primed by social discontents, where nationalist leaderships were able to combine social reform with their programs of self-definition, autonomy, or independence, their chances for success were increased—as in Georgia. Where social, particularly agrarian, reform was delayed or neglected—as in Ukraine—ethnic political aspirations alone did not prove strong enough to sustain nationalist intellectuals in power.

In some regions, like Transcaucasia, the principal lines of conflict during the first revolutionary year were political and social, without much of an ethnic coloration. Though the central state's authority over the non-Russian peripheries eroded quickly, until the October seizure of power by the Bolsheviks most of the borderlands—with the notable exception of Poland, Finland, and Ukraine—did not consider political separation from the new democratic Russia. A broad sense that social issues could be settled within the framework of the new constitutional order as it would be constructed by the Constituent Assembly was complemented by a recognition that raising ethnic issues could have far-reaching and deadly consequences. In Baku, for example, the local Bolshevik leaders remained cautious about accelerating their drive to power precisely because they feared that people would divide along ethnic lines. But after October, and especially after the Bolsheviks dispersed the elected Constituent Assembly in early January 1918, the ties that bound many of the borderlands to the center were torn asunder. For the next three years civil war in multiethnic regions often degenerated into bloody ethnic conflict, sometimes between Russians and non-Russians but often between different non-Russian peoples. Azerbaijanis and Armenians slaughtered one another in eastern Transcaucasia, and independent Georgia and Armenia fought a brief war over borders.

This uncivil warfare not only pulverized the remnants of the tsarist political and social structure but left the Soviet regime with a devastated economic and social landscape on which to build its new order. A crisis of authority continued well beyond the civil war years, though far more immediate was the problem of physical survival for tens of millions of people. Ethnically distinct peasants and workers, whatever their particular experiences, shared the collapse of state authority and economic order. In the flux of revolution social categories and identities became even more fluid and overlapping. As I have tried to show in an earlier work,[7] nationalism was for most nationalities still largely concentrated among the ethnic intelligentsia, the students, and the lower middle classes of the towns, with at best a fleeting following among broader strata. Among Belorussians, Lithuanians, and Azerbaijanis, the paramount identification was not with one's nation, but with people nearby with whom one shared social and religious communality. Neither nationalism nor socialism was able to mobilize large numbers of these peoples into the political struggles that would decide their future. For several other nationalities, among them the Latvians and the Georgians, class-based socialist movements were far more potent than political nationalism. Socialism as presented by the dominant intellectual elite answered the grievances of both social and ethnic inferiority and promised a sociopolitical solution to the dual oppression. For still other nationalities, like the Ukrainians and the Estonians, nationality competed with class for the primary loyalty of the workers and peasants, with neither winning a dominant position. In Finland, a deadly polarization between social groups led to a civil war between parts of a population relatively united on the question of national independence and commitment to Finnish culture. For the Armenians, a rather unique case of a people divided between two empires, without a secure area of concentration and facing extermination, a non-class, vertically integrating nationalism overwhelmed all competitors.

The Soviet government inherited a collapsing state structure that was rapidly being replaced by local authority both in Russian and non-Russian regions. The centrifugal flight of authority ended only with the reintegration of regions and independent states by the Red Army. Able to subdue tens of millions of non-Russians with a combination of military force, political repression, and appeals to self-determination, the Soviet government quickly turned to accommodate the great majority of the population with an easier economic policy and concessions to national sentiments and particularities. The experience of the civil war, and the evident power of nationalism, at least among elites, encouraged the Bolshevik leaders to compromise their earlier opposition to federalism. The major consequence of the Russian Revolution for non-Russians was the creation of new national "states" within a new multinational federation. Rather than full political independence or forced assimilation into the greater Russian population, non-

Russians were given administrative distinction, national cultural promotion, and a kind of affirmative action program for the indigenous peoples (*korenizatsiia*). At least for the first fifteen years after the revolution a socialist form of nation-building took place in the Soviet republics. New "nations" were created, as in Central Asia, where they had never existed, and smaller peoples were given alphabets and cultural institutions that they had never before enjoyed. All within the limited and confining framework of "socialist construction," to be sure, but this national formation created national intelligentsias and working classes, national Communist elites and reading publics that at the end of the Soviet period would be coherent and conscious enough to be mobilized or mobilize themselves against the decaying center of the empire of republics.[8]

Out of chaos and collapse, in conditions of international and even domestic isolation, the Soviet government built a new state, won the civil war, pacified a resistant peasantry, and, by 1926, restored the prewar economy. At the same time it rebuilt a multinational polity that soon took on the characteristics of a new empire. Perhaps the most unique empire in the twentieth century, the Soviet Union was at one and the same time by its own understanding an anti-imperialist state, a federation of sovereign states, and a voluntary union—all claims that its opponents could easily dismiss as self-serving and disingenuous. In the minds of its designers the Soviet Union was something more than a normal state; it was the prefiguration of a future non-state dedicated initially, at least in Lenin's view, as an example of equitable, non-exploitative relations among nations, a model for further integration of the other countries and the fragments of the European empires. Anti-imperialism, then, was both a model for the internal structure of the USSR and a posture to attract supporters from abroad. Like Woodrow Wilson, Lenin was a major contributor to the delegitimizing of imperialism and empires, and anti-imperialism remained until the end of the USSR a major element in Soviet rhetoric.

But from its inception the Soviet Union replicated imperialist relations. The regathering of Russian lands was an effort carried out in conditions of civil war, foreign intervention, and state collapse by a relatively centralized party and the Red Army. The power of the center (the metropole), as well as its demographic weight, was far greater than any of the other units (the periphery) of the new state. Concessions were made to the perceived power of nationalism, which it was believed was appropriate for a certain stage of history soon to be superseded. It was assumed that political and cultural rights for non-Russians and the systematic constraint of Russian nationalism, along with the development of a socialist economy, would be sufficient to solve the "national question." While creating national territorial units with broad cultural privileges, the new government's overwhelming concern was that the new multinational federal state be a single integrated economy. On this point there was to be no compromise. Economic policy was statewide, and each federal unit was bound to others and to the center by economic ties and dependencies. Relations between the metropole and periphery thus were different on the political, cultural, and economic levels. Politically, certainly most pronouncedly in the first decade of Soviet rule, power was somewhat defused, with bargaining taking place between the center and the republics and autonomies. Culturally, the policy of *korenizatsiia* ("rooting") stressed indigenization of the local culture and the local elites. The new state attempted to incorporate elites that were not hostile to Soviet power and to allow the development of "nations" within the Soviet federation, but the political order, in which a single party monopolized all decision-making everywhere, undermined from the beginning local centers of power. As the regime became ever more centralized and bureaucratized in Moscow, the inequitable, imperial relations between center and peripheries became the norm until actual sovereignty existed only in the center. Economically the emphasis was on efficiencies that in general disregarded ethnocultural factors. Economic regionalization was usually an extra-ethnic practice, and cadre policy in the economy, even in the 1920s, was supposed to consider specialization, education, and training over ethnic qualifications.

The effect of this dualistic policy, which at one and the same time stressed a kind of ethnically blind modernization and promoted ethnocultural particularism and local political power within bounds, was to create increasingly coherent, compact, and conscious national populations within the republics while promising an eventually supra-ethnic future, full of material promise. In this new imperial arrangement the agenda was ultimately set in Moscow; the relationship between center and republics was therefore imperial, for important issues of politics and the economy were not decided at the republic level. Like other great empires the Soviet Union legitimized its subordination of the colonized through a rhetoric of developmentalism and progress. Modernization justified the forced surrender of self-determination.

The imperial aspects of the Soviet system became clearer in the early 1930s as Stalin moved steadily away from the more radical aspects of *korenizatsiia* and gave a much more positive valence to Russian language and culture. Stalinism attempted in a haphazard way to rethink the idea of the Soviet "nation" by using a non-ethnic Russian culture as a unifying idiom for the whole country. While nations continued to be promoted on the periphery of the empire, effective participation in the political, economic, or cultural elite of the country required a cultural competence in Russian and a loyalty to the entire Soviet project that superseded local identities and loyalties. Through generous rewards of power, prestige, and influence, along with severe punishments, the Soviet center attracted "the best and the brightest" among the national elites, many of which were created during Soviet times, to collaborate with the all-Soviet rulers. The costs of refusing to work in this way, of displaying "local nationalism," were extraordinarily severe—imprisonment or even death.

World War II was the moment when a political integration took place between the Soviet Union and *rodina* (motherland), not only Russia, not only the Soviet *rodina*, but also those of the other nationalities—the Georgian *samshoblo* or the

Armenian *hairenik*. Stalin combined the appeals of nationalism with support of socialism, blending the two indistinguishably. For several decades thereafter it was nearly impossible for many, perhaps most, people to imagine their homeland without the Soviet Union. A shared rite of passage had bound the pieces into a provisional whole, with a certain degree of officially sanctioned local nationalism permitted. Only in the 1960s and afterwards did dissidents move beyond the official bounds and propose much more threatening alternatives to the Soviet idea of a cultural nation without full political sovereignty.

There are many ironies to Soviet history. Certainly a principal one must be that a radical socialist elite that proclaimed an internationalist agenda that was to transcend the bourgeois nationalist stage of history in fact ended up by making nations within its own political body. Another is that the very successes of the Soviet system, not least this making of nations, but also the industrialization, urbanization, and mass education of the country, made the political system that had revolutionized society largely irrelevant. Instead of legitimizing the system, as it had done earlier, modernization undermined it at the end by creating the conditions and the actors that were able to act without the direction of the Communist Party. This might be called the "dialectic" of the Russian Revolution: whatever the intentions of the Bolsheviks they succeeded only too well in creating the conditions for their ultimate demise. Like other great empires in the modern world, the Soviet Union was a modernizing state. It was not interested in preserving, but in transforming social and cultural relations. But at the same time it built and then petrified a hierarchical, inequitable, non-democratic political structure that progressively became a fetter on further political—and to a large extent, social, economic, and cultural—development. This state structure became increasingly irrelevant, setting the stage for decay and ultimately a crisis of legitimacy. The time arrived when the political structure had to change or society and the economy would simply continue to stagnate and decline.

Too successful for its own good and not successful enough to satisfy the expectations it aroused, the authoritarian Soviet state created by the revolution and Stalinism constrained the creative potential of an ever more educated and mobile Soviet people. Though it is perhaps too much to claim that the articulate, educated urban society, with its talented and sophisticated intelligentsia, that had emerged in the course of seventy years was the "civil society" of liberal and Marxist expectations, it is possible to characterize late Soviet society as having a "public sphere," an arena of educated public opinion, *obshchestvennost'*, with which the geriatric Soviet leaders had to contend. Even less well recognized by the leadership was the parallel "achievement" of creating new nations within the pseudo-federal structure of the Soviet Union. The powerful emergence of compact, coherent, nationally conscious nations in many of the union republics and several of the autonomous republics and regions placed a formidable task before the last Soviet leaders: how to create democratic, egalitarian relations between the formerly subordinated peoples of the peripheries, while maintaining a united federation; how to go beyond empire and form a multinational democracy. Gorbachev believed that such a revolutionary decolonization of the Soviet state structure was possible while maintaining the country as a single state. His radical opponents around Yeltsin and in many of the republics came to believe otherwise. Holding the Soviet state together, a difficult task in any circumstances, turned out, after the seismic intervention of the August 1991 coup, to be a task that neither the leaders nor what the system had become were up to.

Notes

1. Marc Raeff, "Patterns of Russian Imperial policy Toward the Nationalities," in ed. Edward Allworth, *Soviet Nationality Problems* (New York: Columbia University Press, 1971), 22–42; Idem, "In the Imperial Manner," in ed. Marc Raeff *Catherine the Great: A Profile* (New York: Hill & Wang, 1972), 197–246; S. Frederick Starr, "Tsarist Government: The Imperial Dimension," in ed. Jeremy Azrael, *Soviet Nationality Policies and Practices* (New York: Praeger, 1978), 3–38.

2. See his *Russkaia revoliutsiia, 23 fevralia–25 oktiabria 1917*, 2 vols. (Prague: Institut istorii sotsializma, 1968).

3. For an excellent treatment of the agrarian revolution and the Soviet state in the early Soviet period, see Orlando Figes, *Peasant Russia, Civil War* (Oxford: Oxford University Press, 1989).

4. Sheila Fitzpatrick, *Education and Social Mobility in the Soviet Union, 1921–1934* (Cambridge: Cambridge University Press, 1979); Idem, *The Russian Revolution* (New York: Oxford University Press, 1982).

5. A. J. Polan, *Lenin and the End of Politics* (Berkeley: University of California Press, 1984).

6. William G. Rosenberg, "Russian Labor and Bolshevik Power After October," *Slavic Review* 44, no. 2 (Summer 1985): 213–238.

7. Ronald Grigor Suny, *The Revenge of the Past: Nationalism, Revolution, and the Collapse of the Soviet Union* (Stanford, Calif.: Stanford University Press, 1993).

8. Ibid.

12

AFTERMATHS OF EMPIRE AND THE UNMIXING OF PEOPLES

ROGERS BRUBAKER

Migration has always been central to the making, unmaking, and remaking of states. From the polychromatic political landscapes of the ancient world, with their luxuriant variety of forms of rule, to the more uniform terrain of the present, dominated by the bureaucratic territorial state, massive movements of people have regularly accompanied—as consequence and sometimes also as cause—the expansion, contraction, and reconfiguration of political space.[1]

This paper addresses the intertwined dynamics of migration and political reconfiguration in the aftermath of the collapse of the Soviet Union. Substantial migrations within and from Transcaucasia and Central Asia have already occurred in connection with the progressive erosion and eventual collapse of Soviet authority and the incipient reorganization of rule along national lines.[2] But it is the potential for much vaster migrations, rather than the scale of existing flows, that has focused attention and concern on migration in the last few years.

That potential has been viewed with special alarm in northwestern and Central European capitals and in Moscow, the former envisioning a mass westward exodus of millions, perhaps tens of millions of ex-Soviet citizens, the latter fearing a vast, chaotic, and brutal "unmixing of peoples" entailing, in particular, an uncontrollable influx into Russia of the Russian and Russophone population from the non-Russian successor states. Articulated in crude and undifferentiated fashion, these fearful visions, jointly propagated by Western, Soviet, and post-Soviet journalists and politicians, have done more to obscure than to enhance our understanding of the actual and prospective dynamics of post-Soviet migrations. The former vision, to be sure, seems recently to have lost its hold on European public opinion. The alarmist rhetoric, sensationalist headlines, and cataclysmic imagery of 1990 and 1991, warning of the imminent inundation of Western Europe, have all but disappeared—no doubt because the expected onslaught failed to materialize. The vision of mass ethnic unmixing, however, remains powerful. Its plausibility is enhanced by the Yugoslav refugee crisis, which resulted directly from the dissolution of a multinational state and the incipient reconfiguration of political authority along national lines.[3] It is thus understandable that the specter of an analogous "unmixing of peoples" in post-Soviet Eurasia—the specter of "ethnic cleansing" on a vaster canvas—haunts discussions of post-Soviet migration.

Without belittling the potential dangers of a chaotic and brutal unmixing of peoples in certain parts of the former Soviet Union, I seek in this paper to provide a more nuanced and differentiated analysis of the relation between political reconfiguration and migrations of ethnic unmixing in post-Soviet Eurasia. Although such migrations are likely to be highly variegated, potentially involving scores of ethnonational groups and migration trajectories, I focus here on a single set of flows—on the actual and potential migration to Russia of ethnic Russians and other Russophone residents of the non-Russian successor states.[4] I restrict the scope of the discussion in this manner for both analytical and substantive reasons. Analytically, this will permit a more sustained and differentiated discussion of the migratory dynamics of this group. Substantively, not only do the 25-million-odd Russians represent by far the largest pool of potential ethnomigrants,[5] but the manner in which and extent to which they become involved in migrations of ethnic unmixing will be fraught with consequences for Russian domestic politics and for relations between Russia and the non-Russian successor states.

I analyze the reflux of Russians from the ex-Soviet periphery in broad historical and comparative perspective, considering them alongside earlier post-imperial migrations that ensued when a ruling ethnic or national group in a multinational empire was abruptly transformed, by the shrinkage of political space and the reconfiguration of political authority along national lines, into a national minority in a set of new nation-states. Three such cases are examined: Balkan Muslims during and after the disintegration of the Ottoman empire, Hungarians after the collapse of the Habsburg empire, and Germans after the collapse of the Habsburg empire and the German Kaiserreich.[6] From this excursus into comparative history I extract four general analytical points, and bring them to bear on the post-Soviet migration of Russians to Russia. I adopt this historical and comparative approach not because the past offers precise analogs of the present—it does not—but because consideration of a variety of partially analogous cases can enrich and improve our understanding of the intertwined dynamics of migration and political reconfiguration.

Muslim/Turkish Migration from the Balkans

Consider first the Ottoman case. The protracted disintegration of the Ottoman empire spanned well over a century, from the late eighteenth century to the aftermath of the First World War. Throughout this period, and even earlier, the shrinkage of Ottoman political space was accompanied by centripetal migration of Muslims from the lost territories to remaining Ottoman territories.[7] But it was the last half-century of Ottoman disintegration and the formation of national states in its wake that produced mass displacements. This unprecedented wholesale restructuring of populations, linked to the transformation of multinational empires into nation-states, led Lord Curzon to speak of the "unmixing of peoples."[8]

While the details of these migrations are far too complex—and too contested[9]—to analyze here, a few general points should be emphasized. The first concerns the magnitude of the unmixing. Several million people were uprooted from Bulgaria, Macedonia, Thrace, and western Anatolia alone in the last quarter of the nineteenth and first quarter of the twentieth century. The migrations radically simplified the ethnic demography of these regions, constructing relatively homogeneous populations where great heterogeneity had been the norm. In 1870, for example, Muslims (Turks, Bulgarian-speaking Pomaks, and Circassian and Crimean resettlers from Russia) were at least as numerous as Orthodox Christian Bulgarians in most of what would later become Bulgaria. By 1888, however, the Muslim share of the population of Bulgaria (including eastern Rumelia) had fallen to roughly a quarter, and by 1920 Muslims comprised only 14 percent of the population.[10] Similarly, between 1912 and 1924 the intricately intermixed population of Macedonia and Thrace—comprised mainly of Turkish-speaking Muslims, Greeks, and Slavs identifying themselves mainly as Bulgarians, with none of these constituting a majority—was sifted, sorted, and recomposed into relatively homogeneous blocks corresponding to state frontiers: northern Macedonia became solidly Slavic, southern and western Macedonia predominantly Greek, and eastern Thrace (along with western Anatolia) purely Turkish.[11]

The unmixing of peoples initially followed ethnoreligious rather than ethnolinguistic lines, with Muslims moving south and east and Christians moving north and west.[12] It was thus not only ethnic Turks who retreated toward core Ottoman domains, but also other Muslims, notably Bulgarian-speaking Pomaks and Serbo-Croat-speaking Bosnians as well as Circassians and Crimean Tatars who had earlier fled from Russia to the Ottoman Balkans.[13] Language became more important over time as the Ottoman rump state increasingly assumed an ethnically Turkish identity and as the Orthodox Christian Balkan successor states came into increasing conflict with one another. As a result, there was secondary intra-Christian ethnic unmixing, primarily between Greeks and Bulgarians, superimposed on the primary Muslim-Christian unmixing. But even as late as 1923, the Lausanne Convention providing for a massive and compulsory Greco-Turkish population exchange defined the population to be exchanged in religious rather than ethnolinguistic terms.[14]

War was central to the mass unmixing of Balkan peoples.[15] Beginning with the Russo-Turkish War of 1877, intensifying in the Balkan wars of 1912–13, and culminating in the aftermath of the First World War, almost all of the large-scale migrations occurred in direct or indirect connection with military campaigns. This is true, most obviously and directly, of spontaneous flight before advancing armies, in the wake of retreating ones, or as a result of attacks on civilian populations—depressingly prevalent in all the military campaigns of this period, and often intended precisely to provoke mass migration.[16] But other migrations, too, were indirectly caused by war. This is true, for example, of the Muslim migration to Turkey under the terms of the Greco-Turkish population exchange mandated by the Lausanne Convention. Its counterpart—the million-strong Orthodox Christian migration from Turkey to Greece in 1922, which had already been virtually completed by the time the Lausanne Convention was signed—was directly engendered by war: Greeks fled in panic amidst the violence and terror accompanying the Turkish counteroffensive of 1922, which drove the Greek armies in a rout from the regions of western Anatolia and eastern Thrace that they had occupied since the Greek invasion of 1919. Because Turkey did not wish to allow these refugees to return en masse to Turkey, fearing that this would only help perpetuate Greek irredentist ambitions, it agreed to accept in return the compulsory resettlement in Turkey of the (mostly ethnic Turkish) Muslim citizens of Greece.[17] Thus although the latter were not directly uprooted by war, their migration was nonetheless an indirect product of the Greek invasion of Turkey and the Turkish counteroffensive; it would not have occurred in the absence of the Greco-Turkish war.

To underscore the centrality of war to mass migrations of ethnic unmixing in the Balkans between 1875 and 1924 is not to suggest that it was war as such that was responsible for these migrations. It was rather a particular kind of war. It was war at the high noon of mass ethnic nationalism, undertaken by states bent on shaping their territories in accordance with maximalist—and often fantastically exaggerated—claims of ethnic demography and committed to molding their heterogeneous populations into relatively homogeneous national wholes. Not all wars entail the massive uprooting of civilian populations. But wars fought in the name of national self-determination, where the national "self" in question is conceived in ethnic rather than civic terms, but where the population is intricately intermixed, *are* likely to engender ethnic unmixing through migration, murder, or some combination of both. Migrations of ethnic unmixing were thus engendered not by war as such, but by war in conjunction with the formation of new nation-states and the ethnic "nationalization" of existing states in a region of intermixed population and at a time of supercharged mass ethnic nationalism.

Despite their paroxysmal intensity and "finality" at particular places and times, Balkan migrations of ethnic unmixing have been protracted. This holds particularly for the emigration of Muslim Turks from the Balkan successor states. The major phase of unmixing lasted fifty years, from 1875 to 1924, coinciding with the progressive disintegration of the Ottoman state and its final demise in the Kemalist uprising in the aftermath of the First World War. But the emigration of Turks (though no longer of large numbers of non-Turkish Muslims) continued thereafter, albeit more intermittently and on a smaller scale. Bulgaria, in particular—the Balkan state with the largest ethnically Turkish minority—has experienced, in fits and starts, a substantial ongoing "repatriation" of ethnic Turks to Turkey. Nearly 100,000 left under administrative pressure from the Bulgarian side in 1934–1939;[18] another 155,000 were pressured to leave in 1950–51.[19] The most recent, and most massive, exodus occurred in 1989, a few years after the extremely harsh assimilation campaign of 1984–85, in which public use of the Turkish language was banned and Turks were forced to adopt Bulgarian names; when the borders were suddenly opened in 1989, 370,000 Bulgarian Turks fled to Turkey, more than 40 percent of the total Bulgarian Turkish population (although 155,000 returned to Bulgaria within a year).[20]

Finally, the fluctuating but generally favorable policies of the Ottoman government towards the immigration of Balkan Muslims and of the Turkish government towards the immigration of Balkan Turks have significantly shaped the incidence, volume, and timing of the migrations. The openness to immigration had economic-demographic roots: both the Ottoman state and the Turkish republic through the interwar period viewed their territories, and Anatolia in particular, as underpopulated, and sought to encourage immigration in order to promote demographic growth and economic development.[21] But there was also an ideological and cultural dimension to late Ottoman and Turkish immigration policy. In the mid-nineteenth century, the Ottoman government was still largely indifferent to the cultural characteristics of potential immigrants, welcoming, and even seeking specifically to induce, the immigration of non-Muslims.[22] But as the late Ottoman empire came to view itself as a specifically Muslim state (and in its last few years as an incipient Turkish national state), and as the Turkish successor state, defining itself as a nation-state, sought to weld its population into a homogeneous nation, the general openness to immigration was succeeded by a selective openness to Muslims (especially, though not exclusively, those from former Ottoman domains) and, in the Turkish Republic, by a still more selective openness to ethnic Turks from Balkan successor states, who, as Interior Minister Sukru Kaya Bey put it in 1934, could scarcely be expected to "live as slave where the Turk previously was the master."[23]

Magyar Migration from Hungarian Successor States

Our second case is that of ethnic Hungarians after the collapse of the Habsburg empire in the First World War. That sudden collapse differed sharply from the protracted decay of the Ottoman empire. Hungarian rule in the Hungarian half of the empire, far from decaying, had become increasingly consolidated in the half-century preceding the outbreak of war. Unlike the decentralized Austrian half of the empire, the Hungarian half, although ethnically heterogeneous (Magyars comprised only about half the population), was politically unitary, ruled by a centralized, fiercely nationalistic, and almost exclusively Magyar bureaucracy.[24] This internally autonomous quasi-nation-state was dismembered by the postwar settlement. The shrinkage of political space was dramatic. The 1920 Treaty of Trianon stripped Hungary of two-thirds of its land and three-fifths of its prewar population (though in so doing it largely confirmed a de facto state of affairs, the territories in question having been occupied and controlled, with tacit Allied backing, by Romanian, Czech, and Serbian forces since the winter of 1918–19).[25] Although about 70 percent of the lost population was non-Magyar, over three million Magyars suddenly became national minorities in neighboring nation-states, including most importantly 1.7 million Magyars in Transylvania, which was awarded to Romania; 1 million in Slovakia and Ruthenia, which went to Czechoslovakia; and 450,000 in Voivodina, which became part of Yugoslavia.[26]

These new minorities emigrated in substantial numbers in the years immediately following the First World War. But the post-Habsburg migration of Hungarians was quite different from the late- and post-Ottoman migrations of Turks. In the first place, a far smaller share of the Hungarian population migrated. In the six years immediately following the First World War, when most of the migration occurred, about 424,000 Hungarians migrated to Hungary from territories ceded to Romania, Czechoslovakia, and Yugoslavia, representing 13.4 percent, 13.7 percent, and 9.5 percent respectively of the ethnic Hungarian population of the lost territories.[27] Thereafter, apart from a renewed surge in the aftermath of the Second World War—including an organized Hungarian-Slovak population exchange at the insistence of Czechoslovakia, bent on ridding the country of its troublesome minorities[28]—there was little Magyar migration to Hungary from neighboring states until the late 1980s.[29] Although we lack directly comparable figures, Balkan Turkish/Muslim migrations to remaining Ottoman domains and Turkey were undoubtedly much larger, both in absolute numbers and in proportion to the Balkan Turkish/Muslim population.

Ethnic Hungarian migration from the lost territories remained comparatively limited in scope, chiefly because it was primarily an elite migration, confined for the most part to the upper and middle classes. The migration had three analytically distinct phases.[30] First to flee were those most closely identified with the repressive and exploitative aspects of Hungarian rule—and therefore those with the most to fear from a new regime. This group, many of whom fled before Romanian, Czechoslovak, and Serbian/Yugoslav rule were consolidated, included great landowners, military men, and state and county officials connected with the courts and the police. Second, de-Magyarization of public administration, state employment, and education deprived many middle-class Hungarians of their positions as officials, teachers, railroad and postal employees, etc., and engendered a second group of refugees, who fled less in fear than because of economic displacement and loss of social status. Third, agrarian reform, by breaking up the great

Hungarian-owned estates, displaced and pushed toward emigration not only the landowners themselves but the larger category of managers and employees whose livelihood depended on the estates. The peasant masses, however, who made up the large majority of the ethnically Hungarian population in the lost territories, did not migrate in significant numbers. Neither their interests nor their identities were immediately threatened by the change in sovereignty; indeed Hungarian peasants in areas ceded to Romania and Czechoslovakia actually benefitted modestly from land distributions attendant on agrarian reform.[31]

About 85 percent of the 1918–1924 migrants arrived in rump Hungary between late 1918 and the end of 1920.[32] The steep tapering off of the influx thereafter no doubt reflected a declining demand for resettlement on the part of those remaining in the ceded territories. But it also reflected efforts by the Hungarian government, beginning in 1921, to stem the influx by granting entry permits only in exceptional cases. This restrictive policy reflected the economic cost of supporting the refugees, a very large number of whom remained on the bloated state payroll. But it also reflected ideological concerns: the government did not want its revisionist case to be weakened by the mass emigration of Magyars from the lost territories.[33]

The Magyar exodus from the lost territories to rump Hungary, then, was numerically limited by the fact that it remained an essentially middle- and upper-class phenomenon. But it amounted nonetheless to a substantial influx into Hungary, increasing the size of the post-Trianon Hungarian population by about 5 percent in a few years. And the refugees' impact on interwar Hungarian politics—magnified by the predominance of déclassé gentry among them and by their concentration in cities, especially Budapest—was much greater than these numbers would suggest. Radicalized by their traumatic territorial and social displacement, the refugees played a key role in the counter-revolutionary movements of 1919–20 and the White Terror of 1920. Throughout the interwar period, they buttressed right-wing forces, exercising an influence disproportionate to their numbers in parliament and public life. Above all, their zealous, uncompromising, and integral revisionism, demanding the full restoration of the lost territories, powerfully constrained interwar Hungary's foreign policy, preventing any reconciliation with neighboring states and making more likely the fateful alignment with Fascist Italy and Nazi Germany.[34]

Just as the great 1989 exodus of Bulgarian Turks to Turkey marked the continuation of an intermittent process of unmixing that had spanned more than a century, so too the centripetal migration of ethnic Hungarians resumed, forty years after the last significant episode, in the late 1980s.[35] The flow began well before the fall of the Ceaușescu regime; some 36,000 Romanian citizens—three-quarters of them ethnic Hungarians—who fled to Hungary during the late 1980s were residing in Hungary by the end of 1989.[36] Since the fall of Ceaușescu, definitive resettlement has been overshadowed by informal labor migration, made possible by the much greater freedom of movement between the two countries (and by the lax enforcement of work-permit requirements). If the literature on labor migration in other settings is any guide, however, this migration is likely to lead to substantial permanent resettlement, especially on the part of ethnic Hungarians. Romanians, too, have been drawn to Hungary by its relatively attractive labor market. Yet this is by no means a purely economic migration. For Hungarians from Romania—but not for their Romanian neighbors and fellows citizens—ethnic nationality functions as a form of social capital, generating superior migration opportunities. Their language skills and extended family ties give them access to richer networks of information about migration and employment opportunities; and their ethnic nationality may secure them preferential treatment in encounters with border guards and customs officials, with interior-ministry bureaucrats having discretionary authority to grant permanent residence permits and citizenship, with labor inspectors checking workers' documents at work places, or with policemen checking documents on the street.

Since 1991, when war broke out in Yugoslavia, Hungarians from Romania have been joined by migrants (again mostly ethnic Hungarians) from Serbian Voivodina (home, before the war, to some 300,000 Hungarians) and from the Croatian region of eastern Slavonia, fleeing war, conscription, and economic crisis. In some cases, Voivodina Hungarians have been pressured to leave their homes by Serb refugees who had been resettled in their midst. From the Transcarpathian region of southwestern Ukraine, where there are about 170,000 Hungarians, there has been little resettlement (and that mainly on the part of intellectuals); migration has instead taken the form of cross-border petty commerce, exploiting the huge economic disparities between the two states. In Slovakia, the southern part of which is home to some 600,000 Hungarians, nationalizing policies have heightened ethnic tensions; but these have to date been played out much more strongly at the elite level than in everyday life. In the absence of significant economic incentives, there has been little migration to Hungary.

German Migration from Habsburg and Hohenzollern Successor States

Our final comparative case is that of ethnic Germans. After World War I, some four and a half to five million Germans were suddenly transformed from ruling nationality or *Staatsvolk* in the Austrian half of the Habsburg empire and in some eastern, predominantly Polish districts of the German Kaiserreich into beleaguered national minorities in the new and highly nationalist nation-states of Czechoslovakia and Poland as well as in equally nationalist Italy. Another two million Germans from the Hungarian half of the Habsburg empire, while not, in the last decades of the empire, a ruling nationality in the same sense, had nonetheless enjoyed a secure status; apart from the 220,000 Germans of the western Hungarian Burgenland, ceded to Austria after the war,[37] they too suddenly became national minorities—albeit initially less embattled and beleaguered ones—in Hungary, Romania, Yugoslavia, and Czechoslovakia. Altogether, some six and a half million Germans became national minorities including well over three million Sudeten Germans in Czechoslovakia, over a million and a quarter Germans in the territories ceded by Germany and Austria-Hungary to Poland, half a million in territory ceded by Hungary to Romania, half a million in territory ceded by Austria and Hungary to Yugoslavia, half a million in rump Hungary, and a quarter million in the newly Italian South Tyrol.[38]

In response to this great status transformation, there appears to have been negligible migration of Germans from the Hungarian half of the former Habsburg empire, and relatively little migration from the non-German parts of the Austrian half of the empire, yet very heavy migration to Germany from the territories ceded by Germany to Poland. The lack of migration of Germans from former Hungarian territories is understandable. Their status changed least in the aftermath of empire. Ever since the Compromise of 1867 gave Hungarians a free hand in their half of the empire, they, not Germans, had been the ruling nationality. It was Hungarians, not Germans, who were the large landowners, judges, prosecutors, bureaucrats, teachers, and postal and railway employees in the non-Magyar areas, and who fled in fear or emigrated after losing their livelihoods when these areas passed to the non-Hungarian successor states. Germans, by contrast, suffered no such dramatic status reversal with the dismemberment of Hungary, and had no special impetus to flee. In rump Hungary, relatively homogeneous ethnically and preoccupied with territorial revisionism and with the fate of fellow Magyars in the neighboring states, German-Hungarian relations were not particularly tense. Nor were Germans (unlike Hungarians) centrally implicated, in the early interwar years, in the national conflicts of Romania or Yugoslavia. It is therefore not surprising that the Germans of the Hungarian part of the Habsburg empire remained in place after its dissolution.

For Germans from Hohenzollern Germany and the Austrian half of the Habsburg empire, the abrupt transformation from ruling nationality to beleaguered national minority was much more drastic, and these new minorities were immediately plunged into harsh national conflicts in the successor states. At first glance, one might have expected similar post-imperial migration patterns on the part of these ex-Hohenzollern and ex-Habsburg Germans. Yet there were sharp differences. Adequate Austrian statistics are lacking for the crucial first few years after the breakup of the empire.[39] Yet while there appears to have been considerable migration of former imperial civil servants and military personnel from the successor states to Vienna,[40] there was certainly no mass influx. And while Austrians were unhappy with the peace settlement—with the exclusion of the Sudeten and South Tyrolean Germans from the Austrian successor state, and even more with the prohibition of *Anschluss* into Germany—the migrants that did arrive in Vienna, quite unlike their politically powerful and radically irredentist

Hungarian counterparts in Budapest, do not seem to have been strongly committed to recovering lost territories or to have had any impact on interwar Austrian politics.[41]

From the territories ceded to Poland by Germany, on the other hand, there was a mass exodus of ethnic Germans—some 600,000 to 800,000 in the immediately postwar years.[42] The large majority of these came from Posen and Polish Pomerania and resettled in the immediate aftermath, and even in anticipation, of the transfer of sovereignty.[43] Another substantial group arrived somewhat later from the portion of Upper Silesia that was awarded, after the 1921 plebiscite, and accompanying violent struggles, to Poland. More than half of the ethnic German population of the formerly Germany territories that were incorporated into interwar Poland had migrated to Germany within ten years.[44] The exodus was even heavier from urban areas in the lost territories. Ethnic German "public officials, schoolteachers, members of the liberal professions, and [unskilled and semiskilled] workmen [but not artisans] disappeared almost entirely from the towns of the Western Polish provinces."[45] By 1926 the German urban population of Posen and Polish Pomerania had declined by 85 percent.[46]

Why was ethnic German emigration in the aftermath of empire so much heavier from the formerly German territories of Poland than from Habsburg successor states? Why, in particular, was there mass emigration from western Poland but no substantial emigration from interwar Czechoslovakia? The three million Sudeten Germans of Bohemia, Moravia, and Czech Silesia, after all, were among the most politically alienated of successor-state Germans. Highly nationalistic, and looking down on Czechs, over whom they felt destined by history to rule, they were initially unwilling to live as minorities in a Czechoslovak state. Clearly desiring, and formally proclaiming, unification with Austria, and assuming that the Paris peacemakers would recognize their asserted right to self-determination, they were bitterly disappointed when it became clear that the historic frontiers of the Habsburg provinces would be maintained, and the Sudeten territories incorporated into Czechoslovakia.[47] Yet no substantial emigration ensued; nor did large-scale migration occur later in response to what Sudeten Germans interpreted as a government policy systematically favoring Czechs in economic and cultural matters and aimed at weakening the ethnodemographic position of Germans.

The mass ethnic German emigration from western Poland but not from the Sudeten lands shows that the sudden transformation from ruling nationality to beleaguered and politically alienated national minority does not in and of itself generate migrations of ethnic unmixing. Two other factors shaped these strikingly different patterns of post-imperial migration. First, migration to Germany was less of a displacement for the ethnic Germans of the new Polish state than migration to Austria would have been for their Sudeten counterparts. Germany had been defeated in war, diminished in territory, and transformed into a republic; but it was still "the same" state, one to which ethnic Germans who found themselves under unwelcome Polish jurisdiction could plausibly return. The state of the Sudeten Germans, however, had vanished; there was no state for them to return to. Rump Austria was not "their" state; it was not a diminished and transformed Habsburg empire but rather a completely different state.[48]

Second, Sudeten Germans were much more deeply rooted and compactly settled than the Germans of western Poland. Germans comprised—and had for hundreds of years—the overwhelming majority (over 95 percent of the population) throughout most of the Sudeten lands on the northern, western, and southern perimeter of Bohemia and Moravia.[49] Ethnic Germans were in the minority, however, in the territories ceded by Germany to Poland after the First World War. More important, they had been an embattled, demographically eroding, and artificially sustained minority even before the war, when the territories still belonged to Germany. The Prussian and German governments had made strenuous efforts to assimilate the ethnic Poles and to induce ethnic Germans to settle and remain in these frontier districts, but to little avail. The harsh efforts to Germanize the Polish population were counterproductive, alienating the Poles and reinforcing their Polish-national identity.[50] The region's ethnic Germans, moreover, participated disproportionately in the heavy east-west internal migration from the agrarian east to the industrial west in the late nineteenth and early twentieth century, thereby weakening the ethnically German element in the east in spite of massive state efforts to sustain it. Having thus had a precarious and embattled existence even before the war, under German sovereignty, the ethnic German population of these territories lacked the rootedness and firm attachment to the region of their counterparts in the Sudeten region. And they had every reason to expect the new Polish government to attempt just as vigorously and heavy-handedly to Polonize its western borderlands as the German government had sought to Germanize the same territories before the war. That expectation was not disappointed: the policy of the Polish government towards the ethnic German minority was considerably harsher than that of the Czechoslovak government.[51] They were therefore much more likely to emigrate once sovereignty passed to Poland, and even, in substantial numbers, in anticipation of the transfer of sovereignty.

The migration of ethnic Germans from the western provinces of the new Polish state was heavier, both in absolute numbers and in proportion to the size of the new minorities, than any migration from ex-Habsburg lands, including the migration of ethnic Hungarians to rump Hungary. German migration to Germany involved at least half of the German population of the ceded territories, while the Hungarian migration to Hungary only about 13 percent of the ethnic Hungarian population of the ceded territories. Yet although nationalist publicists accused Poland of deliberately driving out Germans from the border areas,[52] and although the resettlers (including small but vigorous nationalist groups from Czechoslovakia, the Baltics, and other areas of German settlement) did become active participants in various homeland nationalist associations, German migration does not seem to have had the political impact of its Hungarian counterpart. This was partly because German losses—of territory and of ethnic brethren—

were much less extensive than Hungary's, and resettlers from lost territories comprised a much smaller fraction of the population of interwar Germany than of interwar Hungary. The German resettlers, moreover, more closely approximated a cross-section of the German population of the lost territories than did their Hungarian counterparts, whose predominantly elite composition amplified their voice in interwar politics.

For Germans, then, little ethnic unmixing occurred in the aftermath of the collapse of the Habsburg empire. The overwhelming majority of the more than five million Germans who became national minorities in the successor states remained in those states throughout the interwar period. Yet mass ethnic unmixing in this region was only postponed, not forestalled. Today there are scarcely any Germans in Czechoslovakia or the former Yugoslavia, and there are only small residual communities of Germans in Hungary and Romania. Of ex-Habsburg Germans in successor states other than Austria, only those of the Italian South Tyrol survive today as a relatively intact community (despite a harsh Italianization campaign in the interwar period and a 1939 German-Italian agreement, at Mussolini's request, to resettle them in Germany).[53] Most of the ex-Habsburg Germans—including virtually all of the Sudeten Germans—were expelled, with Allied acquiescence, in the final stages and immediate aftermath of the Second World War (along with an even larger group of Germans from the eastern provinces of interwar Germany, who fled the advancing Red Army or were driven out in the aftermath of the war). By 1950 there were in the Federal Republic and German Democratic Republic some 12 million ethnic German *Vertriebene* or expellees. Of these about 7 million were German citizens from the eastern territories of interwar Germany, now annexed by Poland and (in the case of the area around Königsberg/Kaliningrad) the Soviet Union. The remaining 5 million were citizens of other—mainly Habsburg successor—states.[54] Between 1950 and 1987, another million and a half ethnic Germans from Eastern Europe and the Soviet Union were resettled in the Federal Republic, over half of them from Poland.[55] Since then, with the liberalization of travel and emigration, nearly two million *Spätaussiedler*[56] have settled in the Federal Republic, lured by its fabled prosperity, and taking advantage of the automatic immigration and citizenship rights that continue to be offered to ethnic Germans from the so-called *Vertreibungsgebiete*, i.e., the territories from which Germans were driven out after the war.[57] As a result, the once vast German diaspora of Eastern Europe and Russia is today undergoing a rapid, and probably final, dissolution.

Ethnic Unmixing in the Aftermath of Empire: Some General Characteristics

From this excursus into comparative history four general analytical points emerge. The first concerns the great variation in the degree, timing, and modalities of ethnic unmixing in the aftermath of empire—variation between the three cases we have considered, but also, and equally important, variation within each case over time, across regions, and among social classes. Consider just a few of the more striking dimensions of variation. In some regions (for example, the Sudeten German lands of Bohemia and Moravia) unmixing has been virtually complete; in others (notably the Hungarian successor states) only a relatively small minority of the former dominant group has migrated. In some cases (for example, that of Germans in provinces ceded after World War I to Poland) large-scale migration occurred in the immediate aftermath of political reconfiguration or (in much of the Balkans) in the course of wars that produced the reconfiguration; in other cases (the ex-Habsburg Germans) mass migration occurred only much later. In many cases migrants fled actual or immediately feared violence (for example, Muslims and others in the Russo-Turkish and Balkan wars, and millions of Germans in the final stages of the Second World War) or were compelled to move by the state (Turks from Greece in 1923–24, Germans in the aftermath of the Second World War); in other cases (German *Spätaussiedler* and the recent Hungarian migrants to Hungary) migrations occurred in more deliberate fashion, as the aggregate result of innumerable individual calculations of well-being.

A corollary of the first point is that there was nothing foreordained about post-imperial migrations of ethnic unmixing. The reconfiguration of political space along national lines did not automatically entail a corresponding redistribution of population. Neither migration nor even the propensity to migrate was inexorably engendered by the status transformation from dominant, state-bearing nationality in a multinational state to national minority in a successor state. Much depended on the manner in which political reconfiguration occurred (notably the extent to which it is effected through or accompanied by war or other types of organized or disorganized violence); on the ethnodemographic characteristics, especially the rootedness, of the new minority; on the anticipated and actual policies of the successor states toward the minority; on the availability and quality of the resettlement opportunities in an external national "homeland"; on the plausibility and attractiveness of mobilization as an alternative to migration, of "voice" as an alternative to "exit"; and so on.

Second, post-imperial ethnic unmixing has been a protracted, if intermittent, process,[58] spanning three-quarters of a century for Hungarians and Germans, and more than a century for Turks. And it continues today: it is striking that all three ethnonational groups have experienced dramatic new waves of migratory unmixing in the last five years. One should think about ethnic unmixing in the aftermath of empire not as a short-term process that exhausts itself in the immediate aftermath of political reconfiguration, but rather as a long-term process in which, according to political and economic conjuncture in origin and destination states, migratory streams may dry up altogether for a time, persist in a steady trickle, or swell suddenly to a furious torrent.

Third, in the protracted course of post-imperial migratory unmixings, the phases of greatest intensity have for the most part been closely linked to actual or threatened violence, especially during or immediately after wars. I emphasized above the importance of war as a direct and indirect cause of the Balkan migrations. And the bulk of the ethnic German migration occurred in the final stages of the Second World War and in the mass expulsions immediately following the war. Yet the centrality of war and, more generally, violence does not mean that post-imperial ethnic unmixing can be neatly subsumed under the rubric of "forced migration." That rubric is in fact too narrow and misleading. Some such migrations were, of course, directly compelled or forced in the most literal sense, and others, while not quite so literally coerced, were nonetheless powerfully induced by credible threats or well-grounded fears of imminent force or violence. But other cases do not satisfy even this expanded, looser definition of forced or coerced migration. This is the case for the great majority of Germans leaving the western provinces of Poland after the First World War, although Nazi propaganda claimed otherwise, and for Germans leaving Eastern Europe and the Soviet Union after 1950; it is also the case for most of the Hungarian migration in the aftermath of the Habsburg collapse and for almost all of the Hungarian migration from Romania in the last decade. Even the mass Turkish exodus from Bulgaria in 1989, while certainly provoked by the communist government of Bulgaria during its last months in power, is not adequately characterized as a forced migration.[59] More generally, even where fear is a central motive of the migrants, it is not always appropriate to speak of forced migrations. Many German migrants from territories ceded to Poland after the First World War, and many Hungarian migrants from Habsburg successor states were no doubt moved in part by diffuse fears and anxieties about their future well-being in the new states; but they were not thereby forced migrants. Fear is a capacious concept: there is a great distance between migration arising from a sharply focused fear of imminent violence and migration engendered by a diffuse fear, concern, or anxiety about one's opportunities, or the opportunities of one's children, in the future. Forced migration is simply not very useful as an umbrella concept here; it is insufficiently differentiated, and it obscures the fact that there is almost always, even in the case of flight from immediately threatening violence, a more or less significant element of will or choice involved in the act of migration. To question the usefulness of an insufficiently differentiated, overextended concept of forced migration, needless to say, is not to deny the importance of intimidation and violence as means deliberately employed to provoke migration.

Fourth, except where whole communities were indiscriminately targeted for removal (as in the Greco-Turkish transfers of 1922–1924 or in the expulsion of Sudeten Germans), there was a pronounced social selectivity to post-imperial migrations of ethnic unmixing (as there is to many other migrations). Most vulnerable to displacement were groups dependent, directly or indirectly, on the state. This included first and foremost military, police, and judicial personnel, bureaucrats, and teachers, but also postal and railway employees and workers in enterprises owned by the state or dependent on state subsidies or contracts. This selectivity of ethnic unmixing was apparent in all the migrations we considered but was demonstrated most dramatically in the Hungarian migrations after the First World War, where the peasant majority remained entirely in place, while the Magyar state-dependent stratum virtually disappeared from the successor states. The reasons for this differential susceptibility to emigration are obvious. The new nation-states were all nationalizing states, committed, in one way or another, to reversing historic patterns of discrimination by the former imperial rulers and to promoting the language, culture, demographic position, economic flourishing, and political hegemony of the new state-bearing nation. Short of enacting overtly discriminatory legislation, one of the main instruments available to the new states in pursuit of these goals was control over recruitment to state employment.

Russian Migration from Soviet Successor States in Comparative and Historical Perspective

In the light of the foregoing, how best can we think about the actual and potential migration to Russia of the twenty-five million successor-state Russians? To begin with (and following the same four points), we should not think of it as a unitary process, evincing the same patterns and following the same stages and rhythms throughout the former Soviet Union. Instead we should think of it as a congeries of related but distinct migrations (or lack thereof, as may be the case for some successor states), exhibiting distinct patterns and rhythms. We should expect, that is, great variation in patterns of post-Soviet Russian migration— variation both among and within successor states.

It follows that we should not think of the reflux of Russians to the Russian Federation as an automatic process, inexorably accompanying the breakup of the Soviet Union. We must avoid conceiving the causes of migration in overgeneralized terms. It is not adequate, for instance, to conceive of Russians leaving the successor states simply because they have been transformed from dominant nationality throughout the Soviet Union to national minorities in the non-Russian successor states. The forces, processes, and conditions engendering Russian migration need to be conceived in much more specific and differentiated terms. It then becomes apparent that what is in general terms a uniform process—the transformation of Russians from dominant state-bearing nationality into national minorities in successor states—is in fact highly variegated and uneven, and that the specific migration-engendering forces, processes, and conditions are unevenly and contingently, rather than uniformly and automatically, associated with the reconfiguration of political authority along national lines in post-Soviet Eurasia.

Earlier post-imperial migrations of ethnic unmixing, we have seen, were protracted; indeed they continue to this day. A broad time horizon seems advisable in thinking about post-Soviet migrations as well. This means looking back as well as forward, for the present Russian reflux toward Russia is not new and unprecedented. Selective ethnic unmixing began long before the explosion of nationalist protest under Gorbachev. The centuries-old current of Russian migratory expansion into non-Russian areas slowed and, in some cases, reversed itself during the last three decades. There was a substantial net Russian outflow from Georgia and Azerbaijan during each of the last three Soviet intercensal periods (1959–1970, 1970–1979, and 1979–1989), and from Armenia in the 1979–1989. During the last intercensal period there was also a net outflow of Russians, for the first time, from Moldova, Kazakhstan and each of the Central Asian republics. And even though net Russian immigration continued, during the last intercensal period, to the Baltics and the Slavic west (Ukraine and Belarus), the rates of such Russian immigration declined over the last three intercensal periods in each of these republics except Lithuania.[60] The current and future phases of the Russian reflux towards Russia should therefore be understood not as initiating but as continuing and reinforcing a reversal of historic Russian migration patterns—a reversal the origins of which long antedate the breakup of the Soviet Union.[61] A broad time horizon also requires that we try to look beyond the immediately visible problems, crises, and migration currents to think, in an admittedly speculative mode, about the longer-term dynamics of political reconfiguration and ethnic unmixing in post-Soviet Eurasia.

The historically crucial role of war and, more broadly, violence in engendering post-imperial migrations of ethnic unmixing, especially the most intense phases of such migrations, holds out the possibility that ethnic Russians might avoid being swept up by the kind of cataclysmic mass migrations that are almost invariably driven by war or at least by actual or threatened violence. Even in the absence of war or significant violence *directed against Russians*, to be sure, many Russians from Transcaucasia and Central Asia have been moving, and will no doubt continue to move, to Russia. But these migrations have not been, and need not be, cataclysmic, even if—to take a hypothetical limiting case—the entire Russian population of Central Asia (excluding Kazakhstan) and Transcaucasia were to migrate to Russia over, say, a ten-year period. Nor can recent and current migrations of Russians from these and some other regions be conceived as forced (*vynuzhdennyi*) migrations, although they are often referred to as such in Russian discussions. The fact that such migrations have been *induced* by political reconfiguration and changes in the political, economic, and cultural status of Russians does not mean that they have been *forced*. Even so, as I argue below, substantial Russian resettlement from these regions would significantly strain the Russian Federation. Yet it is important to distinguish between this mode of non-forced, non-cataclysmic unmixing and the vastly more disruptive and dangerous migrations that could ensue should ethnopolitical conflict in Kazakhstan or Ukraine become militarized or otherwise linked to large-scale violence.

One specific migration-engendering process central to earlier aftermaths of empire was that of "ethnic succession" among officials and other state employees. It was this that accounted for the pronounced social selectivity of those earlier migrations of ethnic unmixing, with the state-dependent stratum of the former *Staatsvolk* heavily overrepresented among emigrants. Here the implications for post-Soviet migration are mixed. On the one hand, almost everyone is dependent, directly or indirectly, on the state, increasing the scope for ethnonational conflict. Although privatization may eventually reduce this dependence, it is itself a state-dependent process, affording ample occasion for ethnonational conflict over modes of appropriation of public assets and enterprises. But while the scope for ethnic conflict over jobs and resources is greater in the post-Soviet than, say, the post-Habsburg case, given the near-universal dependence on the state, the opportunities for ethnic succession *in its classic sphere*, namely public administration, are smaller. The Soviet Union was unlike earlier multinational empires in its deliberate cultivation and institutional empowerment, in the peripheral republics, of numerous non-Russian national intelligentsias—coupled, of course, with harsh repression of deviant political behavior.[62] As a result, the administrative apparatus of the periphery—monopolized by members of the imperial *Staatsvolk* in the old multinational empires, and consequently a prime target for ethnic succession in their aftermath—was already staffed largely by members of the titular nationalities. Public administration therefore does not provide the successor states with comparable opportunities for the wholesale promotion of the new state-bearing nation at the expense of the former ruling nationality.[63] Nonetheless, competition for jobs in all sectors of the economy is bound to intensify as economic restructuring generates higher levels of unemployment, especially in regions where the labor force of the titular nationality is growing extremely rapidly.[64] Given the persisting centrality of the state in economic life, as well as the institutionalized expectations of "ownership" of "their own" polities held by titular elites, such competition is sure to be politicized along ethnonational lines, albeit to differing degrees in differing successor states. Intensifying labor market competition in the Soviet southern tier already contributed to gradual Russian emigration during the last decade,[65] and it will no doubt continue to do so, although specifically political factors will probably become increasingly important in generating emigration from those regions. The extent to which conflict over jobs and resources will generate emigration of Russians from other regions, however, rather than ethnopolitical mobilization on their part, remains to be seen, and will depend on a variety of other factors, some of them sketched below.

A Selective and Uneven Unmixing[66]

To understand the dynamics of the current and future Russian reflux towards Russia, it is not enough to point to the transformation of Russians from confident *Staatsvolk* into beleaguered minority. Nor can one appeal in sweeping terms—as do Russian nationalists—to the persecution of and discrimination against Russians in the successor states. The most salient fact about Russian migration from the successor states is its unevenness, and we need an analytical framework that can help explain this unevenness.

The response of the Russian diaspora to political, cultural, and economic reconfiguration in the aftermath of Soviet disintegration has been strikingly varied.[67] Emigration from non-Russian territories is only one of an array of possible responses. Other responses include individual assimilation, or at least acculturation, to the dominant local population, and collective mobilization for equal civil rights, for special cultural or linguistic rights, for territorial political autonomy, for secession, or even for the restoration of central control. The extent of Russian emigration thus depends in part on the plausibility, feasibility, and attractiveness of alternative responses.

Ethnodemographic variables such as the size, concentration, and rootedness of the Russian populations in the territories in question, as well as the trajectory of these variables over time, comprise a first set of factors governing the relative attractiveness of migration. Where the Russian population is small, scattered, or weakly rooted, and especially when it has already been shrinking, the prevailing response to local nationalisms is likely to be emigration, together with a certain amount of apolitical individual acculturation or assimilation. A large, concentrated, and deeply rooted Russian population, on the other hand, is more likely to remain in place and engage in collective political action. Duration of residence obviously contributes to rootedness—not only how long a given individual or family has resided in the territory, but also how long the community has existed. Past and present ties to the land also contribute to rootedness: peasant communities, and to a lesser extent even the urban descendants of such peasant settlers, are ordinarily more deeply rooted than historically purely urban settlements. Among Russian diaspora communities, rootedness may be greatest in northern and eastern Kazakhstan[68] and in eastern and southern Ukraine;[69] it is probably weakest in the historically purely urban settlements of Central Asia. In wider historical and comparative perspective, however, it should be noted that none of the successor state Russian communities is as deeply rooted as peasant communities have tended to be.

A second set of factors includes the terms of membership and the texture of everyday life for Russians in the new nation-states. By terms of membership I mean the extent to which the rewritten rules of the political game in the new nation-states—especially those bearing on the language of education, the language of public life, the criteria of citizenship, and the rights of permanent residents who are not granted, or do not seek, citizenship in the new states—impose cultural, economic, or political costs on the local Russian populations. More important than formal legislation, however, will be the everyday experience of successor state Russians. Actual or feared violence, in particular, will stimulate emigration from weakly rooted Russian communities, and it will stimulate demands for restoration of central control, or for territorial autonomy, in deeply rooted Russian communities. Informal hostility towards Russians, even without the threat of violence, may have the same effects. Anti-Russian attitudes and practices are particularly important in Central Asia, given the high degree of segregation between Russians and indigenous nationalities and the more classically colonial character of Russian domination there. The great question mark is northern and eastern Kazakhstan, where the same segregation and quasi-colonial situation has existed, yet where the Russian settler population is more deeply rooted, dating from massive rural colonization in the late nineteenth century. Russians in Kazakhstan might be compared in this respect with French settler colonists in Algeria,[70] while Russians in the cities of Central Asia might be more aptly compared with urban Europeans in colonies without deeply rooted European rural settlements.

A further set of factors likely to shape the Russian response to political reconfiguration concerns the prospective economic or political advantages that might induce Russians to remain in a successor state despite anti-Russian sentiment and nationalistic language and citizenship legislation.[71] Such advantages are likely to be especially relevant in the Baltic states, which may be seen as having more favorable prospects than other successor states for economic integration into Europe and for maintaining public order and establishing liberal institutions.

A final set of factors concerns the orientation and policies of the Russian state toward the various communities of diaspora Russians. These include not only "domestic" policies toward immigrants and refugees from the successor states in matters of citizenship, immigration, and relocation or integration assistance (housing, employment, etc.), but also Russian "foreign policy" initiatives vis-à-vis the successor states, seeking either to forestall repatriation to Russia or, if repatriation cannot be forestalled, to regulate it. Russia might seek to prevent a potentially destabilizing massive influx of Russians by negotiating favorable conditions for the diaspora communities, for example, in matters of citizenship and cultural facilities. In a harsher mode, it might engage in coercive diplomacy or even intervene with military force to reassert control over all or part of a refugee-producing successor state, say, a hypothetically radically nationalist Kazakhstan.[72] In general, differential policies of the Russian state toward the various diaspora communities may differentially affect the propensity of diaspora Russians to emigrate.

On the basis of these considerations, we can expect sharply differing rates of migration to Russia on the part of different diaspora groups.[73] Migration will probably be the dominant Russian response to non-Russian nationalisms in Central Asia (excluding Kazakhstan) and Transcaucasia. The Russian population of Central Asia, although large, is exclusively urban and not deeply rooted; and it faces the greatest informal hostility from the indigenous nationalities. The Russian population of Transcaucasia is small and rapidly shrinking. Already during the 1980s, as we have noted above, there was substantial Russian emigration from Central Asia and Transcaucasia, and the rate of emigration has increased since the collapse of Soviet authority. Russian emigration rates are likely to remain much lower from areas with territorially concentrated and historically rooted Russian populations such as eastern and southern Ukraine, northern and eastern Kazakhstan, Moldova east of the Dniester, and northeastern Estonia. There, we are more likely to see—and in some cases, of course, already are see-ing—collective political responses on the part of Russians to non-Russian nation-alisms. Elsewhere in the Baltics, comparatively bright medium- and long-term economic prospects can be expected to limit the scale of emigration.

This means that of the twenty-five million Russians in the non-Russian suc-cessor states, only a small fraction—if nonetheless a large group in absolute num-bers—is at high risk of being induced or forced to flee to Russia in the next few years. The Russians most likely to resettle in Russia are those in Central Asia (3.3 million in 1989) and Transcaucasia (785,000). Many of these—though we do not have a very precise idea how many—have already moved, with the heaviest pro-portional outflow from violence-torn Tajikistan.[74] This pool of actual and poten-tial migrants amounts to less than 3 percent of the total population of Russia. In principle, the resettlement of even a substantial fraction of this migrant pool might benefit Russia. For decades, demographers and economic planners have been concerned about rural depopulation in central Russia and about labor deficits in areas of Russia that were targeted for development projects. In practice, how-ever, it will be difficult for the state to steer resettlement in accordance with demo-graphic and economic needs. Far from benefiting Russia, the migration to Russia in the next few years of a substantial fraction of Central Asian and Transcaucasian Russians would probably place a significant strain on the Russian state, which, in the throes of economic crisis, and having no experience with immigration or refugee flows, is largely unprepared to handle a substantial influx of resettlers or refugees.

Such migration would pose a greater strain on the Central Asian societies, given the Russian or European monopoly or quasi-monopoly of many techni-cal occupations in these countries. The outflow of skilled specialists in the last few years has already disrupted enterprises. Fearing further, more serious dis-ruptions, ruling elites of the Central Asian successor states have urged, and sought to induce, Russians and other Europeans to remain. How successful they will be remains to be seen. Retaining Russians and other Slavs will cer-tainly be easier than retaining those with more attractive resettlement oppor-tunities (especially Germans and Jews, whose Central Asian settlements have been rapidly shrinking). Much will depend on the ability of successor state gov-ernments to maintain public order and on the overall social and political atmosphere in these states.

Much more serious than even a near-complete Russian exodus from Central Asia would be a massive Russian exodus from the core areas of Russian settlement in the non-Russian successor states, Ukraine and Kazakhstan, with some 11.4 and 6.2 million Russians, respectively, in 1989, accounting for 70 percent of the total Russian diaspora.[75] With large, territorially concentrated, and historically rooted communities in these states, Russians are unlikely to leave in large numbers unless (1) government policies and popular practices in Ukraine and Kazakhstan take on a much more sharply anti-Russian orientation than they have at present, and (2) intensifying ethnonational conflict is militarized or otherwise linked with actual or threatened violence. Although there is no immediate prospect of this occurring, it must be reckoned a real possibility over the longer term, especially in Kazakhstan, given the potent historical memories that can be mobilized around the tremendous suffering inflicted by the Soviet state, with whose projects Russian settlers—at least in the case of Kazakhstan—can be all too easily identified.

Besides the tremendous economic problems it would entail, large-scale resettlement of Russians from Ukraine or Kazakhstan to Russia could also be politically destabilizing. The still-modest reflux of Russians to Russia—represented as forced migration—already provides abundant grist for the mills of Russian nationalists. A much larger Russian exodus from these core areas of Russian settlement in the near abroad, especially one occurring in response to sharply anti-Russian state policies or instances or threats of violence, would further strengthen the nationalists, and the refugees could form key constituencies for radical nationalists committed to recovering control of what they claim are "historically Russian" territories. In other instances, including, as we saw above, interwar Hungary, displaced and dispossessed refugees have provided constituencies for extreme nationalist parties and programs.

Conclusion

Post-Soviet Eurasia has entered what is likely to be a protracted period of political reconfiguration, involving simultaneously the reconstitution of political authority, the redrawing of territorial boundaries, and the restructuring of populations. These multiple reconfigurations, together with massive economic transformations, have already entailed considerable migration, and will no doubt entail considerably more, possibly on a scale unseen since the aftermath of the Second World War. The largest of these migrations—and one particularly fraught with political implications—has been and will continue to be that of successor-state Russians to Russia. Surveying earlier instances of ethnic unmixing in the aftermath of empire, this paper has sought to come to grips analytically with the patterns and dynamics that are likely to characterize that migration. Arguing against overgeneralized explanations or prognostications of ethnic unmixing, it points to the need for a more nuanced, differentiated approach that would take systematic account of the varied and multiform conditions facing successor state Russians and their varied and multiform responses, including migration, to those conditions.

Notes

This paper was originally commissioned by RAND for a Conference on Migration from and Within the Former USSR, The Hague, March 1993. It was published by Routledge in *Ethnic and Racial Studies* 18, no. 2 (April 1995) and as a chapter in my book *Nationalism Reframed* (Cambridge University Press, 1996). It is reprinted here in slightly altered form by permission of Routledge and Cambridge University Press.

    1. See, for example, Aristide R. Zolberg, "Contemporary Transnational Migrations in Historical Perspective: Patterns and Dilemmas," in *U.S. Immigration and Refugee Policy*, ed. Mary M. Kritz (Lexington, Mass.: D. C. Heath, 1983); Aristide R. Zolberg, Astri Suhrke, and Sergio Aguayo, *Escape from Violence: Conflict and the Refugee Crisis in the Developing World* (New York: Oxford University Press, 1989); Michael R. Marrus, *The Unwanted: European Refugees in the Twentieth Century* (New York: Oxford University Press, 1985); Myron Weiner, "Security, Stability and International Migration" and "Rejected Peoples and Unwanted Migrants in South Asia," both in *International Migration and Security*, ed. Myron Weiner (Boulder, Colo.: Westview, 1993).

    2. Zhanna Zaiontchkovskaia, ed., *Byvshii SSSR: Vnutrenniaia Migratsiia i Emigratsiia* (Moscow: Rossiiskaia Akademiia Nauk, 1992); G. C. Vitkovskaia, *Vynuzhdennaia Migratsiia: Problemy i Perspektivy* (Moscow: Rossiiskaia Akademiia Nauk, 1993).

    3. Robert M. Hayden, "Constitutional Nationalism in the Formerly Yugoslav Republics," *Slavic Review* 51, no. 4 (1992): 654–673.

    4. In what follows, I use the term "Russians" for convenience, on the understanding that it includes not only the 25 million residents of non-Russian republics who identified themselves as Russian in the 1989 census but also certain other Russophone residents of the non-Russian successor states whose migration behavior is likely to be similar—above all, the roughly 1.4 million Ukrainian and Belorussian residents of non-Slavic successor states who, in 1989, identified their native language as Russian (calculated from Gosudarstvennyi Komitet po Statistike, *Natsional'nyi Sostav Naseleniia SSSR* [Moscow: Finansy i Statistika, 1991].)

    5. To these one might add the more than five million Russians living in autonomous formations of the Russian Federation in which Russians comprised less than 50 percent of the population in 1989 (calculated from *Natsional'nyi Sostav Naseleniia SSSR*, pp. 34–48). But the problem of unmixing within the Russian Federation, while deserving analysis in its own right, lies beyond the scope of this paper.

    6. Migrations of ethnic unmixing in the aftermath of empire, of course, do not involve only, or even most importantly, the former ruling groups. One need think only of the murderous deportation of Armenians from northeastern Turkey, to say nothing of the centrality of deportation to the genocidal policies and practices of the Nazi regime. This paper focuses on migrations of former dominant nationalities because these are most closely analogous to post-Soviet migrations of Russians to Russia—a phenomenon that, because of its potential magnitude and the dangers associated with it, deserves investigation in its own right.

7. Kemal Karpat, *An Inquiry into the Social Foundations of Nationalism in the Ottoman State* (Princeton: Center of International Studies, 1973), 106.

8. Marrus, *Unwanted*, p. 41.

9. Kemal Karpat, *Ottoman Population, 1830–1914: Demographic and Social Characteristics* (Madison: University of Wisconsin Press, 1985).

10. Joseph Rothschild, *East Central Europe Between the Two World Wars* (Seattle: University of Washington Press, 1974), 327; Karpat, *Ottoman Population*, pp. 50–51.

11. A. A. Pallis, "Racial Migrations in the Balkans During the Years 1912–1924," *Geographical Journal* 66 no. 4 (1925): 316.

12. Marrus, *Unwanted*, p. 41.

13. Karpat, *Inquiry*, pp. 1–2; Karpat, *Ottoman Population*, pp. 65ff.

14. Stephen P. Ladas, *The Exchange of Minorities: Bulgaria, Greece and Turkey* (New York: Macmillan, 1932), 377ff.

15. Marrus, *Unwanted*, pp. 42ff, 96ff.

16. Karpat, *Ottoman Population*, pp. 71ff; Marrus, *Unwanted*, pp. 45, 98ff.

17. Marrus, *Unwanted*, p. 102. The question of who was responsible for the compulsory rather than voluntary character of the Greco-Turkish population exchange is much disputed. For a balanced account, see Ladas, *Exchange of Minorities*, pp. 335ff, 725.

18. Joseph B. Schechtman, *European Population Transfers, 1939–1945* (New York: Oxford University Press, 1946), 493–494.

19. Alexandre Popovic, *L'Islam Balkanique: les Musulmans du sud-ost européen dans la période post-ottomane* (Berlin: Osteuropa-Institut, 1986), 100.

20. Darina Vasileva, "Bulgarian Turkish Emigration and Return," *International Migration Review* 26 (1992): 348.

21. Schechtman, *European Population Transfers*, pp. 488ff; Karpat, *Ottoman Population*, pp. 61ff.

22. Karpat, *Ottoman Population*, pp. 62ff.

23. Qtd. in Schechtman, *European Population Transfers*, p. 490.

24. C. A. Macartney, *Hungary and Her Successors: The Treaty of Trianon and its Consequences, 1919–1937* (London: Oxford University Press, 1937), 20–26; A. J. P. Taylor, *The Habsburg Monarchy, 1809–1918* (London: Hamish Hamilton, 1948), 185ff.

25. Macartney, *Hungary and Her Successors*, p. 1; Istvan Mocsy, "Radicalization and Counterrevolution: Magyar Refugees from the Successor States and Their Role in Hungary, 1918–1921," Ph.D. Diss., University of California, Los Angeles, 1973, ch. 2; Rothschild, *East Central Europe*, p. 155.

26. Rothschild, *East Central Europe*, p. 155.

27. Mocsy, "Radicalization and Counterrevolution," pp. 8–9.

28. Kalman Janics, *Czechoslovak Policy and the Hungarian Minority, 1945–48* (New York: Columbia University Press, 1982); Dariusz Stola, "Forced Migrations in European History," *International Migration Review* 26 (1992): 337; László Szőke, "Hungarian Perspectives on Emigration and Immigration in the New European Architecture," *International Migration Review* 26 (1992): 306.

29. I do not include wartime Hungarian-Romanian population exchanges within Transylvania, for this territory reverted to Romanian control at the end of the war (on these exchanges see Schechtman, *European Population Transfers*, pp. 425ff).

30. Mocsy, "Radicalization and Counterrevolution."

31. Ibid., pp. 96ff.

32. Ibid., p. 9.

33. Ibid., ch. 10.

34. Ibid.

35. My account of the most recent phase of ethnic unmixing involving Hungarians is based on interviews with officials of the Office for Transborder Hungarians in summer 1994 and 1995 and on discussions with ethnic Hungarians in Cluj, Romania (the largest city in Transylvania), in August 1995.

36. See Szőke, "Hungarian Perspectives on Emigration and Immigration," p. 308.

37. Alfred Bohman, *Bevölkerung und Nationalitäten in Südosteuropa* (Cologne: Verlag Wissenschaft und Politik, 1969), 36.

38. Robert A. Kann, *The Multinational Empire: Nationalism and National Reform in the Habsburg Monarchy, 1848–1918*, 2 vols. (New York: Columbia University Press, 1950), vol. 2, pp. 301ff; Walter Kuhn, "Das Deutschtum in Polen und sein Schicksal in Kriegs- und Nachkriegszeit," in Werner Markert, *Polen* (Cologne and Graz: Bohlau, 1959); Werner Nellner, "Grundlagen und Hauptergebnisse der Statistik," in ed. Eugen Lemberg and Friedrich Edding, *Die Vertriebene in Westdeutschland*, ed. Eugen Lemberg and Friedrich Edding (Kiel: Ferdinand Hart, 1959), vol. 1, p. 67.

39. Alfred Bohman, *Bevölkerung und Nationalitäten in der Tschechoslowakei* (Cologne: Verlag Wissenschaft und Politik, 1975), 146.

40. Marrus, *Unwanted*, p. 74.

41. Some Sudeten German nationalists, to be sure, did move to Germany, where they became part of the Weimar nationalist scene and, at the radical end of the spectrum, conducted an irredentist campaign urging the incorporation of Sudeten German lands into the Reich. Their numbers were small, however, and they had no appreciable influence on Weimar politics. Radical emigré nationalists were more significant players in the homeland nationalist field in the Nazi period; see Ronald M. Smelser, *The Sudeten Problem, 1933–1938: Volkstumspolitik and the Formulation of Nazi Foreign Policy* (Folkestone, U.K.: Dawson, 1975), esp. pp. 29ff.

42. Eugene M. Kulischer, *Europe on the Move: War and Population Changes, 1917–47* (New York: Columbia University Press, 1948), 175; Richard Blanke, *Orphans of Versailles: The Germans in Western Poland, 1918–1939* (Lexington, Ky.: University of Kentucky Press, 1993), 32ff.

43. Martin Broszat, *Zweihundert Jahre deutsche Polenpolitik* (Frankfurt: Suhrkamp, 1972), 212.

44. Schechtman, *European Population Transfers*, pp. 259ff; somewhat higher estimates are given in Broszat, *Zweihundert Jahre deutsche Polenpolitik*, p. 212.

45. Schechtman, *European Population Transfers*, p. 261.

46. Blanke, *Orphans of Versailles*, p. 34.

47. Bohman, *Bevölkerung und Nationalitäten in der Tschechoslowakei*, pp. 39ff; Rothschild, *East Central Europe*, pp. 78–81; Ronald M. Smelser, *The Sudeten Problem, 1933–1938: Volkstumspolitik and the Formulation of Nazi Foreign Policy* (Folkestone, UK: Dawson, 1975), 8–9.

48. Interwar Hungary, on the other hand, *was* essentially a (much) diminished and transformed version of pre-war Hungary; it was in an important sense "the same" state. For this reason, among others, migration to rump Hungary on the part of ethnic Hungarians from the successor states was no doubt more plausible than migration to rump Austria on the part of ethnic Germans.

49. Bohman, *Bevölkerung und Nationalitäten in der Tschechoslowakei*, p. 117.

50. Broszat, *Zweihundert Jahre deutsche Polenpolitik*; Hans-Ulrich Wehler, "Polenpolitik im Deutschen Kaiserreich," in *Krisenherde des Kaiserreichs*, 2nd ed., ed. H.U. Wehler (Gottingen: Vandenhoek and Ruprecht, 1979); Richard Blanke, *Prussian Poland in the German Empire (1871–1900)* (Boulder, Colo.: East European Monographs, 1981).

51. Blanke, *Orphans of Versailles*.

52. Schechtman, *European Population Transfers*, pp. 259–260.

53. Schechtman, *European Population Transfers*, pp. 48–65.

54. Nellner, "Grundlagen und Hauptergebnisse der Statistik," pp. 122ff.

55. Jürgen Pusskepeleit, "Zugangsentwicklung, Ungleichverteilung und ihre Auswirkungen auf die Kommunen," in *Westwärts-Heimwärts? Aussiedlerpolitik zwischen "Deutschtümelei" und "Verfassungsauftrag"* (Bielefeld: AJZ, 1990), 165.

56. In German usage, *Aussiedler* (ethnic German resettlers from Eastern Europe and the former Soviet Union) were distinguished from *Übersiedler* (Germans who moved from East to West Germany). *Spätaussiedler* ("late resettlers") are those who have come recently from Eastern Europe and the former Soviet Union, decades after the post-war expulsion of Germans from these territories.

57. See my *Citizenship and Nationhood in France and Germany* (Cambridge, Mass.: Harvard University Press, 1992), 168ff.

58. Aristide Zolberg, "The Formation of New States as a Refugee-Generating Process," *Annals of the American Academy of Political and Social Science* 467 (1983): 37.

59. Vasileva, "Bulgarian Turkish Emigration and Return."

60. Barbara Anderson and Brian Silver, "Demographic Sources of the Changing Ethnic Composition of the Soviet Union," *Population and Development Review* 15 (1989): 640–642. Migratory unmixing also involved other nationalities. For three decades, for example, there has been substantial net migration of Armenians from Georgia and Azerbaijan to Armenia, and a modest net migration of Azeris from Georgia and Armenia to Azerbaijan. For these nationalities, the refugee flows of the last few years, following the outbreak of Armenian-Azeri ethnic violence in 1988, have only reinforced a long-term trend towards ethnic unmixing in Transcaucasia (ibid., 638–640; Brian Silver, "Population Redistribution and the Ethnic Balance in Transcaucasia," in *Transcaucasia: Nationalism and Social Change*, ed. Ronald Grigor Suny [Ann Arbor: Michigan Slavic Publications, 1983], 377).

61. Zhanna Zaiontchkovskaia, "Effects of Internal Migration on the Emigration from the USSR," in *RAND Conference on Prospective Migration and Emigration from the Former Soviet Union* (Santa Monica, Calif.: November 17–19, 1991).

62. On the early Soviet policy of *korenizatsiia* and subsequent modes of preferential treatment, in higher education and state employment, for members of titular nationalities, see Gerhard Simon, *Nationalism and Policy Toward the Nationalities in the Soviet Union* (Boulder, Colo.: Westview Press, 1991); Philip G. Roeder, "Soviet Federalism and Ethnic Mobilization," *World Politics* 43 (1991).

63. Indeed in comparative perspective, it is misleading to speak of Russians as the "ruling nationality" in the Soviet Union. They were a favored nationality in certain respects, and they were clearly the *Staatsvolk*, the state-bearing nationality, of the Soviet Union, but they were not a ruling nationality in the same sense as were Muslim Turks in the Ottoman Balkans, Hungarians in their half of the Habsburg empire in its last half-century, or Germans in the heavily Polish Prussian east before the First World War.

64. Zaiontchkovskaia, "Effects of Internal Migration on Emigration."

65. Ibid.

66. This section draws on part of my "Political Dimensions of Migration from and among Soviet Successor States," in *International Migration and Security*, ed. Myron Weiner (Boulder, Colo.: Westview, 1993).

67. For an overview see Paul Kolstoe, *Russians in the Former Soviet Republics* (London: Hurst, 1995).

68. Already in 1911, 40 percent of the population of an area roughly approximating the northern two-thirds of present-day Kazakhstan were peasant colonists from European Russia. By contrast, only 6 percent of the population of the remaining parts of Russian Central Asia (today's southern Kazakhstan, plus the four republics of Central Asia proper) were Russians. See Richard Pierce, *Russian Central Asia, 1867–1917* (Berkeley: University of California Press, 1960), 137.

69. In 1897, ethnic Russians comprised 12 percent of the population of the nine Ukrainian provinces of the Russian empire, and a much higher fraction of the population in the industrialized Donets region and elsewhere in southern Ukraine; see Paul Robert Magocsi, *Ukraine: A Historical Atlas* (Toronto: University of Toronto Press, 1985), commentary to Map 18.

70. On settler colonialism, see Ian Lustick, *State-Building Failure in British Ireland and French Algeria* (Berkeley: Institute of International Studies, University of California, 1985).

71. By political advantages I understand here greater security or stability.

72. On coercive diplomacy, see Myron Weiner, "Security, Stability, and International Migration," pp. 23–24.

73. Besides the contextual variables sketched here, characterizing successor states, their Russian communities, and Russian state policy, a set of individual-level variables will be important determinants of Russian emigration. These include age, professional or occupational qualifications, language knowledge, family connections in Russia, and so on.

74. Statistics on migration flows in recent years are derived from bureaucratic procedures (registering with local authorities or applying for special status as a refugee or forced migrant). With the withering away of the state, many migrants avoid such procedures. Statistics thus capture only a part of the flow, by most estimates only a relatively small part (Vitkovskaia, *Vynuzhdennaia Migratsiia*, p. 3).

75. In the case of Ukraine, the precision suggested by census figures, even when rounded to the nearest hundred thousand, is entirely spurious. For while the boundary between Russians and other Slavs on the one hand and Kazakhs on the other is sharp in Kazakhstan, the boundary between Russians and Ukrainians in Ukraine is anything but that. The very categories "Russian" and "Ukrainian" as designators of ethnic nationality rather than legal citizenship are, from a sociological point of view, deeply problematic in the Ukrainian context, where rates of intermarriage are extremely high, and where nearly two million of those designating their ethnic nationality as Ukrainian in the 1989 census admitted to not speaking Ukrainian as their native language *or* as a second language they could "freely command"—a figure many consider to be greatly underestimated (for the data on language, see Gosudarstvennyi Komitet po Statistike, *Natsional'nyi Sostav Naseleniia SSSR*, pp. 78–79). A self-conscious ethnically Russian minority *as distinct from the Russophone population* may emerge in Ukraine, but it cannot be taken as a given. For an argument that political cleavages in Ukraine will follow linguistic rather than ethnic lines, see Dominique Arel, "Language and Group Boundaries in the Two Ukraines," paper presented at conference on *National Minorities, Nationalizing States, and External National Homelands in the New Europe*, August 22–24, 1994, Bellagio Study and Conference Center, Italy.

13

CONCLUSION

KAREN BARKEY AND MARK VON HAGEN

The breakup and threatened breakup of multinational states at the end of the twentieth century, most notably the Soviet Union and Yugoslavia, have revived interest in the three historical, traditional, continuous land-based dynastic empires that most recently occupied much of the territory of the former Soviet bloc: the Habsburg, Ottoman, and Russian empires. Over centuries those empires devised strategies—with varying degrees of success—to rule over their vast domains and diverse peoples in an era before the nation-state and nationalism had triumphed as the "modern" form of political organization. When all three failed to survive the cataclysm of World War I and the challenges of modern nationalist movements, they were succeeded by experiments in the adaptation of the nation-state model to east central and southeastern Europe and the Middle East, or, in the case of the Soviet Union, a new form of multinational existence which was intended nonetheless to accommodate the principle of national self-determination that had received sanction from both the anti-imperialist socialist movements and Wilsonian liberalism.[1]

Although the Great War saw the beginnings of modern practices of ethnic cleansing in the targeting of large communities with discriminatory measures, deportation, even murder, most of the newly minted successor states still remained far from the ideal of one nation / one state, and all had to contend with large populations which were reconceptualized as "national minorities." The League of Nations devoted much of its time and resources to overcoming or mitigating the seemingly intractable dilemmas which flowed from these new arrangements. In large measure our sense of the failure of the League of Nations system derives from that organization's inability to thwart new forces of national irredentism and the rise of crudely xenophobic and chauvinist ideologues to state power across Europe. Whereas World War I and the civil wars that followed in its wake and against its backdrop legitimized state policies of ethnic cleansing, it was World War II however that saw its application in this region of the world with unparalleled murderousness and savagery. Hitler and Stalin were the most enthusiastic practitioners of this "nationality policy," but the victorious Allies enshrined the practice as well with a host of postwar border adjustments and population transfers. The United Nations was proclaimed by those same victorious allies, naively in retrospect, as the triumph over nationalism and ethnic hatred.

Despite this long and violent history of nationalist ideas and nationalizing states in the region[2], many of the popular media and academic accounts of post-Soviet politics have stubbornly treated recent events as unique in time and space; moreover, they have overemphasized the role of nationalism as an autonomous force in state collapse and invoked primordial ethnic hatreds to explain post-imperial conflict. As Katherine Verdery has reminded us, these accounts are often ideology masking itself, whether innocently or not, as analysis; such ideologies have often found themselves realized in foreign policies that tolerate or exacerbate violent conflict.[3] This volume was conceived in part as a response to those mainstream accounts of the consequences of state breakup on the politics of nation-building in east central and southeastern Europe.

Our intention in bringing together the authors was to build a comparative, historical framework in which to explore several key issues in the scholarly literature of historical sociology and conceptually enriched comparative history. We felt a need to reconsider the histories of the major empires in the region because the nation-state has enjoyed such hegemonic status in the organization of the historical and social sciences that scholars have tended to be prejudiced against the study of empires.[4] Yet in contrast to the longer life span of the empires of the region, the nation-state's relatively brief record in this part of the world that succeeded to the traditional empires has often been one of tragic failures in the management of interethnic relations. But any effort to compare the experiences of the empires with those of the successor states confronts the fact that the literature on empires generally fails to explore how empires managed multiethnicity for so long; moreover, whereas the traditional empires managed this complex task for centuries, the Soviet Union was less successful in this comparative perspective. Additional "world-historical" forces that have stimulated social scientists to begin to question the "self-evident" character of the nation-state, and at the least to begin historicizing it, have come from the various efforts at economic and political integration, especially the European Union,[5] but also the continued vitality of separatist regional movements, whether the Catalunyans in Spain or the Quebeqcois in Canada.

We structured this volume along several axes of comparison. First, we are comparing three traditional empires with the Soviet Union, a modern version of their efforts to hold together and rule over multinational societies. Certainly the ideology and political institutions of the Soviet Union distinguished it from the traditional empires in many ways; still the persistent ethnodemographic character and the "nationality policies" of the Soviet state set it apart from the classic nation-states of the modern period and suggest fruitful comparisons with the Ottoman, Habsburg and Russian empires. A second set of comparisons embraces the diverse sub-imperial communities that comprised the multinational societies that serve as the largest units of comparison. For example, we observed a wide range of policies toward ethnic and religious groups and looked for patterns that might suggest how to explain that diversity, whether it be the different treatment of Jews, Finns, and Poles, say, in the Russian Empire, or Christians, Jews, and Muslims in the Ottoman Empire, or Czechs, Hungarians, and Germans in the Habsburg lands. A third implicit comparison is with modern west European cases of state and nation-formation, most especially France and Britain, which have attained the status of ideal-type in theory.[6] Fourthly, another implicit comparison for the traditional empires that are the primary focus of this volume is that with the "classic" colonial empires of Britain and France. Insofar as the literature on empires and imperialism has been developed with any sophistication, it is most certainly true for these two empires. Finally, certain pairs of comparisons were structured around particular dimensions to highlight other issues of importance for post-imperial nation-building. For example, the Ottoman and Habsburg empires shared borderland populations over which they occasionally competed and even waged war. These onetime cross-border populations later served as the cores for unified nation-states, whose elites in turn had to incorporate two different imperial legacies in their emerging national political culture. Another such comparison across time is the Ottoman empire and the Soviet Union, which managed their populations through socially engineered religious (the Ottoman *millet*) and national (the Soviet *korenizatsiia*) administrative systems. Whereas the Soviet state pursued this policy far more intensively than did the Ottoman elites, still both stand out in contrast with the administrative practice of the Habsburg and Romanov empires.

Although all the authors address themselves to the variables of war, nationalism, and the state, the ways in which they are featured in the two parts of the volume can be very different. For example, state-seeking nationalisms are considered as factors in the collapse of the states in the first part; in the second half, nationalism is seen to function as the ideology of state- and nation-building in some instances, but elsewhere again as state-seeking minority nationalism it can contribute to the fragmentation of those post-imperial societies. War, too, functions in a variety of ways throughout the analyses in the volume. Of course, wars can make nations[7] and the legends and myths of struggles for national defense and national liberation are constituent elements in the patriotic rhetoric that helps sustain modern states; but, alternately, the stresses that states subject their populations to in the name of national security and the mass mobilizations needed to sustain the modern wars of the twentieth century create a context in which states collapse. In still other complicated ways wars can have domestic consequences that intensify or mitigate ongoing processes of social transformation and change important aspects of social structure and the relations among dominant and subordinate groups. This was certainly true for the Russian, Ottoman, and Habsburg empires, whose wartime transformations have been suggestively compared to economic and political modernization before their collapse.[8] On the other hand, the Soviet Union and Yugoslavia collapsed as multinational states without being involved in a major international war, but both have experienced bloody conflicts since their collapse.

Above all, we wish to restore an important sense, missing in much of the popular literature, of the dynamic interactions of agency, structure, and historical contingency in the transformations of the several societies. In our essays, it is states and their ruling elites that emerge as key actors and factors in the processes we treat here. Of course, states cannot be presumed to operate with constant levels of autonomy to shape or intervene in their societies; nor can they be assumed to be monolithic entities that execute their will from above, with impunity, and unhesitatingly upon a malleable society. Curiously, the traditional empires and the Soviet Union, despite the fierce reputations of feudal militaristic and barbarian despotisms that their nationalist and socialist opposition spokespeople succeeded in bequeathing to later generations, must be characterized as weak states when judged by the criteria of modern western Europe. State strength here is measured by the degree of bureaucratic penetration of society, political "efficiency," integration and centralization of the nation via uniform standard languages and common markets.[9] Certainly, these transformationalist proclivities, whether they be the Tanzimat of the Ottoman bureaucracy or the Great Reforms of the Romanovs' enlightened bureaucrats, arrived belatedly in the traditional empires and were met with determined resistance from entrenched if declining elites.

However we understand the character of both the traditional empires and the Soviet Union, they now all share a common historical fate of defeat by the principle of national self-determination and the albeit still poorly understood model of the nation-state in the region. Although the relative success of the empires in sustaining extensive land-based multiethnic domains should not be forgotten, the more immediate fact of their collapse should not fail to occupy a central place in our discussions. Alexander Motyl poses the argument, in a comparison that focuses primarily on the Soviet Union and Habsburg empire, that imperial states inevitably collapse because of their political and bureaucratic overextension; but how do we account for the different timing and nature of the collapses, not to mention the wide range of legacies bequeathed by those Old Regimes? In response to this provocative hypothesis of internally driven decline, we find not only similarities, but also important variations in the trajectories of imperial state collapse and a very important role for international forces. The traditional empires in any case operated for centuries before they began their decline, whereas the Soviet Union existed only 70 years.

To return to the function of national ideas, the debate is whether nationalism caused the breakup of the empires or whether the breakup of imperial states "raised the lid from the primordial hatreds." Our four contributions on imperial decline and collapse express a consensus that nationalism was one of the major ideological repertoires of the twentieth century; as such, it was available to challengers of the Old Regimes, but nowhere was it the primary cause of imperial collapse. There is some consensus however that Old Regimes' (including the Soviet Union) state strength declined in relation to the capacity to manage social, economic, and political tensions during the final decades of their existence.[10]

We are also concerned with the place of ideologies and identities, primarily but by no means exclusively national ones, in these transformations. Each of our four states, faced with ever more powerful challenges to its principles by nations to the west and east (Japan in particular), recognized a need to adapt some of the successful ingredients of British, French, German or, eventually, American success. Their efforts ranged from novel ways of organizing their armies to permitting greater involvement by society in local government to expanding education beyond the privileged classes to reorganizing economic activity around the market or capitalism. They all made considerable efforts to hold things together while reforming and to transform bases of legitimacy without sacrificing transnational loyalties to rulers. In response to the powerful pull of nationalism and the triumph of the model of the nation-state in modern Europe, the traditional empires all experimented with new attempts to ground their regimes in the legitimacy of popular sovereignty without ceding the prerogatives of autocracy. In the Russian Empire, official nationality was promoted by the reforming bureaucracy and the Imperial court steadily Russified itself even as the 1897 census showed Russians to constitute less than half the Empire's population. In the Habsburg Empire, beginning with Joseph II, the dynasty embarked on a Germanization of its central administration and promoted a German high culture even while it was compromising with new forms of local rule in the non-German lands. The Ottomans too, perhaps much less ambitiously than the previously mentioned empires, advanced an idea of Ottoman identity that contained important elements of Turkishness, but exacerbated the sense of national discrimination expressed by the non-Turkish nations of their vast holdings. Finally, the Soviet Union as well during its last decades trumpeted the creation of a historically new social formation, the Soviet people, which operated largely however through the Russian language and came to be viewed as Russification by the non-Russian peoples of the Union even while frustrating the efforts of ethnic Russians themselves to forge a national identity of their own. In each of the four cases, then, the imperial or Soviet elites pursued policies that, on the one hand, thwarted the emergence of modern national identities in the name of multinational or transnational harmony, while making still enough concessions to the national principle in other spheres to encourage the rise of anti-state national movements.

The comparative historical perspectives on state collapse in the traditional empires and the Soviet Union provide some backdrop to the next set of issues that center on state- and nation-building after the breakdowns. The historical record reveals a wide range of very diverse experiences of the transition from empire to nationalizing state, but certain commonalities offer much material for productive comparisons. Once again, the processes under consideration involve several levels of comparison: first and most obviously, the nation-building efforts of the states that succeeded to the three traditional empires and the Soviet Union that are the central focus of this volume's studies; second, the post-imperial experiences are compared to the trajectories of west European states; third, the nation-state projects that were forged out of the collapse of our empires are compared to those of the colonial empires; finally, several authors hint at comparisons between the empires themselves and the nation-states or nationalizing states that succeeded them in a consideration of elements of continuity and discontinuity in their patterns of rule.

The processes of transformation at the heart of our enterprise occurred against backdrops of major changes in the international system and in a general context of national, social or political revolutions. The three traditional empires fell during a war that pitted them against their more advanced challengers to the west, but even the Soviet Union's collapse seems to be fatally linked to the terms of international competition set by the non-Soviet world.[11] Rogers Brubaker also frames his discussion of the transformation of the traditional empires in the relationship between war, ethnic unmixing and nation-building. This relationship is present in every case, but different in its outcomes. He compares the migrations of Balkan Muslims, Hungarians and Germans out of the Ottoman, Habsburg, and German empires and draws analytic principles that he then applies to the post-Soviet migrations of Russians back to the Russian Federation from the post-Soviet successor states. The long-term, protracted aspects of these processes which actually started during the decline of the empires in many senses continue until today. The more homogeneous a population is, the easier the task of nation-building; homogeneity is attained fastest during times of war because wartime policies in the twentieth century have often included forced migration or the outright annihilation of groups and even the threat of war has provided a rationale for ethnic cleansing. The lands ruled by the Habsburg, Ottoman and Romanov empires were no strangers to such violence. A related issue is the degree to which the imperial states practiced ethnodemographic surgery as a technique of rule and thereby created the context for the outbreaks of ethnic violence that followed in the wake of their collapses. We need to look not only to the institutional legacies but also to the conditions of exit from the Old Regimes and to the intervention of foreign powers and the international community generally.

Brubaker stresses the diversity in the outcomes of the processes of transformation, and this is a theme that we wish to underline in our discussion of the other contributions as well. How do we begin to account for some of the more fundamental differences? Historically the processes of state- and nation-building that followed in the wake of our empires and the Soviet Union differ radically from the known records of west European state- and nation-formation in their timing and the character of their elites. Certainly all states must engage in similar actions to consolidate their territories and to engage in nation-building, but the European states, unlike the states of east central, southeastern Europe and the Middle East, did not emerge overnight after the breakup of a multinational state; instead they took long centuries to consolidate their rule and build their nation around this rule.[12] State-building generally preceded nation-building, whereas the post-imperial elites under consideration in the second half of our volume were forced to consolidate states and build nations overnight and in highly unpropitious circumstances. The very urgency of the post-imperial processes has encouraged scholars to emphasize the role of contingency in framing actors' possible choices of action.

Another major and directly related difference between the state- and nation-building processes in western Europe and eastern and southeastern Europe was the character of interaction of state and society. In western Europe the process of nation-building went hand in hand with democratization, a constant, gradual, and always contested extension of the franchise.[13] In the post-imperial settings, civil societies were either barely established or largely mimicked, while conservative, often aristocratic or corporatist, elites continued to rule. Whereas in western Europe, the process of nation-building can be seen as a product of continual negotiation between states and societies, in the states under consideration here the nation-building process was carried out largely from above with very little input from social groups and their institutions. The consequences of this pattern of nation-building are to be seen today in the relatively fragile, mutable, and wavering definitions of nationhood, in the absence of a sense of unity in a common project, and in the vulnerability of the societies to find appeal in particularly militant variants of communist or nationalist ideologies.

If the experiences of post-imperial states in eastern Europe and the Middle East diverge in significant ways from the west European trajectory, perhaps the history of the transformation of colonial empires, primarily the British and the French cases, offers other prospects for productive comparison. Hobsbawm argues that colonial empires are also quite different from the traditional empires at the center of this volume; nonetheless we can observe a commonality in the character of the post-imperial and post-colonial elites. In both sets of cases most of the leaders of the new states were revolutionaries who were defined by their opposition to multinational (meaning foreign) rule and who appealed via their fervent nationalism to a highly mobilized and charged population. They deployed a discourse of national oppression, persecution, and liberation which vilified the imperial in order to construct a new and different future, to build a new nation free of "foreign" rule or influence. The transformation of nationalist revolutionaries into nation-builders was certainly not the experience of western Europe, but it was very much the experience of the countries built out of the demise of west European colonial empires.

But this is where the similarities with the post-colonial states reach their limits. And this is because, as Hobsbawm argues, the breakup of traditional empires was made easier by the fact that there were in fact "obvious inheritors" in most cases, whereas the colonial empires restructured most of the preexisting political arrangements in the colonies to such a degree that there were no clear-cut inheritors left after decolonization. Generally, the post-colonial states of Africa and Asia were saddled with territorial and social boundaries that bore little resemblance to preexisting lines of demarcation; even a more "successful" case such as India endured two breakups and civil war (Pakistan and Bangladesh) since winning independence from Britain and continues to be plagued by communal and religious conflict. Among our empires Habsburg rule generally provided the conditions for the easiest transition to independent state existence, with the Czechs and Hungarians standing out as nations with relatively well established historical borders and even experienced elites; in the Russian Empire, the Finns were probably the most successful successors, while in the Ottoman Empire it was the Greeks. Even here, however, the record reveals a great range of outcomes. The Arab nations fared very poorly in the first post-Ottoman decades, as did the populations of Ukraine and Central Asia in the post-Romanov era. In these cases, there was far less achieved by way of consensus on territories or preparation of new nationalizing elites.

Despite the fact that the repertoires of nationalist and nationalizing discourse of post-imperial nation-builders have been remarkably similar, in fact the outcomes of the post-imperial and post-colonial transformations show a great deal of variation. This is due in large measure to the very different legacies left by the two types of empires. While this line of comparison was not pursued further by the contributors to this volume, it is clear that sustained analytic comparisons between colonial rule and traditional imperial rule with an eye to post-imperial nation-state building would be quite valuable. How these two types of empire differed in their rule and administrative practices and how they broke down could help refine our knowledge of nation-state formation. It also suggests the weakness of limiting our approaches in these matters to an analysis of discourse without grounding that analysis in the structural complexities of imperial rule.

Finally, certain of the authors drew comparisons between the empires and successor states to highlight possible features of continuity between empire and nation. Continuities manifest themselves at many levels: the more straightforward infrastructural legacies, the administrative-bureaucratic legacy, and the more elusive political cultural continuities. Continuity is perhaps easiest to chart between imperial cores and rump states, as Serif Mardin does in his study of the transformation of the Ottoman Empire into the Republic of Turkey. He stresses however that such continuities are not straight lines, but rather jagged or zigzag in their character. A rump state after all cannot fully repudiate its past, at least not for very long. Such patterns have begun to emerge in the relationship of the new Russian state to the legacies of its Soviet predecessor. Some spheres of imperial rule that are less politicized in the context of the nationalizing project might survive virtually intact into the rump successor state; these might include local administration, finances, even diplomatic service. Others, however, that are more central to the nationalizing agendas of the new elites, whether they be culture, education or religion, will not transfer so smoothly from one state to the next. The bottom line is that there is no historical guarantee that alternatively all or none of the imperial legacies will be rejected or accepted by the new elites, but that nonetheless fascinating patterns emerge in our reflections that are the outcomes of political contestation, agency and contingency interacting with the constraints imposed by structures. If there is one lesson to be learned from these explorations of imperial collapse and post-imperial state- and nation-building it is precisely this.

Notes

1. Arno J. Mayer, *Wilson vs. Lenin: Political Origins of the New Diplomacy, 1917–1918* (New York: Meridian Books, 1964).

2. Rogers Brubaker, "National Minorities, Nationalizing States, and External National Homelands in the New Europe," *Daedalus* 124, no. 2 (1995): 107–132.

3. A recent trenchant critique of this approach is Katherine Verdery, "Nationalism and National Sentiment in Post-Socialist Romania," *Slavic Review* 52, no. 2 (1993): 185–196.

4. See Michael Mann, *The Sources of Social Power: A History of Power from the Beginning to A.D. 1760* (Cambridge: Cambridge University Press, 1986) for a complaint about the nation-state principle of organization of the social sciences.

5. Michael Geyer, "Historical Fictions of Autonomy and the Europeanization of National History," *Central European History* 22 (1989): 316–343.

6. Gianfranco Poggi, *The State: Its Nature, Developments and Prospects* (Stanford, Calif.: Stanford University Press, 1990).

7. Charles Tilly, "Reflections on the History of European State-Making," in ed. idem, *The Formation of National States in Western Europe* (Princeton: Princeton University Press, 1975), 73–76.

8. Norman Stone, *The Eastern Front, 1914–1917* (London: Hodder and Stoughton, 1975), 285.

9. Poggi, *The State*; Anthony Giddens also discusses these processes in *The Nation-State and Violence* (Berkeley: University of California Press, 1987).

10. The consensus on imperial decline has been challenged on occasion. On the economic vigor of the Habsburg empire in its final decades, see David F. Good, *The Economic Rise of the Habsburg Empire, 1750–1914* (Berkeley: University of California Press, 1984). On a more "optimistic" reading of the final prewar decade in the Russian empire, see the historiographical review essay by Arthur Mendel, "On Interpreting the Fate of Imperial Russia," in ed. T. Stavrou, *Russia under the Last Tsar* (Minneapolis: University of Minnesota Press, 1969), 13–41.

11. Theda Skocpol, in *States and Social Revolutions* (Cambridge: Cambridge University Press, 1979), highlights the intersection of international and domestic processes in her explanation of the French, Russian and Chinese revolutions.

12. See Daniel Chirot, "Nationalist Liberations and Nationalist Nightmares: The Consequences of End of Empires in the Twentieth Century," in ed. Beverly Crawford, *Markets, States, and Democracy: The Political Economy of Post-Communist Transformation* (Boulder: Westview, 1995), 43–68.

13. Charles Tilly, *Popular Contention in Great Britain, 1758–1834* (Cambridge, Mass.: Harvard University Press, 1995); and idem, *Coercion, Capital and European States, 990–1990 A.D.* (Oxford: Blackwell, 1990).

ABOUT THE BOOK AND EDITORS

The Soviet Union was hardly the first large, continuous, land-based, multinational empire to collapse in modern times. The USSR itself was, ironically, the direct result of one such demise, that of imperial Russia, which in turn was but one of several other such empires that did not survive the stresses of the times: the Austro-Hungarian Empire of the Habsburgs and the Ottoman Empire.

This ambitious and important volume brings together a group of some of the most outstanding scholars in political science, history, and historical sociology to examine the causes of imperial decline and collapse. While they warn against facile comparisons, they also urge us to step back from the immediacy of current events to consider the possible significance of historical precedents.

Is imperial decline inevitable, or can a kind of imperial stasis be maintained indefinitely? What role, if any, does the growth of bureaucracies needed to run large and complex political systems of this type play in economic and political stagnation? What is the "balance of power" between the center and the peripheries, between the dominant nationality and minorities? What coping mechanisms do empires tend to develop and what influence do these have? Is modernization the inexorable source of imperial decline and ultimate collapse? And what resources, including the imperial legacy, are available for political, social, and economic reconstruction in the aftermath of collapse? These are just a few of the tantalizing questions addressed by the contributors to this fascinating and timely volume.

Karen Barkey is associate professor of sociology at Columbia University. She is author of *Bandits and Bureaucrats: The Ottoman Route to State Centralization* (1994). **Mark von Hagen** is associate professor of history and the director of the Harriman Institute at Columbia University. He is author of *Soldiers in the Proletarian Dictatorship: The Red Army and the Soviet Socialist State, 1917–1930* (1990).

About the Contributors

Rogers Brubaker is professor of sociology at the University of California at Los Angeles.

István Deák is the Seth Low Professor of History at Columbia University.

E. J. Hobsbawm is emeritus professor of history at Birbeck College, University of London, and emeritus university professor of politics and society at the New School for Social Research.

Caglar Keyder is professor of sociology at the State University of New York at Binghamton and Bogazici University.

Serif Mardin is professor of Islamic studies at the American University.

Alexander J. Motyl is associate director of the Harriman Institute at Columbia University.

Ronald G. Suny is professor of political science at the University of Chicago.

Charles Tilly is Joseph L. Buttenwieser Professor of Social Science at Columbia University.

Solomon Wank is Lewis Audenreid Professor Emeritus of History at Franklin and Marshall College.

Victor Zaslavsky is professor of sociology at the Libera Università Internazionale degli Studi Sociali, Rome.

INDEX